Supporting the Mental Health and Wellbeing of Learners in Post-16 Education

This comprehensive guide provides practical strategies and essential insights for anyone working with young adults, revealing the importance of nurturing mental health and wellbeing needs of students in the post-16 education sector.

An invaluable resource for understanding and addressing the unique challenges faced by learners, many of whom will be transitioning into adulthood, this book covers key areas such as stress management, building resilience, and fostering positive self-esteem, and equips readers with the knowledge and practical strategies needed to support the mental health and overall wellbeing of post-16 learners. It offers detailed real-life case studies, practical advice and the latest research to support academic and student-services staff to effectively engage with students. It also addresses issues such as anxiety, depression, exam stress and peer pressure and provides evidence-based strategies that can be implemented in both the classroom and one-to-one settings. This text supports the reader in understanding what can be done to support learners' mental health and wellbeing both across the college and in individual classrooms.

With its accessible language and actionable advice, this book is an essential toolkit for all those concerned with the wellbeing needs of students.

Paul Demetriou is an educational consultant who has worked for over 35 years with young people and adults in the FE sector with mental health issues and learning needs.

Supporting the Mental Health and Wellbeing of Learners in Post-16 Education

Paul Demetriou

LONDON AND NEW YORK

Designed cover image: © Getty Images

First published 2025
by Routledge
4 Park Square, Milton Park, Abingdon, Oxon OX14 4RN

and by Routledge
605 Third Avenue, New York, NY 10158

Routledge is an imprint of the Taylor & Francis Group, an informa business

© 2025 Paul Demetriou

The right of Paul Demetriou to be identified as author of this work has been asserted in accordance with sections 77 and 78 of the Copyright, Designs and Patents Act 1988.

All rights reserved. No part of this book may be reprinted or reproduced or utilised in any form or by any electronic, mechanical, or other means, now known or hereafter invented, including photocopying and recording, or in any information storage or retrieval system, without permission in writing from the publishers.

Trademark notice: Product or corporate names may be trademarks or registered trademarks, and are used only for identification and explanation without intent to infringe.

British Library Cataloguing-in-Publication Data
A catalogue record for this book is available from the British Library

Library of Congress Cataloging-in-Publication Data
Names: Demetriou, Paul, author.
Title: Supporting the mental health and wellbeing of learners in post-16 education / Paul Demetriou.
Description: Abingdon, Oxon ; New York, NY : Routledge, 2024. | Includes bibliographical references and index. | Identifiers: LCCN 2024018368 (print) | LCCN 2024018369 (ebook) | ISBN 9781032543376 (hardback) | ISBN 9781032543369 (paperback) | ISBN 9781003424376 (ebook)
Subjects: LCSH: Counseling in higher education. | College students--Mental health. | Adult students--Mental health.
Classification: LCC LB2343 .D377 2024 (print) | LCC LB2343 (ebook) | DDC 378.1/97--dc23/eng/20240429
LC record available at https://lccn.loc.gov/2024018368
LC ebook record available at https://lccn.loc.gov/2024018369

ISBN: 978-1-032-54337-6 (hbk)
ISBN: 978-1-032-54336-9 (pbk)
ISBN: 978-1-003-42437-6 (ebk)

DOI: 10.4324/9781003424376

Typeset in Galliard
by SPi Technologies India Pvt Ltd (Straive)

Contents

Introduction	1
1 Colleges and mental health	5
2 Main issues related to social and emotional wellbeing faced by young people	30
3 Approaches to effective college wellbeing systems	60
4 The relationships between social and emotional wellbeing and learning and attainment	92
5 Approaches to pastoral care when supporting social wellbeing and emotional health issues in Further Education	123
6 The development and usage of basic helping skills to support students' mental health and wellbeing needs	152
7 Harnessing the power of thoughts and feelings: Supporting young people with social and emotional issues through identification and monitoring	181
8 Approaches to teachers' wellbeing	200
9 Whole college approaches to mental health and wellbeing	224
10 General mental health and wellbeing services	238
Index	*241*

Introduction

Welcome to 'Supporting the Mental Health and Wellbeing of Students in Post-Compulsory Education.' This book is designed to provide educators, counsellors, and individuals working in the post-compulsory education sector with valuable insights, practical strategies, and resources to promote the mental health and wellbeing of students. This introductory chapter will outline the structure of the book, highlight the use of case studies, questions, and reflective tools throughout, and discuss what the readers will gain from this book and why it is important.

Structure of the book

This book is organised into three main sections, each exploring different aspects of supporting student mental health and wellbeing.

Section 1

This section delves into the theoretical foundations of student mental health, exploring concepts such as resilience, self-esteem, and stress management. It aims to provide a comprehensive understanding of the factors influencing mental health in post-compulsory education. In addition, it will cover approaches to effective college wellbeing systems and the relationships between social and emotional wellbeing and learning and attainment.

Section 2

This section provides evidence-based strategies and interventions that can be implemented in educational settings to support student and staff mental health and wellbeing. It examines approaches to pastoral care when supporting social wellbeing and emotional health issues in further education (FE) and covers topics like mindfulness, self-care, promoting healthy coping mechanisms, and identifying and responding to mental health concerns.

Section 3

Here, I focus on the role of educational institutions and educators in creating a supportive and inclusive environment for students' mental health. This section will address topics such as building positive relationships, promoting inclusion, and implementing effective communication strategies. In essence it will look at a whole college approach to social and emotional wellbeing.

Use of case studies, questions, and reflective tools

Throughout this book, I have incorporated real-life case studies to illustrate the challenges and successes in supporting student mental health. These case studies will leave open questions, encouraging readers to think critically and engage in reflective exercises. Additionally, each chapter includes thought-provoking questions and reflective tools to facilitate self-reflection and application of the concepts discussed.

Effective support necessitates a deep understanding of individual experiences and context. To facilitate this understanding and encourage active engagement, the book incorporates case studies, questions, and reflective tools throughout its content. These elements play a vital role in enhancing the learning experience and applicability of the material.

Case studies provide real-life scenarios, allowing readers to connect theory with practice. They offer a glimpse into the challenges faced by students helping learners to develop empathy and a nuanced perspective. By examining these case studies, practitioners can also develop critical thinking skills and creative problem-solving approaches, preparing them to address diverse situations. Importantly, the book intentionally includes case studies that leave open questions. This deliberate choice aims to promote discussion and encourage readers to explore various possibilities and outcomes. By leaving these questions unresolved, the book invites readers to reflect on their own biases, assumptions, and prior knowledge, fostering a deeper understanding of the complexities inherent in mental health and wellbeing support.

The inclusion of thought-provoking questions is another essential aspect of this book. Beyond simply presenting information, these questions challenge readers to critically analyse concepts, apply principles to practical scenarios, and consider multiple perspectives. By engaging with the questions, practitioners are encouraged to reflect on their own practices, explore alternative approaches, and develop a more comprehensive understanding of mental health and wellbeing support.

In addition to case studies and questions, reflective tools are incorporated throughout the book. These tools help practitioners to introspect, evaluate their own beliefs and practices, and identify areas for growth. Reflection is a valuable process that stimulates self-awareness, enhances professional development, and supports the ongoing improvement of one's support services.

Thus, the case studies, questions, and reflective tools utilised in this book serve as essential components that foster active learning, critical thinking, and self-reflection. Together, they provide a comprehensive and holistic approach to understanding and supporting the mental health and wellbeing of students in the post-compulsory education setting.

What you will gain from this book

My hope is that this book will serve as a valuable resource for all individuals invested in the mental health and wellbeing of students in post-compulsory education. By providing practical strategies, real-life examples, and reflective tools, we aim to empower readers to create supportive environments and implement effective interventions in their educational practice. Ultimately, I believe that prioritising student mental health is not only crucial for their overall wellbeing but also for their academic success and personal growth.

Why this book is important

The mental health of students in post-compulsory education is a pressing concern that cannot be ignored. Research consistently highlights the prevalence of mental health challenges among students and the negative impact it can have on their educational experience. This book seeks to address this issue by equipping educators and professionals with the knowledge and skills needed to support student mental health effectively. By prioritising mental health and wellbeing, we can foster a positive and conducive learning environment that enables students to thrive academically and personally.

A note to the readers of this book,

It is crucial to remember that you are not expected to handle every situation alone. There may be instances where you encounter complex mental health issues that surpass your qualifications or expertise. In such cases, it is essential to seek additional support and involve professionals with specialised training.

Within your institution, there may be dedicated mental health teams, counsellors, or pastoral care support staff who can provide guidance and advice. Make use of these available supports and trust in their experience.

Additionally, many external organisations and networks are specifically designed to support FE practitioners in promoting student mental health and wellbeing such as educational associations, professional bodies, or local authorities that provide training programmes, workshops, and conferences focused on mental health.

Moreover, establishing connections with peers within the education sector can be invaluable. Online forums, social media groups, or professional networks can be excellent platforms to establish connections and find support outside of your immediate environment.

My hope is that this book serves as a comprehensive resource to support you in your journey to promote student mental health and wellbeing. While I aim to provide practical strategies, case studies, and reflective tools that can inform your practice, it is crucial to remember that every situation is unique. This book aims to equip you with knowledge, but it is essential to adapt the information to suit your specific context and seek additional support when necessary.

1 Colleges and mental health

What is mental health? And does it matter?

There are many definitions of mental health, one of which is:

> 'Mental health is defined as a state of well-being in which every individual realises his or her potential, can cope with the normal stresses of life, can work productively and fruitfully and is able to make a contribution to his or her community.'
>
> (WHO, 2001)

Mental health is more than the state of mind; it is about emotional resilience, self-esteem, and confidence. It affects our ability to communicate, to build and sustain relationships, to learn and work, and to achieve our potential and aspirations.

What are mental health difficulties and who has them?

The social context

Everyone experiences distress, anxiety, worry and grief. For many, these difficulties are temporary. Sometimes, if our emotional resilience (our mental immune system) is low, recovery may take longer or require more support. People may need medication, counselling, or interventions like cognitive behavioural therapy to help them make a full recovery.

Recovery may also be affected by other personal and social factors like the support available to us, the strength of our relationships, our financial or housing situation, or our physical health. We may be more vulnerable to developing mental health difficulties during times of transition, both positive and negative, or stress or when dealing with prolonged illness or disability. Socio economic disadvantages expose people to even greater risk. According to research by Marmot et al. (2010) children and adults living in households in the lowest 20% income bracket in Great Britain are two to three times more likely to develop mental health problems than those in the highest.

DOI: 10.4324/9781003424376-2

No-one is immune from difficulties with mental health, potentially we can all develop them just as we can all develop difficulties with physical health.

A continuum of mental health

It is useful to see health, whether physical or mental, as a continuum. At one end is good health, where a person is able to communicate and work effectively to sustain positive relationships and build good social networks. At the other end is poor health or illness and its negative impact on daily functioning, work and relationships and there is a range of experience in between. There is, however, a second aspect of the continuum which is to do with a sense of wellbeing rather than our actual state of health. The key point is that we all move up and down on this continuum of mental and physical health.

Two case studies illustrating the mental health continuum

Figure 1.1   Self-reflective task

Jayden: 'I have been on medication for arthritis for a year now but I would say that my health has improved over that period. Before Christmas I never felt right with myself and with life in general, probably because of all the pressure to get everything done, all the expense, end of another year, terrible weather, kids under my feet and all that. Since the new year I have felt better though my actual health hasn't changed and I still need the tablets. I feel better in myself though, more comfortable with things, I'm generally more able to just get on with stuff.'

Winston: 'I feel pretty bad at the moment, no particular reason. I have problems sleeping, gone off my food, but I can't put my finger on anything specific. I keep myself fit, go to the gym regularly and I play football. Maybe I just need a change, a new girlfriend or something.'

Self-reflect on the following issues and then look at how do the issues explored in these case studies impact on your professional practice and how would you support students who came to you with these thoughts.

- Identify personal experiences that help you distinguish between your state of health and your sense of well-being.
- Identify examples that illustrate this distinction for both physical and mental health and well-being.
- Design a visual representation of the continuum that can help you to understand it using these experiences and/or the cases above.

Why does mental health matter to teachers?

Mental health matters fundamentally to teachers for the following reasons:

- Most teachers will, at some point, work with learners who experience mental health difficulties that impact their ability to learn, whether they are identified or not
- Some learners are particularly vulnerable to developing mental health difficulties (e.g. those who also experience another disability, young people, offenders, care leavers and carers, and those who experience poverty, homelessness, unemployment, crime, abuse, racism or other forms of discrimination) (Newton et al., 2021). This point is developed in more depth later in the chapter
- It is estimated that by 2025 the incidence of depression will be second only to chronic heart disease. In autumn 2022, around 1 in 6 (16%) adults aged 16 years and over reported moderate to severe depressive symptoms (ONS, 2022)
- People with mental health difficulties are the key focus of many government policies and the social inclusion agenda
- Learners and staff who experience mental health difficulties have rights under the Equality Act 2020
- Engagement in learning is proven to support the recovery process, build confidence and enhance mental wellbeing in students
- Teachers have a crucial role to play in creating positive and healthy learning environments, in challenging the stigma and prejudice that still surrounds mental health, in promoting positive mental health and wellbeing, and improving employability
- The mental wellbeing of staff is fundamentally important as it impacts on their performance as educational support.

(Glazzard and Rose, 2019)

Figure 1.2   Self-reflective exercise

Consider the following statements and decide how many of them you agree with. Record and keep your personal responses for future reference.

1 People with a diagnosed mental illness are not well enough to be in learning or work
2 Mental health difficulties are the same as learning difficulties
3 Mental illness is an illness like any other
4 People with serious mental illness are likely to be aggressive

> 5 One of the causes of mental illness is a weakness of character or will power
> 6 Students with mental health needs often use them as an excuse to get extensions for their assignments
> 7 Learners with mental health needs are more demanding than other learners
> 8 If I take on a student or apprentice who has a mental health issue they are likely to disrupt lessons or the workplace
> 9 Having students or employees who experience mental health difficulties may bring benefits for other learners and/or employees
> 10 Having students or colleagues who have a mental health issue will involve a lot of extra work for me
> 11 Young people today are just 'snowflakes' and they need to become more resilient
> 12 I am confident in my ability to respond to someone who has mental health difficulties

Attitudes to mental health issues

People who experience mental health conditions often say that stigma and the discrimination that results from it are more damaging and difficult to deal with than the actual health issues themselves. For many, their perception of themselves and their mental health difficulties, their self-esteem and confidence can all be damaged by negative attitudes. Their ability to manage their difficulties, to openly discuss their needs or seek support can also be further impaired by the negative perceptions and attitudes that they experience.

The effects of stigma and discrimination can be felt by those experiencing mental health difficulties long after the actual symptoms have been managed or resolved. And yet research consistently indicates that one in four of us experience some kind of mental health difficulty and one in six people report experiencing a common mental health problem (like anxiety and depression) in any given week in the UK (Mc Manus et al., 2016).

Language has long been a key indicator of stigma, prejudice and discrimination whether with regard to age, race, gender, sexual orientation or disability. This applies also to mental health. Language is very powerful in conveying messages whether intended or not. Commonly used terms like 'mentally ill', 'mental illness' and 'mental health problems' can carry negative or unhelpful connotations. They may indicate an inappropriate degree of severity or permanence or may be dismissive or disempowering of people who experience difficulties with their mental health (Richards, 2018).

When asked to estimate what proportion of people in the UK might have a mental health problem at some point in their lives, respondents to a 2009 survey tended to underestimate – only 13% of respondents correctly stated one in four, whilst the majority, 65%, thought it was one in ten or even less (24% thought one in ten, with 41 % thinking it was less than this).

Changing attitudes towards mental health conditions

According to a survey conducted by Public Health England in 2015 the levels of knowledge about mental health issues were quite high. For example:

- 63% of people were confident they know what it means to have good mental wellbeing. People are aware of different factors that impact on their mental wellbeing and the things they can do to improve it. Two-thirds spend at least "quite a lot" of time thinking about their own mental wellbeing, and a majority feel they know what to do to improve their mental wellbeing and have the time to do
- Spending time with friends and family (76%), going for a walk or getting fresh air (63%), and getting more sleep are widely regarded by people as activities which help them feel more positive (54%)

The same survey suggested that attitudes to mental health improved in some respects since 1994 which is illustrated by the following statistics:

- The belief that virtually anyone can become mentally ill increased from 89% in 2008 to 91% in 2009
- People with mental health problems should have the same rights to a job as anyone else increased from 66% in 2008 to 73% in 2009
    However, there have also been reverse trends, for example, the belief that one of the main causes of mental illness is a lack of self-discipline and will-power increased from 14% in 2008 to 18 % in 2009 and that
- There is something different about people with mental illness that makes it easy to tell them from normal people increased from 17% in 2008 to 21% in 2009

Complex and enduring mental health conditions are usually well managed. Most people who experience them continue to lead active and purposeful lives and many recover completely (CFL, 2021). Whilst the PHE survey found that levels of understanding and tolerance of people with mental illness seemed generally high, since 1994 the proportion of respondents voicing more tolerant opinions has actually decreased from 92% to 85%.

The survey also notes attitudinal differences by age group, gender and social grade. It showed that consistently throughout the survey, those expressing the most negative attitudes towards mental illness were men rather than women, those in the youngest age group (16–34), those in semi-/unskilled manual occupations and people dependent on state benefits.

These findings are important for those working throughout the FE sector because:

- They help us to understand why so few people declare their mental health difficulties or seek support
- The age and social groups found generally to be the least tolerant are those who are themselves amongst the most vulnerable in terms of mental health and also those often most in need of good learning opportunities
- The FE sector can have a major impact not only in providing positive learning experiences but also in being an agent for attitudinal change

Figure 1.3   Case study

Laeticcia has started a childcare course at her local college. It took a lot of courage to get over her anxieties about it. She has been honest with the college about her past mental health difficulties and has been well supported so far by her tutors. She is doing very well with the course and on her first work placement. She was really enjoying it but one of the other people working there overheard a conversation between Laeticcia and her tutor in which her past difficulties were mentioned. Since then she has heard a few of them talking about her and questioning whether she should be working there.

Laeticcia is understandably becoming more and more uncomfortable at her placement and is feeling quite stressed. She believes that her work is beginning to suffer and she is concerned that, although she has been fine for a few years now, her previous difficulties will return.

Think about the following:

- *How far is Laeticcia being disabled by the attitudes around her rather than by any actual difficulties with her health?*
- *What might have been done to prevent this situation arising?*
- *To what extent is she possibly being affected by past experiences, a lack of confidence and/or negative self perception?*
- *If you were her tutor, how could you support her?*
- *Would you know where you or she could get further advice or support?*
- *If you were her employer/placement supervisor how would you approach this issue?*
- *What support could you offer?*
- *What could be the impact of this situation on Laeticcia, in the short and longer term?*

Factors which impact particularly upon the mental health of young people in education who are 16 plus

Recent research suggests that there is an increasing level of mental health need in young persons. Some of this stems from improvements to culture as it has become more acceptable to talk about mental health and also from earlier identification of needs but services to address these needs are scarce and hard to access (Crenna-Jennings 2021).

The onset of mental health issues tends to first occur at a young age and as students age into their late teens, their understanding of mental health increases and there is greater awareness of the importance of looking after their own mental health. The FE sector's diverse intake of students means that it includes both substantial numbers of younger students who may experience symptoms for the first time, as well as older students who are more likely to have an established mental health condition, and who may be undertaking learning for the positive impact it can have on mental health and wellbeing.

Despite its potential to provide positive support, in general, the post school context can also introduce pressures that negatively impact upon students' mental wellbeing, specifically associated with transition to new, often larger, more populous learning environments, and the expectation for students to be more autonomous and able to manage their own learning experience (Crenna-Jennings, 2021).

Social connections are affected in these transitions, which again can increase anxiety causing a negative effect on mental health. Research also suggests that workload is higher in the 16–19 phase, leading to stress and concerns amongst students about managing this and passing assessments. Where students need to re-sit exams such as English and Maths in the UK, until they pass these exams is an additional stress. Other risk factors include the following (Newton et al., 2021):

- People from Black, Asian, and Minority Ethnic backgrounds face multiple risk factors for poor mental health related to economic disadvantage, struggles in attainment at FE and experiences of racism both in society in general and in the education system (Bains and Gutman, 2021)
- Women are more likely to experience a mental health issue than men. Young women are also at higher risk for developing a mental health issue, in particular anxiety, than young men. The onset of mental health issues also tends to be later in young women than young men, with boys aged 11–16 more likely to have a mental health disorder than girls, and girls most likely to have a mental health disorder at age 17–19
- Being lesbian, gay, bisexual or trans (LGBT+) increases likelihood to experience poor mental health. Nearly 35% of young people who identified as lesbian, gay, bisexual or another sexuality had a mental health disorder, compared to 13% of young people who identified as heterosexual.

Discrimination and harassment contribute to mental health issues for the LGBT+ community (Ellis et al., 2015)
- Poor mental health is more common in children from lower income households. Young people's feelings about their family's socioeconomic status (SES) wishing they could afford more and feeling poorer compared to their peers – are associated in a graded fashion with both lower wellbeing and higher levels of psychological distress, while feeling poorer than peers is also associated with lower self-esteem (Krauss and Park, 2014)
- There is a clear relationship between unemployment and poor mental health. Unemployment negatively affects self-esteem and increases feelings of distress; an estimated 34% of unemployed people have mental distress, compared to 16% of those employed. There is also an association between unemployment and suicide (Reiss, 2013)
- Job insecurity also increases the risk of depressive symptoms (Kim and von dem Knesebeck, 2016), and adult unemployment can have a negative effect on children's mental health as those living with socioeconomic disadvantage are two to three times more likely to develop mental health problems (Reiss, 2013)
- Support services are also under resourced and inadequate in the first place, particularly those for young people and a lack of diversity within the workforce of support services can be off-putting for people from Black, Asian and Minority Ethnic backgrounds (CFL, 2021)
- Transition from primary into secondary school tends to reflect a decline in feelings of wellbeing and continues to drop as children move through secondary school. As children get older, the decline in median wellbeing scores is greater for girls than for boys. In focus groups, young people highlighted the transition to secondary school as being particularly hard on their self-esteem due to increased concerns about being judged and not fitting in
- During adolescence levels of distress and issues with poor self-esteem seems to rise with girls starting off at age 14 with higher scores and, on average, seeing a larger rise as they move into late adolescence. As levels of worry and pressure increase whilst they moved through secondary school (Robins and Trzesniewski, 2005)
- Health and activities in childhood, including physical activity and social media habits, are important for all three outcomes : wellbeing, distress and self-esteem. There is a clear relationship between frequency of exercise and scores on all three outcomes at age 17, in both males and females (Singh et al., 2023). Being overweight in childhood is also found to be associated with worse mental and emotional health (MEH) outcomes for both boys and girls, showing a lasting impact of negative body image and related social interactions throughout adolescence
- International research has suggested that heavy social media use is associated with worse scores on all outcomes in girls age 14 and 17, but only worse wellbeing for boys at age 14 demonstrating that peer influence is particularly important at this time of life (Long and Cheng, 2007)

- The social dimension of life, including quality of relationships with parents and peers, is highly important for young people's mental and emotional health. The following have negative effects on both sexes during adolescence; being bullied, -frequent arguing with parents, parental breakups. being placed in the bottom stream in school, poor maternal health and safety at home (Crenna-Jennings, 2021)

The impact of the pandemic on mental health in the UK between 2019 and 2022

These factors have been exacerbated since 2019 because of the pandemic which research by Newton et al. (2021) suggests has had significant impacts on mental health amongst young students in the capital. These include the following:

- Although even before the pandemic this generation of young people was experiencing high levels of mental health issues, and in particular post-traumatic stress disorder and self-harm according to the Mental Health Foundation (MHF, 2020) young people aged 18–24 were more likely to report this as a result of the pandemic than the UK population as a whole
- They also found that 18–24 year-olds were more likely than any other age group to report hopelessness, loneliness, issues with coping, and suicidal thoughts/feelings
- A study conducted by YoungMinds (2020) noted that young people with a history of mental health issues had concerns over losing connection with friends, non-immediate family, and other trusted adults
- According to research by Fancourt et al. (2022) While on average, reports of self-harm thoughts and behaviours did not significantly change during the pandemic, a proportion of our participants reported experiencing psychological or physical abuse, having thoughts of suicide or self-harm, and harming themselves. Young adults, women, those of lower SES, unemployed individuals, and people with disabilities, chronic physical illnesses, and a mental health condition were most at risk
- They further explained that while most people gradually adjusted to the novelty and stresses of the pandemic, groups who suffered disproportionately to others were those in already vulnerable positions before COVID-19. These groups' mental health tended not to recover as quickly as others. They included women, young adults, people of lower educational attainment, and those living alone or with children who had slower rates of recovery (Fancourt et al., 2022)
- They also found that that people from different socio-economic and demographic backgrounds and with different personality traits employed different coping strategies. In general, improvements in mental health were seen among people who spent time outdoors, who had access to green space, who communicated with friends and family or had social contact, who

exercised, pursued hobbies, and engaged in creative activities and more specifically groups that stood out as experiencing psychological challenges during the pandemic included: people of lower SES (people from ethnic minority groups; adolescents (13–18 years old) and young adults (18–29 years old); women; parents of young children; people with health conditions; and key workers. In fact those with lower SES tended to evidence higher levels of mental health symptoms early in the pandemic, and those experiencing financial or employment problems continued to report a decline in their mental health much later in the pandemic

- It was also found that people from ethnic minority backgrounds struggled more with their mental health which was compounded by higher rates of discrimination, loneliness, and barriers to healthcare
- According to OECD (2020) the burden of excess bereavement and trauma fell most heavily on those who are already most disadvantaged
- This was also true of adolescents and young adults who consistently had worse mental health than older age groups, primarily because they were more likely to face significant changes to their education, social lives, and support systems and, they were more likely to use fewer healthy coping strategies such as exercise or the pursuing of hobbies, compared to older age groups whose lives and routines were disrupted less and who could draw on more years of experience to manage the challenges of the pandemic
- According to the study by Daly et al. (2022) younger adults (aged 18–34) experienced an 18.6% increase in risk of mental health problems during the period whereas those aged 50–64 experienced a 9.3% increase.
- Young people were also less likely to ask for mental health support compared to order people. According to Daly et. al (2022) over a quarter (28%) didn't ask for help because they didn't feel they were deserving of it. But of those that did, many felt uncomfortable accessing remote support with 30% saying technology was a barrier, with privacy being a particular concern
- Gender inequalities were also evident from their research as women had a more psychologically challenging experience during the pandemic than men. The reasons for this included having more responsibilities in the home, balancing childcare and professional commitments, experiencing increased domestic violence, or managing pregnancy and motherhood without the support of friends and family
- Daly et al. (2022) suggested that being female and having a higher education or household income level were associated with particularly pronounced increases in mental health problems. Findings that younger adults and females showed particularly pronounced declines in mental health may reflect that these groups are known to have an underlying vulnerability to mental health problems
- Those people who developed long Covid had much higher initial increases in depressive symptoms than those with "short" COVID-19, and also

maintained higher anxiety and depressive symptoms in the months following their infection, with levels of higher depression lasting as long as two years. This was particularly evident in people from lower SES backgrounds who lived in crowded accommodation or with children, or those with lower educational attainment, or with physical or mental ailments (Fancourt et al., 2022)
- People's mental health was worsened by challenges in accessing health services, which meant that some mental health problems that could have been treated early became worse and some physical health deteriorated, causing secondary symptoms of anxiety and depression
- According to Molodynski (2021) over the coming months and years, mental health challenges will likely result from personal and financial losses during the pandemic, as well as the rise in inflation and cost of living, persisting and growing cases of long Covid, and the combination of other forces such as Brexit, global political unrest, and climate change and that consequently without sufficient mental health services and support, people with moderate mental health problems could develop more serious illness

The impact of divorce on young people's mental health and wellbeing

Divorce has both significant physical and emotional impacts on young people. The main psychological impact of parental separation on teenagers is that they are more likely to suffer from mental health-related issues such academic difficulties (e.g., lower grades and school dropout), disruptive behaviours (e.g., conduct and substance use problems), and depression (Lee and McLanahan, 2015). A 2011 study by D'Onofrio et al. (2019) suggested there was a strong correlation between the mental welfare of teenagers and family structure. It showed that teenagers with both biological parents present at the same time tend to be in better mental health than those with separated parents.

Another study by Perales et al. (2017) suggested that children with separated parents are twice as likely to need psychological help than children living in stable family environments. The sane study found that children living in intact, nuclear families are about half as likely as children in step, blended, or one-parent families to have a mental disorder or need psychological help.

Some studies show that the psychological effects and emotional strain of divorce even linger into adulthood. Fuller-Thomson and Dalton (2011) research suggested that men from families that divorced during their childhood were more than three times as likely to consider suicide than men whose parents never divorced and according to a study by Tullius et al. (2022) parental divorce during adolescence increased adolescent's risk to develop both emotional and behavioural problems, and this effect increased even further for an additional four years. Their findings further showed that effects of parental divorce on emotional problems were larger for girls than boys, two years after the event of parental divorce, but did not differ by gender for behavioural problems.

Impact of bullying on MH and well being

Bullying in childhood is a global public health problem that impacts on child, adolescent and adult health and figures suggest that one in three children globally under 16 had been bullied during February 2021 (Armitage, 2021). Being bullied can leave pupils with poor mental health and the effects can continue to adulthood (Garcia et al., 2015) [online].

Research by Lereya et.al. (2015) showed an increased risk of young adult mental health problems such as anxiety, depression, and self-harm or suicidality in children who were bullied by peers and that children and young people who were exposed to bullying, whether previously maltreated or not, were more likely to have mental health problems in adulthood than those not exposed to either bullying or maltreatment.

Research from University College London (UCL, 2022) [online] shows that lesbian, gay, and bisexual young people are at an increased risk of bullying, which could lead to self-harm. Men that have experienced bullying in childhood are linked to worse economic outcomes, for example higher rates of unemployment, sickness, and disability, compared with men that did not experience bullying in childhood (Brimblecombe et al., 2018) [online].

Peer and family factors can impact the risk of bullying victimisation (Biswas et al., 2022) [online]. Coming from a low-income background could increase the risk of being bullied, have negative experiences within school, and higher risk of mental health problems (UCL, 2022) [online], however, interventions were found to improve young people's mental health and help to provide a more positive effect within the school environment.

Cyberbullying has become more prominent since 2010 in global terms. International survey figures suggest that 60% of parents with children aged 14 to 18 reported them being bullied in 2019 (Cook, 2023) (Online). According to a survey conducted by Ditch the Label, a UK-based anti-bullying charity, which took place from September 2019 to March 2020, between March 2019 and March 2020, 19% or one in five children between the age of 10 and 15 in England and Wales experienced at least one form of cyberbullying and that up to 26% of cyberbullying victims had a long-term disability or illness. A single cyberattack can last online for extended periods of time, which therefore, can prolong the harm for the victim (Baldry, Farrington, and Sorrentino, 2015) [online].

The Impact of academic pressure on the mental health of young people

Young people who self-report higher levels of academic-related stress also report lower well-being, measured using psychological social, cognitive, and physical components (OECD, 2020). A systematic review of 13 studies showed that in individuals undertaking higher education, self-reported levels of stress are associated with poorer quality of life and well-being (Ribeiro et al., 2017).

Ongoing stress also triggers the development of more serious mental health issues such as anxiety and depression (Kessler, 1997; Moylan et al., 2013). The prevalence of anxiety is as high as 35% in students in post secondary education (Bayram and Bilgel, 2008; Eisenberg et al., 2007) and of depression is 30% (Ibrahim et al. 2013).

There is a variety of different factors which constitute academic pressure. These include pressure to perform, perceptions of workload, examination, self-perceptions, and time management, finance issues, familial pressures, and adapting to a new environment (Barbayannis et al. 2022).

The perception of academic stress varies among different groups of college students. For instance, female college students reported experiencing increased stress at college more than their male counterparts (Lee et al., 2013). Non-binary students report increased stressors and mental health issues (Tebbe and Budge, 2022). Several studies also indicate that racial/ethnic minority groups of students, including BAME are more likely to experience anxiety, depression, and suicidality than their white peers (Liu, 2015; Kodish et al., 2022).

According to a study by Insight Network in 2019 using data obtained from 38,000 UK students, respondents reported high levels of anxiety, with 42.8% often or always worried. Almost nine in ten (87.7%) said they struggled with feelings of anxiety – an increase of 18.7 percentage points on 2017 figures – and a third (33%) reported suffering from loneliness often or all the time. More than four out of ten (44.7%) admitted using alcohol or drugs to cope with their problems, while one in ten (9.5%) said they did this often or always (Weale, 2019). This was supported by a survey study of 128 Grade 11 students attending competitive private schools in the United States which reported high rates of drug and alcohol use associated with a greater desire for academic achievement, higher perceived stress, less effective coping strategies, and less closeness with parents (Leonard et al., 2015).

Stress is a contributing factor to poor sleep in young people which has been confirmed by many international studies including in the U.S., Saudi Arabia, Portugal and Pakistan, the impact of which can lead to difficulty paying attention in class, lower grades, higher stress, and trouble getting along with other people (Lee et al., 2013; 2017).

People who were stressed, such as during examination periods, were less likely to be physically active, which may lead to the development of noncommunicable diseases, including metabolic syndrome, obesity and reduced insulin sensitivity, resulting from unhealthy lifestyle habits and stress system dysregulation (Pervanidou and Chrousos, 2012) nd higher body weight (Stephens et al., 1995).

The World Health Organisation (1996) states that students must be healthy and emotionally secure to fully participate in education and reports that anxiety about schoolwork, homework and tests has a negative impact on students' academic performance in science, mathematics and reading. The OECD (2020) survey also highlights that top-performing girls report that the fear of making mistakes often disrupts their test performance (OECD, 2020).

Higher perceived stress levels are associated with poorer academic performance. According to OECD figures (2020) students in the bottom 25% of academic performance report feeling far more stressed compared to those in the top quarter of academic performance.

Slimmen et al. (2022) suggest that the degree to which stress is perceived depends on underlying factors or stressors such as loneliness, personality, and coping style. Students who are open to new experiences and environments were found to experience significantly less stress and were more able to adapt to new environments. Their research suggested that academic pressure had the strongest negative impact on mental wellbeing compared to other underlying stressors such as family and money problems but that these could exacerbate the stress produced by academic pressure (Slimmen et al., 2022).

The impact of tests and examinations on Mental Health and Wellbeing

The move to increased, and more difficult, curriculum content that is largely assessed through terminal exams, as in GCSEs, A Levels and BTECs courses has coincided with an increase in the number of students requesting support or counselling to cope with the pressures and reporting adverse effects on mental health (including self-harm, anxiety, depression, and suicidal thoughts) (Putwain, 2022).

Test anxiety encompasses negative physiological, affective and cognitive responses to a test or assessment, where symptoms such as rapid heart rate and breathing, and worry about underperforming, occur before, during or after an assessed performance.

It can be experienced by people of all ages, and in some children and young people across all stages of education. It is difficult to determine the prevalence of test anxiety amongst students. However, it has been argued that females are more likely to experience test anxiety than males (Howard, 2019).

Studies have shown that that higher exam anxiety can result in lower exam performance, through interfering with memory, attention, and the ability to mentally manipulate information in one's mind and can affect students of all aptitudes as much and can impact on exam performance by as much as two grades in UK GCSE examinations (Howard, 2019; Putwain, 2022).

Higher levels of examination or test anxiety are also associated with lower student wellbeing and a high risk of poor mental health. Coroner's reports specifically cited exam pressures as a specific cause in 15% of cases in a study of adolescent suicide in England between 2014–15 (Rodway et al., 2016).

According to research by OECD (2020) students from the UK reported feeling more anxious about studying and assessments than the global average. For example, even if they are well prepared for a test, 72% of students from the UK reported still feeling anxious, whereas the global average was 56%; and 52% of students from the UK reported feeling tense when they study, whereas the global average was 37%. These results suggest that students in the UK may be more likely to report studying- and assessment-related worries than the global average.

Evidence suggests that test anxiety does not have a single cause. Many factors can increase test anxiety or protect against it such as individual differences in beliefs about academic ability whilst social interactions with teachers, parents and peers can also increase test anxiety through fear appeals. Confidence, self-belief and coping mechanisms can mediate the experience of test anxiety. (Putwain, 2022). Age can also impact on test anxiety as there is some evidence that the degree to which students experience it is found to increase with age, (Byrne et al., 2007; Kutsyuruba, et.al, 2015).

Females more likely to report anxiety over sitting tests and with being evaluated by others (von der Embse et al., 2018). Stöber (2004) found that males and females prepare for exams in different ways, with males being less likely to prepare and seek support for studying, and more likely to avoid thinking about the exam through varieties of distractions.

Features of the assessment itself can also influence the degree of anxiety experienced. For instance, responding to multiple-choice questions is reported as being less anxiety-eliciting than writing extended responses. In contrast, performance-based assessments with the social element of an audience (such as oral language presentations and sports or performing arts assessments) are likely to elicit a greater degree of test anxiety than traditional pen and paper exams. Perceptions around difficulty and stakes of the assessment can also contribute towards test anxiety in some students (Howard, 2019).

- Neuro-diversity

Students with special educational needs and disability report greater levels of stress, nervousness, and anxiety in general, and for exams in particular (Heiman and Precel, 2003; Nelson and Harwood, 2011). These worrying thoughts likely result from a perceived importance of reading, writing and maths skills for academic success, alongside the recognition that these skills may be less easily mastered.

Teachers that are experiencing feelings of stress and burnout can transfer this to their pupils in the classroom (Oberle and Schonert-Reichl, 2016). Around 70% of teachers indicated that their stress levels sometimes affect the way that they interact with pupils (Hutchings, 2015). Moreover, teachers may become unable to effectively manage the social and emotional challenges in the classroom, resulting in students being more likely to disengage and underperform (Marzano, Marzano and Pickering, 2003).

Stress and anxiety can also be spread within the student population as a form of emotional contagion. For instance, students report that their concerns are influenced by their peers being worried about assessments, and that this contributes to their own self-reported anxiety. High-achieving females tend to be more susceptible to emotional contagion. This is because they are more likely to discuss school pressures and what is worrying them and compare themselves to one another than boys (Låftman et al., 2013).

> **Figure 1.4 Teaching strategy – Self affirmation exercise worksheet**
>
> *Here is a worksheet that I ask my Level two health and social Care students to complete when they are feeling the pressure of multiple deadlines (Aisha, Health and Social Care lecturer).*
>
> *The human brain is made to adapt and change with thoughts and experiences. This is called neuroplasticity. Self-affirmation is one of the neuroplasticity exercises that you can use to create positive self-talk and bring healthy changes to your thinking process. Self-affirmations impact on your sense of self. When you feel your sense of self falling, you can quickly use self-affirmations to maintain your worth. These are also statements that you can use as reminders to yourself, your goals, your worth, and your values.*
>
> *Positive Affirmation List*
>
> *Create a positive affirmation list or a poster. Take a pen and paper, and list all the positive affirmations you're likely to use. You can also break them down into social, emotional, physical, or intellectual categories. Here are some positive affirmations you can add;*
>
> *I am strong, fit, and healthy*
> *I work out every day*
> *I eat a healthy diet every day*
> *I love myself*
> *I have a strong sense of self-esteem*

Identity and MH and wellbeing

The formation of identity has long been associated with positive mental health and academic outcomes (Tajfel and Turner, 1986; Smith and Silva, 2011; Reynolds et al., 2017). Erikson (1965) understood one of the main psychological functions of identity is to provide a sense of inner self-sameness and continuity, to bind together a person's past, present and future into a coherent whole. Therefore, one of the key developmental tasks in adolescence and young adulthood is to develop a coherent sense of self and identity (1965). During these life-stages, young people seek answers to questions related to who they are and who they would like to be in different life domains (e.g., vocation; relationships; religious beliefs; values) (Schwartz et al., 2013).

According to Erikson successful identity development involves moving from a state of predominant 'identity confusion' (i.e., a sense of inconsistency or uncertainty in one's idea of oneself) towards 'identity synthesis' (i.e., a sense of sameness and continuity of the self; Erikson, 1950). Ongoing identity development may increase vulnerability to social-emotional disorders, whilst such difficulties may also impede identity development (Klimstra and Denissen, 2017).

Some research studies over the past decade have suggested that identity confusion is positively correlated with depressive and anxiety disorder symptoms (Luyckx et al., 2014; Klimstra and Denissen, 2017. Marcotte and Lévesque, 2018). On the whole researchers have suggested that identity development difficulties may increase the likelihood of the emergence of social-emotional disorders, social-emotional disorders may increase the likelihood of identity development difficulties, or both may be the common symptoms of something different (Potterton et al., 2022).

Adolescents and young adults develop a sense of self during a phase of life that involves many role changes. These transitional periods, such as entering tertiary education, initiating intimate relationships, and joining the workforce, may form an important context that increases the salience of identity processes (Heaven and Ciarrochi, 2008), and may go hand in hand with identity change and incidental and stressful life events, such as the death of a relative, a breakup of a relationship, or an accident, can also serve as turning points in the development of identity (Slotter and Gardner, 2011).

Research by Long et al. (2007) suggests that that online communication as an individual experience and as a network of shared group membership is also a key element in the identity development of adolescents and should be regarded as a significant aspect of behavioural growth by parents, health care providers and teachers.

Sexual identity

Adolescents who identify as belonging to a sexual minority (for example, identifying as gay, lesbian and bisexual) are at greater risk of developing mental health problems, such as depression, relative to their heterosexual peers (Lucassen et al., 2017; Luk et al., 2018). Relative to heterosexual adolescents, sexual minority adolescents are also at a greater risk of engaging in a number of these adverse health risk behaviours and of other negative outcomes such as being the targets of peer victimisation (Amos et al., 2020). Peer victimisation has also been linked to an increased risk of developing depression amongst adolescents (Bariola et al., 2016).

The results of research by Nelson and Andel (2019) suggested that LGBTQ+ individuals were almost twice as likely to have ever experienced depression when compared to heterosexual individuals, but LGB individuals were not more likely to report worse memory or health than heterosexual participants, LGBTQ people appear to be at greater risk than heterosexual people of mental disorders and suicidal behaviour. LGB people are subject to institutionalised prejudice, social stress, social exclusion (even within families) and anti-homosexual hatred and violence and often internalise a sense of shame about their sexuality.

LGBTQ people are at higher risk of suicidal behaviour, mental disorder and substance misuse and dependence than heterosexual people. Similarly, depression, anxiety, alcohol, and substance misuse were at least 1.5 times more common in LGBTQ people. Findings were similar in men and women but LB women were at particular risk of substance dependence, while lifetime risk of suicide attempts was especially high in GB men (King et al., 2008).

Research from the National Longitudinal Study of Adolescent Health reveals that this 'perfect storm' of stressors can increase the risk of suicide among LGBT teens. Researchers suggest that teens struggling with sexual identity are more likely to manifest suicidal thoughts and actions. Signs include: obsession with emotional pain and death, withdrawal from family and friends, giving away possessions, reckless behaviour. Increased anger or aggression and excessive sleeping or not getting out of bed (Russell and Joyner, 2001).

Transgender issues

In the UK, the trans population is estimated to be in the region of 300,000; approximately 0.4% of the UK population (see Reed et al., 2009); a large proportion of whom are relatively invisible being not obviously different in social appearance from cisgender1 men and women. Poor mental health and psychological distress are disparately high among transgender people. In the USA, where transgender adults represent an estimated 1·4 million individuals, according to the National Centre for Transgender Equality, 40% report attempted suicide and depression, 33% anxiety, and 26% alcohol or drug misuse. Preliminary research suggests that gender affirmation might improve mental health through the direct effect of affirmation on wellbeing and through reduced exposure to stressors such as discrimination and violence.

Transgender people experience the background rates of common mood disorders, bipolar disorder, schizophrenia etc. that are seen in the general population, as well as a potentially increased rate of some conditions because of chronic minority stress and discrimination (Bockting et al., 2013).

Transgender people are more likely to live in poverty, be discriminated against in employment and be victims of violence than non-transgender people. Transgender people also face higher rates of family loss and homelessness. Transgender people with intersecting identities such as race, ethnicity, or socioeconomic status also face increased living pressures (White et al., 2015).

Transgender women of colour face extraordinarily high rates of social and health disparities [Bauer et al., 2009]. Factors like regular and casual sexual partners, low self-efficacy, and low self-esteem also put transgender women at a higher risk of depressive symptoms (Lin et al., 2021). Transgender women had the highest score for anxiety when compared to heterosexual peers (Zhu et al., 2019), Gender differences were found in suicide ideation and suicide attempt. Chen et al. (2019) research found a higher prevalence of suicide ideation in transgender women than transgender men (60·7% vs 51·5%). Compared with transgender men, the study also showed that transgender women had higher rates of suicide attempt (20·7% vs 11%) and seeking support from mental health services (34·4% vs 20·6%).

According to a study by Ellis et al. (2015) derived from the UK Trans Mental Health Study 2012 (McNeil et al., 2012) – which was the first comprehensive study of trans people's experiences of health care and the first study exploring the mental health experiences of trans people – specifically and separately – in the UK. In total, 621 participants of their research (66%) reported having used mental health services (through NHS, private, or voluntary-sector organisations) for reasons other than accessing gender reassignment medical assistance (e.g. hormones). Many of those respondents suggested that this was prior to transitioning.

References

Amos, R., Manalastas, E. J., White, R., Bos, H., and Patalay, P. (2020). Mental health, social adversity, and health-related outcomes in sexual minority adolescents: A contemporary national cohort study. *Lancet Child & Adolescent Health*, 4(1): 36–45. doi:10.1016/S2352-4642(19)30339-6

Armitage, R. (2021). Bullying in children: impact on child health. *BMJ Paediatrics Open*, 5: e000939. doi:10.1136/bmjpo-2020-000939

Bains, S., and Gutman, Leslie Morrison. (2021). Mental health in ethnic minority populations in the UK: Developmental trajectories from early childhood to mid adolescence. *Journal of Youth and Adolescence*, 50: 2151–65. doi:10.1007/s10964-021-01481-5

Baldry, A., Farrington, D., and Sorrentino, A. (2015). "Am I at risk of cyberbullying"? A narrative review and conceptual framework for research on risk of cyberbullying and cybervictimization: The risk and needs assessment approach Aggressive and violent behaviour [online]. Available from: https://www.sciencedirect.com/science/article/pii/S1359178915000762 [Accessed on 25 Nov 2022].

Barbayannis, G., Bandari, M., Zheng, X., Baquerizo, H., Pecor, K. W., and Ming, X. (2022). Academic stress and mental well-being in college students: Correlations, affected groups, and COVID-19. *Frontiers in Psychology*, 13: 886344. doi:10.3389/fpsyg.2022.886344

Bariola, Emily, Lyons, Anthony, and Lucke, Jayne. (2016). Flourishing among sexual minority individuals: Application of the dual continuum model of mental health in a sample of lesbians and gay men. *Psychology of Sexual Orientation and Gender Diversity*, 4. doi:10.1037/sgd0000210

Bauer, Greta, Hammond, Rebecca, Travers, Robb, Kaay, Matthias, Hohenadel, Karin, and Boyce, Michelle. (2009). "I don't think this is theoretical; this is our lives": How erasure impacts health care for transgender people. *The Journal of the Association of Nurses in AIDS Care: JANAC*, 20: 348–61. doi:10.1016/j.jana.2009.07.004

Bayram, N., and Bilgel, N. (2008). The prevalence and socio-demographic correlations of depression, anxiety and stress among a group of university students. *Social Psychiatry and Psychiatric Epidemiology*, 438: 667–72. Retrieved from https://www.ncbi.nlm.nih.gov/pubmed/18398558

Biswas, T. Thomas, H. J., Scott, J. G., et al. (2022). Variation in the prevalence of different forms of bullying victimisation among adolescents and their associations with family, peer and school connectedness: A population-based study in 40 lower and middle income to high-income countries (LMIC-HICs). *Journal of Child and Adolescent Trauma*, 15: 1029–39. doi:10.1007/s40653-022-00451-8

Bockting, W. O., Miner, M. H., Swinburne Romine, R. E., Hamilton, A., and Coleman, E. (2013). Stigma, mental health, and resilience in an online sample of the US transgender population. *American Journal of Public Health*, 103(5): 943–51. doi:10.2105/AJPH.2013.301241

Branje, S., de Moor, E. L., Spitzer, J., and Becht, A. I. (2021). Dynamics of identity development in adolescence: A decade in review. *Journal of Research on Adolescence*, 31(4): 908–27. doi:10.1111/jora.12678

Branje, S., and Morris, A. S. (2021). The impact of the COVID-19 pandemic on adolescent emotional, social, and academic adjustment. *Journal of Research on Adolescence*, 31(3), 486–499. doi:10.1111/jora.12668

Brimblecombe, N., Evans-Lacko, S., Knapp, M., King, D., Takizawa, R., Maughan, B., and Arseneault, L. (2018). Long term economic impact associated with childhood bullying victimisation. *Social Science & Medicine*, 208: 134–41. doi:10.1016/j.socscimed.2018.05.014

British Social Attitudes. (2015). https://www.gov.uk/government/statistics/british-social-attitudes-survey-2015

Buchanan, D., and Warwick, I. (2020). Supporting adults with mental health problems through further education. *Health Education Journal*, 79(8), 863–874.

Byrne, D. G., Davenport, S. C., and Mazanov, J. (2007). Profiles of adolescent stress: The development of the adolescent stress questionnaire (ASQ). *Journal of Adolescence*, 30: 393–416. doi:10.1016/j.adolescence.2006.04.004

Campaign for Learning. (2021). *Understanding and Overcoming a Mental Health Crisis in 2021 Issues for Post-16 Education, Employment, the World of Work and Retirement*. London: CFL.

Chen, R., Zhu X., Wright, L., Drescher, J., Gao, Y., Wu, L., Ying, X., Qi, J., Chen, C., Xi, Y., Ji, L., Zhao, H., Ou, J., and Broome, M.R. (2019). Suicidal ideation and attempted suicide amongst Chinese transgender persons: National population study. *The Journal of Affective Disorders*. 245: 1126–1134. doi: doi:10.1016/j.jad.2018.12.011

Campaign for Learning (CFL). (2021). *Understanding and Overcoming a Mental Health Crisis in 2021 Issues for Post-16 Education, Employment, the World of Work and Retirement*. London: CFL.

Cook, S. (2023). Cyberbullying facts and statistics for 2018–2023. https://www.comparitech.com/internet-providers/cyberbullying-statistics/ [Accessed on 26 Nov 2022].

Crenna-Jennings, W. (2021). *Young People's Mental and Emotional Health*. Education Policy Institute: Trajectories and Drivers in Childhood and Adolescence.

Daly, M., Sutin, A., and Robinson, E. (2020). Longitudinal changes in mental health and the COVID-19 pandemic: evidence from the UK Household Longitudinal Study. *Psychological Medicine*, 52: 1–10. doi:10.1017/S0033291720004432

Daly, Michael, Sutin, Angelina, and Eric Robinson. (2022). Longitudinal changes in mental health and the COVID-19 pandemic: Evidence from 2 the UK household longitudinal study.

Dantzer, R. (2012). Depression and inflammation: An intricate relationship. [Comment Research Support, N.I.H., Extramural]. *Biological Psychiatry*, 711: 4–5. Retrieved from http://www.ncbi.nlm.nih.gov/pubmed/22137156

Dantzer, R., O'Connor, J. C., Lawson, M. A., and Kelley, K. W. (2011). Inflammation-associated depression: From serotonin to kynurenine. [Research Support, N.I.H., Extramural Review]. *Psychoneuroendocrinology*, 363: 426–36. Retrieved from http://www.ncbi.nlm.nih.gov/pubmed/21041030

D'Onofrio, B., and Emery, R. (2019). Parental divorce or separation and children's mental health. *World Psychiatry*, 18(1): 100–101. doi:10.1002/wps.20590

Eisenberg, D., Gollust, S. E., Golberstein, E., and Hefner, J. L. (2007). Prevalence and correlates of depression, anxiety, and suicidality among university students. *The American Journal of Orthopsychiatry*, 774: 534–542. Retrieved from https://www.ncbi.nlm.nih.gov/pubmed/18194033

Ellis, S., Bailey, L., and McNeil, Jay. (2015). Trans people's experiences of mental health and gender identity services: A UK study. *Journal of Gay & Lesbian Mental Health*, 19(1): 1–17.

Erikson, E. H. (1950). *Childhood and Society*. London: W W Norton & Co.
Erikson, E. H. (1965). *Childhood and Society*. London: Hogarth.
Fancourt, D., Steptoe, A., and Bradbury, A. (2022). *Tracking the Psychological and Social Consequences of the COVID-19 Pandemic Across the UK Population: Findings, Impact, and Recommendations from the COVID-19 Social Study* (March 2020–April 2022). London: UCL.
Fuller-Thomson, E., and Dalton, A. D. (2011). Suicidal ideation among individuals whose parents have divorced: Findings from a representative Canadian community survey. *Psychiatry Research*, 187(1–2): 150–55. doi:10.1016/j.psychres.2010.12.004
Garcia, D., et al. (2015). Predictors of school bully perpetration in adolescence: A systematic review aggression and violent behaviour [online], 23 August 2015. 126–36. Available from: https://www-sciencedirect-com.bathspa.idm.oclc.org/science/article/pii/S1359178915000695?via%3Dihub [Accessed on 25 Nov 2022].
Glazzard, J., and Rose, A. (2019). The Impact of Teacher Well-Being and Mental Health on Pupil Progress in Primary Schools. *Journal of Public Mental Health*. ISSN 1746-5729. doi:10.1108/JPMH-02-2019-002
Heaven, P., and Ciarrochi, J. (2008). Parental styles, gender and the development of hope and self-esteem. *European Journal of Personality*, 22: 707–724. (2008) Published online 5 November 2008 in Wiley Interscience [Accessed on 25 July 2023] (www.interscience.wiley.com) doi:10.1002/per.699
Heiman, T., and Precel, K. (2003). Students with learning disabilities in higher education: Academic strategies profile. *Journal of Learning Disabilities*, 36: 248–58. doi:10.1177/002221940303600304
Howard, E. (2019). *A Review of the Literature Concerning Anxiety for Educational Assessments*. London: OFQUAL.
Hutchings, Merryn. (2015). *Exam Factories? The Impact of Accountability Measures on Children and Young People*. London: Metropolitan University. NUT publications
Ibrahim, A. K., Kelly, S. J., Adams, C. E., and Glazebrook, C. (2013). A systematic review of studies of depression prevalence in university students. *Journal of Psychiatric Research*, 47(3): 391–400. Retrieved from http://www.sciencedirect.com/science/article/pii/S0022395612000357
Kessler, R. C. (1997). The effects of stressful life events on depression. *Annual Review of Psychology*, 48: 191–214. Retrieved from https://www.ncbi.nlm.nih.gov/pubmed/9046559
Kim, T. J., and von dem Knesebeck, O. (2016). Perceived job insecurity, unemployment and depressive symptoms: a systematic review and meta-analysis of prospective observational studies. *International Archives of Occupational and Environmental Health*, 89(4): 561–73. doi:10.1007/s00420-015-1107-1
King, M., Semlyen, J., Tai, S. S., et al. (2008). A systematic review of mental disorder, suicide, and deliberate self harm in lesbian, gay and bisexual people. *BMC Psychiatry*, 8: 70. doi:10.1186/1471-244X-8-70
Klimstra, T. A., and Denissen, J. J. A. (2017). A theoretical framework for the associations between identity and psychopathology. *Developmental Psychology*, 53(11): 2052–65. doi:10.1037/dev0000356
Kodish, T., Lau, A. S., Gong-Guy, E., Congdon, E., Arnaudova, I., and Schmidt, M., et al. (2022). Enhancing racial/ethnic equity in college student mental health through innovative screening and treatment. *Administration and Policy in Mental Health*, 49: 267–82. doi:10.1007/s10488-021-01163-1
Kraus, Michael W., and Park, Jun W. (2014). The undervalued self: Social class and self-evaluation. *Frontiers in Psychology*, 5: 1404.
Kutsyuruba, Benjamin, Klinger, Don, and Hussain, Alicia. (2015). Relationships among school climate, school safety, and student achievement and well-being: A review of the literature. *The Review of Education*, 3: 103–35. doi:10.1002/rev3.3043

Låftman, Sara, Almquist, Ylva, and Östberg, J. (2013). Students' accounts of school-performance stress: A qualitative analysis of a high-achieving setting in Stockholm, Sweden, *Journal of Youth Studies*, 16. doi:10.1080/13676261.2013.780126

Lee, D., and McLanahan, S. (2015). Family structure transitions and child development: Instability, selection, and population heterogeneity. *American Sociological Review*, 80(4): 738–63. doi:10.1177/0003122415592129

Lee, S. Y., Wuertz, C., Rogers, R., and Chen, Y. P. (2013). Stress and sleep disturbances in female college students. *American Journal of Health Behavior*, 37(6): 851–58.

Leonard, N. R., Gwadz, Marya V., Amanda, Ritchie, Linick Jessica, L., Cleland Charles, M., Lereya, Elliott, Copeland, S. T. William E., Costello, E Jane, and Wolk, Dieter. (2015). Adult mental health consequences of peer bullying and maltreatment in childhood: Two cohorts in two countries. *Lancet Psychiatry*, 2: 524–31 Published Online. April 28, 2015. doi:10.1016/S2215-0366(15)00165-0

Lin, Y., Xie, H., Huang, Z., Zhang, Q., Wilson, A., Hou, J., Zhao, X., Wang Y., Pan, B., Liu, Y., Han, M., and Chen, R. (2021). The mental health of transgender and gender non-conforming people in China: A systematic review. *The Lancet Public Health*, 6(12): e954–e969. doi:10.1016/S2468-2667(21)00236-X. PMID: 34838199.

Liu, Y. Y. (2015). The longitudinal relationship between Chinese high school students' academic stress and academic motivation. *Learning and Individual Differences*, 38: 123–126. doi:10.1016/j.lindif.2015.02.002

Long, Janet H., and Chen, Guo-Ming. (2007). "The impact of internet usage on adolescent self-identity development." *China Media Research*, 3(1): 99–109. Available at: http://www.wwdw.chinamediaresearch.net/index.php/back-issues?id=37

Lucassen, M. F., Stasiak, K., Samra, R., and Frampton, C. M., and Merry, S. N. (2017). Sexual minority youth and depressive symptoms or depressive disorder: A systematic review and meta-analysis of population-based studies. *The Australian and New Zealand Journal of Psychiatry*, 51(8): 774–87. doi:10.1177/0004867417713664

Luk, T. T., Wang, M. P., Shen, C., Wan, A., Chau, P. H., Oliffe, J., Viswanath, K., Chan, S. S., and Lam, T. H. (2018). Short version of the smartphone addiction scale in Chinese adults: Psychometric properties, sociodemographic, and health behavioral correlates. *Journal of Behavioral Addictions*, 7(4): 1157–65. doi:10.1556/2006.7.2018.105

Luyckx, Koen, Teppers, Eveline, Klimstra, Theo, and Rassart, Jessica. (2014). Identity processes and personality traits and types in adolescence: Directionality of effects and developmental trajectories. *Developmental Psychology*, 50. doi:10.1037/a0037256

Marcotte, Julie, and Lévesque, Geneviève. (2018). Anxiety and well-being among students in a psychoeducation program: The mediating role of identity. *Journal of College Student Development*, 59: 90–104. doi:10.1353/csd.2018.000

Marmot, M., Allen, J., Goldblatt, P., Boyce, T., McNeish, D., Grady, M., and Geddes, I. (2010). Fair society, healthy lives: Strategic review of health inequalities in England post 2010. Retrieved from https://www.instituteofhealthequity.org/resources-reports/fair-society-healthy-lives-the-marmot-review/fair-society-healthy-lives-exec-summary-pdf.pdf [Accessed 07/11/16].

Marzano, R. J., Marzano, J. S., and Pickering, D. J. (2003). *Classroom Management That Works. Research-Based Strategies for Every Teacher*. New York: Pearson Education.

McManus, S., Bebbington, P. E., Jenkins, R. et al. (2016). *Mental Health and Wellbeing in England: the Adult Psychiatric Morbidity Survey 2014*. Leed, UK: NHS DigitMental Health and Wellbeing in England: the Adult Psychiatric Morbidity Survey 2014. https://openaccess.city.ac.uk/id/eprint/23646/

McNeil, Jay, Bailey, Louis, Ellis, Sonja, Morton, James, and Regan, Maeve. (2012). Trans mental health study. Available from: https://www.scottishtrans.org/wp-content/uploads/2013/03/trans_mh_study.pdf

Molodynski, A. (2021). Mental health care in the UK – a call for urgent action. *Progress in Neurology and Psychiatry*, 25(3): 8–9.

Moylan, S., Maes, M., Wray, N. R., and Berk, M. (2013). The neuro progressive nature of major depressive disorder: Pathways to disease evolution and resistance, and therapeutic implications. *Molecular Psychiatry*, 185: 595–606. Retrieved from http://www.ncbi.nlm.nih.gov/pubmed/22525486

Nelson, C. L., and Andel, R. (2019). Does sexual orientation relate to health and wellbeing? A propensity-score matched analysis. *Innovation in Aging*, 3(Suppl 1): S303. doi:10.1093/geroni/igz038.1111

Nelson, J. M., and Harwood, H. (2011). Learning disabilities and anxiety: A meta-analysis. *Journal of Learning Disabilities*, 44(1): 3–17. doi:10.1177/0022219409359939

Newton, Becci, Patel, Rakhee, Akehurst, Georgie, Alexander, Kate, Byford, Morwenna, Rickard, Catherine, Ebanks-Silvera, De-Jon, Buzzeo, Jonathan, Cook, Joseph, and White-Smith, George. (2021). *Supporting Good Mental Health Amongst London's FE Learners An Assessment of Mental Health Needs and Support Approaches*. London: IES.

Oberle, E., and Schonert-Reichl, K. A. (2016). Stress contagion in the classroom? The link between classroom teacher burnout and morning cortisol in elementary school students. *Social Science & Medicine*, 159: 30–7. doi:10.1016/j.socscimed.2016.04.031

OECD. (2020). PISA 2020 Results (Volume III). Paris, France.

Office of National Statistics (ONS). Cost of living and depression in adults, Great Britain: 29 September to 23 October 2022. https://www.ons.gov.uk/peoplepopulationandcommunity/healthandsocialcare/mentalhealth/articles/costoflivinganddepressioninadultsgreatbritain/29septemberto23october2022

Ozen, N. S., Ercan, I., Irgil, E., and Sigirli, D. (2010). Anxiety prevalence and affecting factors among university students. *Asia-Pacific Journal of Public Health*, 221: 127–133. Retrieved from https://www.ncbi.nlm.nih.gov/pubmed/20032042

Perales, F., Johnson, S. E., Baxter, J., Lawrence, D., and Zubrick, S. R. (2017). Family structure and childhood mental disorders: New findings from Australia. *Social Psychiatry and Psychiatric Epidemiology*, 52(4): 423–433. doi:10.1007/s00127-016-1328-y

Pervanidou, P., and Chrousos, G. P. (2012). Metabolic consequences of stress during childhood and adolescence. *Metabolism*, 615: 611–619. Retrieved from https://www.ncbi.nlm.nih.gov/pubmed/22146091

Potterton, R., Austin, A., Robinson, L., et al. (2022). Identity development and social-emotional disorders during adolescence and emerging adulthood: A systematic review and meta-analysis. *Journal of Youth and Adolescence*, 51: 16–29. doi:10.1007/s10964-021-01536

Putwain, D., and Daly, A. L. (2022). Test anxiety prevalence and gender differences in a sample of English secondary school students. *Educational Studies*, 40(5), 554–570. doi:10.1080/03055698.2014.953914

Reed, B., Rhodes, S., Schofield, P. and Wylie, K. (2009). Gender variance in the UK: Prevalence, incidence, growth and geographic distribution. Retrieved from Gender Identity Research in Education Society (GIRES) website http://www.gires.org.uk/assets/MedproAssets/GenderVarianceUK-report.pdf

Reiss, F. (2013). Socioeconomic inequalities and mental health problems in children and adolescents: A systematic review, *Social Science & Medicine*, 90: 24–31. ISSN 0277-9536, doi:10.1016/j.socscimed.2013.04.026. (https://www.sciencedirect.com/science/article/pii/S0277953613002608).

Reynolds, A. J., Hayakawa, M., Ou, S. R., Mondi, C. F., Englund, M. M., Candee, A. J., and Smerillo, N. E. (2017). Scaling and sustaining effective early childhood programs through school-family-university collaboration. *Child Development*, 88(5): 1453–65. doi:10.1111/cdev.12901

Ribeiro, Í. J. S., et al. (2017). Stress and quality of life among university students: A systematic literature review. *Health Professions Education*. doi:10.1016/j.hpe.2017.03.002

Richards, V. (2018). The importance of language in mental health care. *The Lancet*, 5(6): 460–61.

Robins, Richard W., and Trzesniewski, Kali H. (2005). Self-esteem development across the lifespan. *Current Directions in Psychological Science*, 14(3): 158–62.

Rodway, C., Tham, S. G., Ibrahim, S., Turnbull, P., Windfuhr, K., Shaw, J., Kapur, N., and Appleby, L. (2016). Suicide in children and young people in England: A consecutive case series. *The Lancet Psychiatry*, 3: 699–700.

Russell, S., and Joyner, K. 2001. Adolescent sexual orientation and suicide risk: Evidence from a National study. *American Journal of Public Health*, 91(8): 1271–1281.

Schwartz, H. A., Eichstaedt, J. C., Kern, M. L., Dziurzynski, L., Ramones, S. M., Agrawal, M., et al. (2013). Personality, gender, and age in the language of social media: The open-vocabulary approach. *PLoS One*, 8(9): e73791. doi:10.1371/journal.pone.0073791

Singh, B., and Olds, T., Curtis, R., et al. (2023). Effectiveness of physical activity interventions for improving depression, anxiety and distress: an overview of systematic reviews. *British Journal of Sports Medicine*. doi:10.1136/bjsports-2022-106195

Slimmen, S., Timmermans, O., Mikolajczak Degrauwe, K., and Oenema, A (2022). How stress-related factors affect mental wellbeing of university students A cross-sectional study to explore the associations between stressors, perceived stress, and mental wellbeing. *PLoS One*, 17(11): e0275925. doi:10.1371/journal. pone.027592

Slotter, E. B., and Gardner, W. L. (2011). Can you help me become the "me" I want to be? The role of goal pursuit in friendship formation. *Self and Identity*, 10(2): 231–47. doi:10.1080/15298868.2010.482767

Smith, T. B., and Silva, L. (2011). Ethnic identity and personal well-being of people of color: a meta-analysis. *Journal of Counseling Psychology*, 58(1): 42–60. doi:10.1037/a0021528

Stephens, T. W., Basinski, M., Bristow, P. K., Bue-Valleskey, J. M., Burgett, S. G., Craft, L., ... Heiman, M. (1995). Nature. The role of neuropeptide Y in the antiobesity action of the obese gene product. *Nature*, 377(6549): 530–32. Retrieved from: https://www.ncbi.nlm.nih.gov/pubmed/7566151

Stöber, J. (2004). Dimensions of test anxiety: Relations to ways of coping with pre-exam anxiety and uncertainty. *Anxiety, Stress, and Coping*, 17: 213–26.

Tajfel, H., and Turner, J. C. (1986). The social identity theory of intergroup behavior. In: S. Worchel and W. G. Austin (eds.), *Psychology of Intergroup Relation*. Chicago: Hall Publishers, 7–24.

Tebbe, E. A., and Budge, S. L. (2022). Factors that drive mental health disparities and promote well-being in transgender and nonbinary people. *Nature Reviews Psychology*, 1(12): 694–707. doi:10.1038/s44159-022-00109-0

Tullius, J. M., De Kroon, M. L. A., Almansa, J., and Reijneveld, S. A. (2022). Adolescents' mental health problems increase after parental divorce, not before, and persist until adulthood: a longitudinal TRAILS study. *European Child & Adolescent Psychiatry*, 31(6): 969–78. doi:10.1007/s00787-020-01715-0

University College London. (2022). Study Data from University College London (UCL) update knowledge of bullying (predictors of self-harm and suicide in lgbt youth: the role of gender, socio-economic status, bullying and school experience). Obesity, Fitness & Wellness Week, [online] 09 Apr, 663, Available from: https://link.gale.com/apps/doc/A699214640/AONE?u=bsuc&sid=ebsco&xid=2d216920 [Accessed 23 Nov 2022].

Von der Embse, N.P., Jester, D., Roy, D., and Post, J. (2018). Test anxiety effects, predictors, and correlates: A 30-year meta-analytic review. *Journal of Affective Disorders*, 227: 483–493.

Weale, S. (2019). The Guardian Levels-of-distress-and-illness-among-students-in-uk-alarmingly-high. https://www.theguardian.com/education/2019/mar/05/levels-of-distress-and-illness-among-students-in-uk-alarmingly-high

White, H. J. M., Reisner, S. L., and Pachankis, J. E. (2015). Transgender stigma and health: A critical review of stigma determinants, mechanisms, and interventions. *Social Science & Medicine*, 147: 222–31. doi:10.1016/j.socscimed.2015.11.010

World Health Organisation. (1996). *Health Promoting Schools*. Manilla, Spain: Copyright Cl World Health Organization 1996.
World Health Organization. (2001). *Strengthening Mental Health Promotion*. Geneva: WHO.
Young Minds. (2020). Coronavirus: Impact on young people with mental health needs https://www.youngminds.org.uk/about-us/reports-and-impact/coronavirus-impact-on-young-people-with-mental-health-needs/
Zhu, X., Gao, Y., Gillespie, A., Xin, Y., Qi, J., Ou, J., Zhong, S., Peng, K., Tan, T., Wang, C., and Chen, R. (2019). Health care and mental wellbeing in the transgender and gender-diverse Chinese population. *The Lancet Diabetes and Endocrinology*, 7(5): 339–41. doi:10.1016/S2213-8587(19)30079-8

2 Main issues related to social and emotional wellbeing faced by young people

Depression

Global figures

According to World Health Organization (WHO, 2021):

- Globally, one in seven 10–19 year-olds experiences a mental disorder, accounting for 13% of the global burden of disease in this age group
- Depression, anxiety and behavioural disorders are among the leading causes of illness and disability among adolescents
- Suicide is the fourth leading cause of death among 15–29 year-olds
- The consequences of failing to address adolescent mental health conditions extend to adulthood, impairing both physical and mental health and limiting opportunities to lead fulfilling lives as adults

Depression is estimated to occur among 1.1% of adolescents aged 10–14 years, and 2.8% of 15–19 year-olds. Depression and anxiety share some of the same symptoms, including rapid and unexpected changes in mood. Cumulative rates of depression are higher. For example, academic studies have suggested that over a 12-month period, at least 8% of adolescents will have experienced a depressive episode. Another study has reported that by the age of 18, around 20% of young people will have had a depressive episode (ONS, 2021b).

The NHS Digital survey (2020) collected information on young people's demographics, health, family and socioeconomics to establish any differences between individuals with and without depression. The data showed that depression in young people was more commonly reported in the following groups:

- Older adolescents: Depression rates were highest in 17–19 year-olds (4.8%), followed by 11–16 year-olds (2.7%), and then children aged 5–10 (0.3%)
- Girls: Depression rates were higher in girls (2.8%) than boys (1.3%)
- Special educational needs: Depression rates were higher in young people with special educational needs (3.6%) compared to those without (1.5%)

- Poor general health: Depression rates were higher in young people with fair to very bad general health (7.4%), followed by those with good health (2.6%), and then those with very good health (1.1%)

Depression rates were higher in young people who had a parent experiencing a common mental health disorder, such as anxiety or depression. More young people had depression when living in low-income households or as part of families in receipt of benefits and/or families with unhealthy family functioning. Depression rates did not differ based on ethnic group; neighbourhood deprivation; or different regions of England. Anxiety and depressive disorders can profoundly affect school attendance and schoolwork and this social withdrawal can exacerbate isolation and loneliness and depression which can lead to suicide (WHO, 2021).

Research by World Health Organisation (WHO, 2021) indicates that Depression is estimated to occur among 1.1% of adolescents aged 10–14 years, and 2.8% of 15–19 year-olds. Women are more likely (19%) than men (14%) to report experiencing some form of depression which is consistent across all age groups. Over one in three (35%) women aged 16 to 29 years experienced moderate to severe depressive symptoms compared with 22% of men of the same age.

The Mental Health Foundation (MHF, 2019, 57) has reported that people who are 'socioeconomically disadvantaged were 2–3 times more likely to develop mental health problems'. Such an unequal distribution reflects existing general health inequalities in the UK as identified in study by Marmot (2020), who outlined that people who have a lower level of socio-economic status (SES), will experience more years of depression, ill health and die at an earlier age, than those who have a higher level of SES.

Among working age adults aged 16 to 64 years, those with lower gross personal annual incomes of less than £10,000 a year had the highest rates of moderate to severe depressive symptoms (29%) when compared with all higher income groups, Adults living in the most deprived areas of England (based on the Index of Multiple Deprivation) were twice as likely to experience some form of depression in autumn 2022 (25%) than adults living in the least deprived areas (12%) (Marmot et al., 2020).

Research by Buchanan and Warwick (2020) suggested that depression created barriers to their respondents' learning at times within the classroom. They reported concentration problems due to experiencing fatigue following disrupted sleep, low moods or intrusive auditory hallucinations. This was exacerbated by a lack of feeling safe in the classroom and a sense of fear relating to the stigma of having mental health problems was shared by other students (2021).

Figures can conceal a wide range of differences in age and gender. For example, a 2017 mental health survey conducted in England showed that rates of depression were 9% among 11–16 year-olds and 14.9% in 17–19 year-olds; in the older age group, one in four females (22.4%) had depression. Overall this survey observed an overall prevalence of 2.1% among 5–19 year-olds; in the oldest 17–19 year-old group, the rate was 4.8% (RCPCH, 2020).

It has been hypothesised that social changes, such as greater loneliness, academic strain, widening socio-economic inequality, or a greater willingness to disclose mental health difficulties may account for the rise in depression rates and increased gender gap, but what these factors are remains unknown (Thapar et al., 2022).

According to the Diagnostic and Statistical Manual of Mental Health Disorders (DSM-V. 2023) depression can manifest a variety of symptoms including:

- Low or irritable mood
- Loss of interest or pleasure (Anhedonia)
- Fatigue
- Suicidal thoughts
- Sleep difficulties
- Difficulties with concentration and decision making
- Changes in appetite or weight
- Sluggishness
- Feelings of worthlessness or excess guilt

Combinations of symptoms can vary however in clinical severity, from "mild" to, "moderate" or "severe" depression; age at first onset; comorbidities; and outcomes. Depression can spontaneously remit, recur or persist (persistent depressive disorder) but also herald the onset of later bipolar disorder or schizophrenia (Thapar et al., 2022).

Several risk factors have been identified that help to explain depression's aetiology. These include:

- Genetic factors with genetic risk higher for more severe, recurrent, and early onset depression
- Combined with social stressors such as abuse, bullying, bereavement
- Other mental health issues or learning disabilities such as ADD and ADHD, Bipolar disorder
- Other individual risk factors include temperament (e.g. negative and positive emotionality)
- Potential links between depression and sleep disorder and depression and obesity
- Personality (e.g. neuroticism)
- Certain styles of thinking and behaving (e.g. cognitive rumination)
- A history of anxiety and irritability in childhood
- Chronic physical illness, particularly those that affect the central nervous system (e.g. migraine, epilepsy)
- Having a parent with depression. Approximately 40% of those with an affected parent develop depression
- Problems with the cognitive control of emotion and extreme self-referential thinking. For example, excessive introspection and self-reflection and rumination

- There are also community-level stressors associated with an increased prevalence of depression across age groups include living in poverty, violent neighbourhoods, homelessness, being a refugee or displaced, exposure to war or terrorism and the impact of COVID-19 (Thapar et al., 2022).

Only two-thirds of adolescents with anxiety or depressive disorders seek and access any professional help, and only a minority access specialist mental health support (Radez et al., 2022). Barriers to young people seeking help have been identified as the following:

- Limited-service provision and long waiting times
- A lack of mental health knowledge, including difficulties with mental health problem
- Identification, negative views, and attitudes towards mental health and help-seeking,
- Family circumstances
- Societal views and negative attitudes towards mental health and help-seeking (e.g., stigma and embarrassment), and perceiving help-seeking as a sign of one's weakness
- Making sense of difficulties
- Problem disclosure, ambivalence to seeking help
- The role of others such as peers, teachers etc

A central theme in their research was the struggle in the respondents to find a balance between wanting to be independent and the need for other people's help and support, and commonly relied on adults, particularly their parents and school staff, to access professional help all within the context of the growing need for autonomy and independence that is characteristic of adolescence (Radez et al., 2022).

Figure 2.1 Five ways you can help your students manage their depression

Encourage them to:

- *Stay in touch with friends and family. This can include things like talking to one person about your feelings, spending time with your friends or family or volunteering, meeting new people by joining a club*
- *Do things that make them feel good. Use hobbies, social life, me-time as methods for a quick mood boost*
- *Exercise for 30 minutes a day building up to this from 10 minutes if need be*
- *Eat a healthy, depression-fighting diet reducing their intake of foods that can adversely affect their brain and mood, such as caffeine, alcohol, trans fats, and foods with high levels of chemical preservatives or hormones*

> (such as certain meats). Suggest that they boost their B vitamins. Deficiencies in B vitamins such as folic acid and B-12 can trigger depression so they might want to take a B-complex vitamin supplement or eat more citrus fruit, leafy greens, beans, chicken, and eggs. Alternatively, they could boost their moods with foods rich in omega-3 fatty acids. Omega-3 fatty acids play an essential role in stabilising mood. The best sources are fatty fish such as salmon, herring, mackerel, anchovies, sardines, tuna, and some cold-water fish oil supplements
> - Expose themselves to sunlight on a daily basis for at least 15 minutes per day. Sunlight can help boost serotonin levels and improve their moods and increase the amount of natural light in their homes by opening blinds and drapes and sitting near windows.

The impact of COVID-19 lockdowns on depression in young people

According to Mind's survey of 1917 young people aged 13–24 from 16338 respondents (2020):

- 69% had pre-existing problems with depression
- Two thirds of young people said that their mental health has become worse during the period of lockdown restrictions, from early April to mid-May
- Loneliness and boredom were key contributors to poor mental health. Feelings of loneliness have made nearly two thirds of people's mental health worse during the past month, with 18–24 year-olds the most likely to see loneliness affect their mental health
- One in four young people did not access support during lockdown because they did not think that they deserved support
- Nearly a third of respondents used alcohol or illegal drugs, with 18–24 year-olds using this coping strategy more than over-25s
- A third of young people with existing mental health problems used self-harming to cope
- 63% of women and 67% of non-binary people said their mental health had become worse over this period in comparison to half (51%) of men
- Over half (58%) of under-18s who received free school meals said their mental health was poor or very poor (vs 41% not), with nearly three quarters (73%) of this group saying that it had become worse during lockdown

The impact of the lockdowns and restrictions during the period of between March 2020 and March 2022 was clearly reflected in levels of depression and anxiety which broadly corresponded with COVID-19 waves, lockdowns, and restrictions. By the time the first lockdown was introduced, depression and anxiety levels were already higher than normal levels, driven by fears and stresses relating to the virus and surrounding uncertainty (Fancourt et al., 2022).

According to research by Daley et al. (2022) the increase in mental health problems was largest among those aged 18–34 years and younger adults (aged 18–34) experienced a 18.6% increase in risk of mental health problems whereas those aged 50–64 experienced a 9.3% increase.

During this period young adults, women, those of lower SES, unemployed individuals, and people with disabilities, chronic physical illnesses, and a mental health condition were most at risk of having thoughts of suicide or self-harm, and harming themselves. Suicidal ideation and self-harm have affected on average 20% of young adults since March 2020, and only 10% among the 60+ age group. (Fancourt et al., 2022). Young adults' poor mental health may also be connected to their coping strategies. During the pandemic, they were more likely to use harmful avoidant strategies to cope with the pandemic, such as drinking alcohol, substance use, denial, or withdrawing from others, which can later have negative effects on mental health (Taylor et al., 2021).

The rise in mental health issues was more than twice as large for women, particularly young women aged between18–35, as for men. Research by Etheridge and Spantig (2022) suggested that this was due to a variety of factors including: family and caring responsibilities; financial and work situation; social engagement; health situation, and health behaviours, including exercise and gender differences in personality traits.

According to research by Thapar et al. (2022) the long-term effects of depression on young women can include depression recurrence; the onset of other psychiatric disorders for example, schizophrenia and wider, protracted impairments in interpersonal, social, educational, and occupational functioning.

Figure 2.2 Teachers self-test

How much do you know about young people and depression?
Activities:
Multiple-choice questions:

1 *Which of the following is a core symptom of depression in young people?*

   a *Low mood*
   b *Irritability*
   c *Deliberate self-harm*
   d *Loss of pleasure in life*
   e *Lack of energy*
   f **All the above**

2 *What is the estimated prevalence of depression in adolescents?*

   a *It does not exist*
   b *1%*
   c *5%*
   d *10%*
   e *30%*

3 What are some of the central causes of depression in young people?

   a Over-eating
   b Social media
   c Drug abuse
   d Trauma
   e Course work struggles
   f **All the above**

Figure 2.3 Here's a multiple-choice question (MCQ) that I devised for my students to use during a tutorial about wellbeing (Zoe, Learning coach)

1 What is the most important way to improve mental health and well-being?

   a Exercise regularly
   b Get enough sleep
   c **Spend time with loved ones**
   d Eat healthy food

   Answer: c. Spend time with loved ones

2 What is the most effective way to cope with stress?

   a **Talk to a friend**
   b Listen to music
   c Read a book
   d Take a walk

   Answer: a. Talk to a friend

3 What is the best way to manage anxiety?

   a **Take a deep breath**
   b Take medication
   c Avoid stress
   d Get a massage

   Answer: a. Take a deep breath

4 What is the most important factor for maintaining good mental health?
   a **Positive attitude**
   b Healthy diet
   c Regular sleep
   d Stress management

   Answer: a. Positive attitude

5 What is the best way to reduce the risk of mental health issues?

   a   Exercise regularly
   b   Get enough sleep
   c   Avoid stress
   d   **Talk to a friend**

   Answer: d. Talk to a friend

6 What is the most effective way to manage depression?

   a   **Seek help from a professional**
   b   Exercise regularly
   c   Spend time alone
   d   Talk to a friend

   Answer: a. Seek help from a professional

7 What is the best way to improve mental clarity?

   a   **Meditate**
   b   Exercise
   c   Get enough sleep
   d   Avoid stress

   Answer: a. Meditate

8 What is the most important factor for maintaining good mental health?

   a   **Positive attitude**
   b   Healthy diet
   c   Regular sleep
   d   Stress management

   Answer: a. Positive attitude

9 What is the best way to cope with negative emotions?

   a   **Talk to a friend**
   b   Listen to music
   c   Take a walk
   d   Read a book

   Answer: a. Talk to a friend

10 What is the most important way to improve mental health and well-being?

   a   Exercise regularly
   b   Get enough sleep
   c   **Spend time with loved ones**
   d   Eat healthy food

   Answer: c. Spend time with loved ones

Anxiety

Background

Anxiety disorders are among the most prevalent and earliest developing mental disorders (Beesdo-Baum and Knappe, 2012; Kessler et al., 2010). They frequently take a chronic and impairing course, co-occur with other mental disorders (Beesdo-Baum and Knappe, 2012; Kessler et al., 2010) and can develop into other mental health issues from childhood over adolescence to adulthood (Niermann et al., 2021).

Anxiety disorders are characterised by an uncomfortable emotional state, negative feelings about the future, or distress that triggers a sense of defence that serves as a warning so that the individual can prepare to face a possibly dangerous situation. Anxiety can be a normal reaction or can become pathological (Mondin et al., 2013).

During adolescence and young adulthood young people undergo major physical, cognitive, and psychosocial changes, making them vulnerable to external and environmental pressures and susceptible to the development of anxiety disorders). Anxiety is associated with an increased risk of subsequent onset of anxiety disorders, including depression, substance use disorders and physical health problems (Beesdo-Baum and Knappe, 2012; de Lijster et al., 2018; Holmes et al., 2018).

Research shows that anxiety issues in young adults are the result of a combination of genetic makeup and life circumstances. Between 30% and 40% of the factors related to anxiety disorders are genetic, parental and can be inherited. Life experiences are also significant in determining the likelihood of an anxiety disorder. Early Life Stress (ELS) events, such as abuse, neglect, or the early death of a parent, are risk factors for anxiety and can contribute to the likelihood of anxiety disorders in young adults (Beesdo-Baum and Knappe, 2012).

ONS figures from Spring 2022 suggested young people's levels of anxiety in the UK were still consistently higher post- COVID. Around four in ten (42%) of 16- 29 year-olds questioned said they experienced high levels of anxiety, which was above that of other age groups. For example, 34% of 30- 49 year-olds reported high anxiety 31% of 50- 69 year-olds and 30% of people aged 70 and over. On a scale of 0 to 10, where 0 is "not at all" and 10 is "completely", the average score for people aged 16- 29 in the survey was 4.9. 25% of the respondents in this age group said they felt lonely always, often, or some of the time (ONS, 2022).

The level of anxiety in young women has increased over the past few years in the UK. According to a 2022 survey nearly one-third (31%) women aged 16 to 24 years in the UK reported feeling depressed or suffering from anxiety between 2018 to 2020; this is an increase from the previous year (26%) and the same period five years earlier (26%) (ONS, 2022).

Some explanations may be related to factors such as greater cultural acceptance of fear and avoidance behaviour in women and different adaptive patterns. Young males tend to use substances such as nicotine and alcohol as self-medication, which could mask the primary symptoms of anxiety disorders (Mondin et al., 2013.)

The COVID-19 crisis significantly affected the lives of young people (15–24 year-olds), and research by the OEDC points to a surge in mental health issues among this age group and across many OEDC countries. For example, in Belgium, France and the U.S. anxiety and depression was around 30% to 80% higher among young people than the general population (OEDC, 2021). Research by Racine et al. (2021) confirmed that 25% of young people globally suffered from depression and 20% experienced anxiety symptoms suggesting that youth mental health difficulties during the COVID-19 pandemic probably doubled over the period.

Types of anxiety disorder

- Generalised Anxiety Disorder (GAD) is the most common type of anxiety in young adults. This type of anxiety involves excessive worry and distress over everyday occurrences. GAD affects 3.1% of the UK. population, yet only 43.2% are receiving treatment. Women are twice as likely to be affected as men. GAD often co-occurs with major depression. Even though the age of onset for anxiety disorders is typically in childhood or adolescence, GAD can still be expected in old age (50 years or more (Munir and Takov, 2023).

    GAD is defined as persistent or chronic worry and tension with the most common symptoms being sleep disturbances, diminished concentration, irritability, and restlessness (Dursun et al., 2022). It is the most common mental disorder among children and adolescents with estimated prevalence ranging between 0.9% and 28.3%, 45.82 million incident cases and 301.39 million prevalent cases. Global research on adolescents, including 82 countries with wide geographic variety and cultural background, reported anxiety prevalence ranging from 7% to 12% (Sabbagh et al., 2022)
- Social Anxiety Disorder (SAD), also referred to as social phobia, refers to anxiety triggered by social settings. Therefore, social anxiety in young adults can interfere with everyday activities at work or in school. Social anxiety is defined as fear or anxiety about social situations in which there is possible scrutiny by others (Schneier et al., 2000).

    Individuals who have SAD visibly struggle with social situations. They show fewer facial expressions, avert their gaze more often, and express greater difficulty initiating and maintaining conversations compared to individuals without social anxiety. This can lead to individuals reducing their interactions or shying away from engaging with others (Jefferies and Ungar, 2020). Over 18% of young people may have SAD which may be linked to high usage of social media (Kim et al., 2022)
- Panic Disorder (PD) is a debilitating anxiety disorder, characterised by repeated, unexpected panic attacks, involving physical symptoms, such as a racing heart, dizziness and chest pain, along with a fear of recurring attacks and changes in behaviour to avoid further attacks (Cackovic et al., 2022).

It occurs in 2–3% of the global populationis most common amongst adolescents and is characterised by recurrent, unexpected episodes of intense anxiety for a period of at least one month (Norholm and Ressler, 2009).

PD affects 2.7% of the U.K population. Women are twice as likely to be affected as men. Panic disorder commonly co-occurs with other anxiety disorders, particularly agoraphobia and is more prevalent among girls (1.7%) than boys (0.5%) (Baker et al., 2022)
- Specific Phobias. A phobia, which is considered a type of anxiety disorder, is an irrational fear or aversion to something that poses little or no actual danger, such as spiders, heights, germs, etc. Specific phobias affect 9.1% of the UK. population. The most common phobia types across both community and clinical samples are the animal and natural environment types (Milne et al., 1995). Women are twice as likely to be affected than men. Symptoms typically begin in childhood; the average age of onset is 7 years old (Ollendick et al., 2010).

Figure 2.4   Mental exercises

Use mental exercises to take your student's mind off uncomfortable thoughts and feelings. They are discreet and easy to use at nearly any time or place. Experiment to see which works most effectively for them.

- *Name all the objects you see*
- *Describe the steps in performing an activity you know how to do well. For example, prepare your favourite meal, or doing your make up*
- *Count backwards from 100 by 7*
- *Pick up an object and describe it in detail. Describe its colour, texture, size, weight, scent, and any other qualities you notice*
- *Spell your full name, and the names of three other people, backwards*
- *Name all your family members, their ages, and one of their favourite activities*
- *Read something backwards, letter-by-letter. Practice for at least a few minutes*
- *Think of an object and "draw" it in your mind, or in the air with your finger. Try drawing your home, a vehicle, or an animal*

- Obsessive-Compulsive Disorder (OCD). Obsessive-compulsive disorder (OCD) is characterised by the presence of unwanted, intrusive obsessions (unpleasant thoughts, images or urges) and compulsions (repetitive behaviours which may be covert, e.g. mental counting). OCD in young adults can cause unwanted and disturbing obsessions that create extreme anxiety for them, and to relieve the anxiety they can engage in repetitive thoughts or actions known as compulsions. for example, excessive hand washing, counting, or repeatedly checking that a door is locked (Williams and Shafran, 2015). Research suggests that OCD affects between 0.3 and 5.6% of 5- 18 year-olds and that it increases dramatically in teenage years. It shares symptoms with GAD and with Autism and is often confused with the two (Williams and Shafran, 2015).

There are specific thinking errors in OCD which often need to be challenged when working with individual sufferers. These include thought-action fusion, the belief that thinking about a bad event makes it more likely to happen to another person; sole responsibility, where people with OCD believe that they alone are responsible for the prevention of harm; black and white thinking involving judgment about own behaviour and perfectionism which can result in harsh self-criticism (Williams and Shafran, 2015).

- Post-Traumatic Stress Disorder (PTSD) is seen as unique amongst those classified as anxiety disorders because it is inherently associated with both environmental (e.g. a triggering traumatic event) and genetic contributions (Norholm and Ressler, 2009). PTSD along with depression and GAD is classified as a distress disorder (Slade and Watson, 2006). Research from King's College London suggested one in 13 young people in the UK have had post-traumatic stress disorder before reaching age 18. Of the young people in the study who had PTSD 75% had another mental health condition at age 18, 50% had self-harmed and 20% had attempted suicide since age 12 (Lewis et al., 2018)
- PTSD is defined in DSM-V as the development of symptoms following exposure to an extreme traumatic event in which an individual experienced an actual or perceived threat of death or serious injury or threat to physical integrity; or witnessed an event that involved an actual or perceived threat of death, serious bodily injury or threat to the physical integrity of to another individual (DSM-5-TR).
- The symptoms of PTSD are characterised as belonging to one of three independents, but often interconnected, groupings. These are flashbacks or nightmares, avoidance of trauma related stimuli, irritability, hypervigilance, and consistent episodes of depression. It can also combine with Major Depressive Disorder (MDD), and GAD (Breslau et al., 2000).

Figure 2.5 Self-reflection questions

1. *How do you know when one of your student is anxious?*
2. *Will anyone tell you that they are behaving differently?*
3. *Will you wait before doing anything in the hope that it goes away after a time on its own accord?*
4. *If not what will help it to go away?*

Figure 2.6 Case study

One of my students wanted to be a Reporter when he finished his Media course so I set him this research exercise on a worksheet to understand where their feelings of anxiety might have come from.

Your closest ancestors are your mother, father, grandparents, and great-grandparents on both sides of your family. Interview as many of these people as you can in person, or on the phone. Ask them the following questions and transcribe their answers on separate sheets of paper.

1 Which words would you use to describe anxiety?
2 Would you describe yourself as a highly anxious, moderately anxious, or rarely anxious person, and why?
3 Explain how you experience the feeling of anxiety in your body, mind, and emotions.
4 Explain what you do to manage anxiety when you feel it.
5 Describe how any or all of your responses may have changed over the course of your life.

Now ask yourself the same questions and record your answers here.

Look back over the answers to your relatives' interview questions. Describe any patterns you see in the answers.

How do your relatives' answers compare to your answers?

What, if anything, do you better understand about yourself in relation to anxiety by having learned about your relatives?

Eating issues, eating disorders and mental health

Eating issues

Six in ten (60%) 17-19 year-olds have "possible problems with eating", according to research undertaken by NHS Digital (2022). More than 50% of older teenagers and young adults in England have a problematic relationship with food. 62.3% of 19-23 year-olds have the same issues which include individuals feeling shame about how much they eat, deliberately making themselves vomit or being anxious about their appearance. The problems are more common among girls and young women than their male peers. 75% of girls and young women aged 17- 19 and 45% of boys reported similar feelings or behaviours which has increased from 44% in 2017 to 60% in 2022.

Eating Disorders (ED) can be triggered by a range of factors which include genetics, personality traits such as perfectionism, negative body image, low self-esteem and factors such as grief, abuse or stress which has been compounded by the after effects of the COVID-19 lockdown such as the stress and anxiety induced by young people's inability to go to school, concern about relatives' health, or isolation from friends (NHS Digital, 2022).

According to DSM-5 classification, the most prominent EDs are anorexia nervosa (AN), bulimia nervosa (BN), and binge eating disorder (BED), referred to as the three typical EDs. Other EDs are referred to as "atypical" forms of these disorders or named Other Specified Feeding or Eating Disorders (OSFEDs) (2023).

An eating disorder is a mental health condition where people use the control of food to cope with feelings and other situations. Unhealthy eating behaviours may include eating too much or too little or worrying about weight or body shape. Teenagers between 13 and 17 are mostly affected (NHS Digital 2020). EDs are serious mental illnesses characterised by disturbances of body image and eating behaviour (DSM-5, 2023). They typically have their onset during the transition to adulthood; mean age of onset for AN and BN is between 15 and 19 (Potterton et al., 2020)

A person with an eating disorder is five times more likely to abuse drugs or alcohol than a person without an eating disorder, and a person with a substance abuse problem is 11 times more likely to have an eating disorder. Conversely, 35% of substance abusers have been found to also have an eating disorder, compared to the 3% of the general population diagnosed with an eating disorder (Hudson, et al 2007).

Young people with eating disorders also reported that the COVID-19 lockdown had a negative effective on their EDs, for instance, their thoughts, feelings of anxiety, depression (73%), and isolation and a decrease in motivation to recover (Vitagliano et al., 2021).

Types of eating disorders

The most common eating disorders are:

- Anorexia nervosa which is associated with trying to control weight by not eating enough food, exercising too much, or doing both. It can result in severe weight loss, secondary to distorted body image, intense fear of gaining weight and resultant pathological dieting or food restriction. Anorexia has a lifetime prevalence of 0.9% in women and 0.3% in men (Galmiche et al., 2019)
- Bulimia Nervosa which is associated with losing control over how much is eaten and then taking drastic action to not put on weight. Frequent excessive eating (known as a food binge) followed by inappropriate purging (such as self-induced vomiting, abuse of laxatives and/or excessive exercising) to avoid weight gain. Bulimia has a lifetime prevalence of 1.5% for women and 0.5% for men (Potterton et al., 2020). It is sometimes related to Binge Eating Disorder (BED) which involves episodes of compulsively eating very large amounts of food with a sense of loss of control and is known to effect 3.5% among women and 2% of men (Huryk et al., 2021)

- Other Specified Feeding or Eating Disorders (OSFED). A person may have an OSFED if their symptoms do not exactly fit the expected symptoms for any specific eating disorders. OSFED is the most common eating disorder (Hay et al., 2023)

Figure 2.7 Supporting exercise

Working on concrete goals in eating disorder recovery can be a valuable tool. Here are some example areas for improvement or coping strategies you can try with students:

- *Asserting myself*
- *Being spontaneous*
- *Learning new coping mechanisms*
- *Communicating*
- *Decision making*
- *Eating with others, family and friends*
- *Expression of feelings*
- *Feeling in charge of myself*
- *Having fun*

Figure 2.8 Supportive suggestions

Changing their Mind-sets
   Instead of leaving their thoughts on automatic, encourage your students to recognise and stop the negatives. This could be facilitated by them

- *Practicing different, more positive self-talk through speaking and writing (such as writing positive thoughts in a journal and rehearsing them out loud regardless of whether they really believe them)*
- *Questioning their beliefs systems/When they discover that old ones do not apply to their present lives, it creates a space for them to create new ones*
- *Having discussions with other people about what they believe*
- *Being open to constructive criticism*
- *Redirecting or reframing negative statements. For example, saying out aloud, "I am a great person," even if they don't believe it 100%*
- *Taking quiet time to give their minds a rest and moving "beyond" the chatter. When they quiet their mind, they can more easily listen to their inner voices*
- *Thoughts and feelings are connected and by changing the way they think, and they change the way they feel*

Eating Disorders (EDs) amongst older learners

EDs typically have their onset during the transition to adulthood from 18–25 during periods of demographic change (eg. changes in residence, occupation and relationships) (Potterton et al., 2020).

According to research by Potterton et al. (2020) approximately a quarter of this age group engage in unhealthy weight control behaviours, whilst up to 10% may engage in binge-eating, and between 11 and 20% have probable ED and that possibly 19% meet the criteria for Bulimic Eating Disorder. Binge eating can have a series of psychosocial outcomes in later adulthood including depression (Mason and Heron, 2016).

Figure 2.9   Journal Writing

Helping activity

Encourage your student to do the following activities and feedback on their success when you see them next:

1. *Write in your journal at least once a day*
2. *Check in with yourself through your journal*
    Write when you feel anxious, lonely, afraid, overwhelmed, etc
3. *Write about your goals*
    What DO you hope to accomplish through recovery? Self-respect, nurturing relationships, coping skills, etc. With your list in front of you, ask that this list come true. Repeat this process throughout your eating disorder recovery, as your goals will change as you grow. Asking for what you want will not only point you towards your future, but it will also help you let go of the past.
4. *Eating disorder recovery journal prompts:*
    Write one sentence each about five or ten good things in your life.
    Describe one of the happiest moments of your life. Try to remember why you felt so good about yourself at that time. Hold on to those good feelings for the rest of the day.
    List ten people you admire (five you personally know and five you know from society or history). What attributes do they have that you admire? List your attributes. Which ones do you admire in yourself?
    Pick one family member and write in-depth about your impressions of them as well as your relationship with them. Describe some dramatic experiences you had together. Why were those events so relevant, and how did they make you feel? Choose another family member on another writing occasion.
    Make a list of 5–10 myths and 5–10 rules that you want to change. A myth may be something like, "Skinny people are happier," and a rule might be, "If I eat dessert, I have to do 100 sit-ups."
    Make lists of short-term and long-term goals. Cross out any entries that have to do with losing weight, burning calories, etc.

Self-harming

> **Figure 2.10 Teacher myth buster quiz**
>
> *Test your own understanding of self-harm with these questions:*
>
> 1. Students who self-harm are attempting suicide.
>   True
>   **False**
> 2. Students who self-harm are attention seeking.
>   True
>   **False**
> 3. If you ignore someone's self-harm they'll stop.
>   True
>   **False**
> 4. Only young people self-harm.
>   True
>   **False**
> 5. Everyone who self-harms has been abused.
>   True
>   **False**
> 6. Only people with mental health problems self-harm.
>   True
>   **False**
> 7. Stopping self-harming is easy if the young person really wants to
>   True
>   **False**
> 8. Self-harm is the latest craze with young people.
>   True
>   **False**
> 9. People who self-harm need to be seen by a doctor.
>   True
>   **False**
> 10. Talking about self-harm makes it worse.
>   True
>   **False**
> 11. Cutting is the only form of self-harm.
>   True
>   **False**
> 12. People self-harm when they feel (circle as many as you agree with):
>   Bored Depressed Upset Confident
>   Guilty Frustrated Angry Confused

> *Lonely Anxious Hopeful Tired*
> *Desperate Happy Fulfilled Relaxed*
>
> *Quiz answers*
> 1. to 11. False
> 12 All of them.

Self-harm is used variously as a coping mechanism, a strategy of emotion regulation, self-punishment, or a cry for help, among other things. According to Liu and Mustanski (2012) other reasons for self-harm included pressure, isolation, not fitting in, anger and frustration with themselves, panic attacks, the need to take control of something, the need to escape, bereavement and stress caused by examinations and school. It is associated with poor educational attainment and employment prospects, mental health problems, and increased risk of substance misuse in early adulthood (Compas et al., 2017).

Self-harm affects up to 25% of young people and can result in adverse outcomes including repetition of self-harm, suicide and mortality, mental health morbidity, poorer education and employment outcomes, and overall decreased quality of life, as well as being costly to treat (Mars et al., 2014; Robinson, 2017).

Self-harm is common in young people: at least 10% report having self-harmed. It is more common in females than males, especially in early adolescence. Self-harm is much less frequent in younger children, but under the age of 11 self-harm is more common in boys than in girls. It has been suggested that four times as many girls than boys have direct experience of self-harm (Fox and Hawton, 2004).

Young people who have experienced self-harm are more likely to report suicidal ideation and plans for suicide and to report greater levels of emotional distress, difficulties with anger and low self-esteem, as well as antisocial behaviour and health risk behaviours such as illicit drug use than those that do not (Laye-Gindhu and Schonert-Reichl, 2005 Hetrick et al., 2020). Some of the key groups at risk of self-harm include:

- Young people in institutional or residential settings (including the armed forces, sheltered housing or foyers and boarding schools) (Rouski et al., 2021)
- Young people under the age of 21 in custodial settings. Since 2011, there has been a decline in the rates of self-harm among women, while self-harm among men has risen. The rate per 1000 male prisoners had increased by 90% from 161 incidents per 1000 prisoners in December 2006 to 306 at the end of 2015. The rate of incidents per 1000 male prisoners in 2015 increased by 31% from 2014. However, 25% of prisoners self-harm,

according to research by Pope (2018). This was particularly true of young women; 65% of females under 21 harmed themselves and 10% of young males
- LGBTQ+ young people who report higher rates of self-harm than heterosexual young people (they are two to three times more likely to self-harm). Hatchel et al. (2020) found that 72% of LGBTQ+ young people reported a regular history of absenteeism at school due to homophobic harassment; 50% reported they had contemplated self-harm, and 40% had self-harmed at least once
- There appears to be comparatively little research about the actual experience and needs of young men and women who self-harm from black and minority ethnic groups and communities, in spite of the fact that young people from ethnic minorities face unique socioeconomic and cultural challenges that may contribute to disproportionately higher stress exposure (Coyle and Vera, 2013; Perry-Parrish et al., 2016). Some research suggests the rates of self-harm and eating disorders are believed to be higher among adolescent South Asian girls than their non-Asian counterparts (Soni-Raleigh, 1996)
- Research has suggested that this may be the consequence of a variety of complex and contradictory factors including isolation and despair, forms of abuse within families, conflicts between generations in families but also additional religious and social pressures (Bhardwaj, 2001). A study led by University of Manchester researchers' suggested rates of self-harm could be rising more quickly in children and adolescents from ethnic minority groups than in those from white groups (Farooq et al., 2021). The same study found higher average annual increases among Black and South Asian young people and those from other non-white ethnic groups compared to young white people (2021). Young people from an ethnic minority background were also more likely to live in economically deprived areas, less likely to report mental health issues and less likely to be receiving mental health care than their white counterparts.
- The researchers suggested that increases after 2011 may be associated with deprivation, poverty, and cuts in public services which might have particularly affected those living in poorer communities (2021). According to research by Cooper et al. (2006) the rates of self-harm were highest in young Black females (16–34 years) in the three cities.in the UK surveyed. White females were more likely to present with self-injury (mostly cutting) as a method of harm, compared with South Asian and Black females, who were more likely to self-poison using non-ingestible substances (mostly cleaning fluids). The latter were also more likely to be unemployed and report housing problems compared with Caucasian women (Cooper et al., 2006)
- 40% of young people with learning difficulties are likely to develop a diagnosed mental health problem and although they experience the same range of mental health problems as other young people, they are more prone to

depression and anxiety disorders and these often go unrecognised and untreated which can lead to self-harm (Emerson and Hatton, 2007). According to the National Autistic Society autistic people are more likely to self-harm than non-autistic people and autistic women are more likely to self-harm than autistic men. (NAS, 2021). The most common forms of self-harm amongst young people with learning disabilities include self-hitting, skin picking, self-biting self-cutting and self-burning (Licence et al., 2020)

Figure 2.11 Class exercise to be used in tutorials when discussing self-harm

I find using class discussions in tutorials a good way of teaching sensitive emotional issues. For example, when I am teaching about self-harm and mental health issues, I use a smart board or flip chart on which I have written two headings, "Feelings that are hard to deal with" and the other "Feelings that are easy to deal with". Then I ask my class to begin to identify these feelings and write them down in the appropriate columns. Once we have a list of five or six feelings under both headings, I choose one from each and ask the class to give examples of when they might feel like that. Then we develop this by looking at life events that could trigger both the 'positive' feeling and the 'negative' ones. In our discussions we always make it clear that it is not the feeling that is good or bad but the event that caused it and how it is managed by the person themselves (Jeremiah, Physics teacher).

Self-harm is a continuum of self-harm behaviours including: self-harm as a response to coping with psychosocial stressors associated with developmental milestones, self-harm with clinical symptoms (anxiety and depression are the most common), and self-harm that signals a young person's intent to commit suicide (Bailey and Wright, 2017). Examples of self-harming include:

- Self-cutting
- Taking an overdose
- Swallowing objects or poisons
- Hitting or bruising
- Self-strangulation with ligatures
- Burning

Young people often hide their self-harm, but there are several signs that they may be self-harming. These include:

- Unexplained cuts, burns or bruises
- Keeping themselves covered, avoiding swimming, or changing clothes around others

Signs of self-harm may be similar to signs of physical or other abuse. For example, cigarette burns or bruises could be inflicted by the young person themselves or by someone else, so it may be hard to know the reason behind a given sign.

Other non-specific signs of self-harm (which may also relate to other mental health problems) include:

- Becoming withdrawn or isolated
- Low mood; lack of interest in usual activities; lowering of academic grades
- Sudden changes in behaviour e.g. becoming irritable, angry or aggressive
- Excessive self-blame for problems, expressing feelings of failure, uselessness or hopelessness (Bailey and Wright, 2017).

Research by Hetrick et al. (2020) identified six factors / triggers for self-harm from their qualitative study of seven young people. These were:

- Distressing emotions. These include feelings like helplessness and guilt, unworthiness of being depressed, feeling like a burden on others, Shame, embarrassment, feeling overwhelmed because of lack of control, confused because of mental health and emotions and anxious and angry with themselves because of their bottled up emotions. Research has also found an association between parental criticism and self-harm (Hetrick et al., 2020)
- Sense of isolation. This seems to arise from issues with friends or family and this triggered the urge to self-harm. Young people mention feelings of family conflict, no friends at school, not belonging, stigmatisation because of sexual orientation, people were not accepting of who they were, feelings of alienation and no support and feelings of suicide (Joiner, 2005)
- Exposure to self-harm. Research has shown that graphic images of self harm on social media lead to comparison and competitiveness regarding the severity of wounds, and that graphic images can lead to young people believing self-harm is an acceptable coping method (Lewis and Baker, 2011; Baker and Lewis, 2013)
- Relationship difficulties. Amongst the family feelings included isolation, high parental expectations/disappointing parents, parental lack of understanding, lack of support and lack of communication. Relationship difficulties amongst peers and friends included explaining self-harm scars, sexual harassment, and bullying (including cyber-bullying). With partners, self-harming could be triggered by having a relationship with someone who also engages in self-harm, lack of communication and a relationship break-up (Baker and Lewis, 2013)
- Social comparison. There is a variety triggers involved with social comparison including identifying with others' personal stories, competition with peers on social media, perceived social norms that they do not fit into, pressure from competing with peers' academic performances (Plener et al., 2015)

Main issues related to social and emotional wellbeing 51

- School/work difficulties. These included the following pressures: exams, deadlines Year 12 pressure competing with peers' academic success, hostile work environment, lack of support from colleagues or management
- Research by Madge et al. (2008) suggested that central factors most consistently associated with self-harm, across countries and gender, were attempted suicide or self-harm in a family member, drug use and a low self-image and low self-esteem

---

Figure 2.12   Self- reflection exercise

Here are three comments made by students about the reasons why they harm themselves:

Comment one

Pain works. Pain heals. If I had never cut myself, I probably wouldn't still be around today. My parents didn't help me, religion didn't help me, school didn't help me, but self-harm did. And I'm doing pretty well for myself these days. Don't get me wrong, not in a heartbeat do I think that self-harm is a healthy coping mechanism, but it saved me."

Comment two

There is no better way for me to release the intense emotions I feel than through self-harm. It's like a release valve for all the pain inside me. I know it's not the best solution, but during those moments, it's the only thing that helps.

Comment three

Self-harm gives me a sense of control and distraction from overwhelming emotions. It's the only way I know how to cope when things get too much.

If these were made to you as their teacher, how would you respond to them?

Possible response to comment one

I'm sorry to hear that you haven't received the support you needed from various sources, but I want to emphasize that self-harm is not a healthy coping mechanism. While it might have provided some temporary relief, it is important to seek healthier and safer alternatives to deal with emotional pain. There are professionals who can offer you support to explore healthier coping strategies.

> **Possible response to comment two**
>
> *I hear that self-harm feels like a release for you during intense emotional moments, but it's crucial to consider the potential harm and risks associated with it. It is understandable that you may feel that it's the only thing that helps, but I encourage you to reach out to a mental health professional who can assist you in finding healthier coping mechanisms that provide long-term relief without causing harm.*
>
> **Possible response to comment three**
>
> *I understand that self-harm might give you a sense of control and temporary distraction from overwhelming emotions, but it is important to remember that self-harm is not a sustainable or healthy solution. It's essential to explore alternative coping strategies that can help you manage your emotions in a healthier and safer way. Seeking support from therapists or counsellors can be beneficial in finding alternative techniques that provide a sense of control without causing harm*

According to Bailey and Wright (2017), there are a series of misleading myths and stereotypes associated with the behaviour of young people who self-harm, some of which are reinforced by public opinion and the media. This can result in lack of understanding, negative judgments, and deprivation of service. These myths and caricatures include that self- harm is:

- Manipulative attention seeking for pleasure
- A group activity only carried out by those who are interested in 'Goth' sub-culture
- A failed suicide attempt
- Evidence of borderline personality disorder

Suicidal ideation amongst young people

The term 'suicidal ideation' refers to thoughts that life isn't worth living, ranging in intensity from fleeting thoughts through to concrete, well thought-out plans for killing oneself, or a complete preoccupation with self-destruction. Globally there is evidence to suggest that between 45% and 60% of adolescents have experienced suicidal thoughts at least once in their lifetime. The overall rate of suicide attempts among young people is three times higher than the rate among adults over 30 years of age and globally among those aged between 10 to 24 years, suicide is the second most common cause of death, after road traffic accidents. It is estimated that approximately 164,000 self-inflicted deaths occur among people aged under 25 years. Most suicide deaths among young people occur within the age of 15–24 years (Basu et al., 2022).

In 2021, there were 5583 suicides registered in England and Wales, equivalent to a rate of 10.7 deaths per 100,000 people; while this was statistically significantly higher than the 2020 rate of 10.0 deaths per 100,000 people, it was consistent with the pre-coronavirus (COVID-19) pandemic rates in 2019 and 2018 (ONS, 2021a). Between the ages 15–24 in the UK, male suicides were three times more common than female suicides.

Since 2013, suicide rates have also risen among younger males aged 10–14, and among females across all ages. Females aged 24 years or under however have seen the largest increase in the suicide rate since ONS time series began in 1981. In England, a quarter of 11–16 year-olds, and nearly half of 17–19 year-olds (46.8%), with a mental disorder reported that they have self-harmed or attempted suicide at some point in their lives (ONS, 2021b).

In 2018 and 2019, in 30% of counselling sessions provided by Childline (NSPCC) the primary concern was identified as mental/emotional health. Since 2009 and 2010, there has been a sharp increase in the total number of referrals Childline counsellors have made to external agencies where there have been suicidal concerns with a total of 3518 referrals made in 2018and 2019. (RCPCH, 2020). The number of young people being referred to Child and Adolescent Mental Health Services (CAMHS) in the UK has also reached a record high, with NHS figures showing a 23% rise in the number of under-18s needing NHS treatment than at the same point last year (ONS, 2022).

Most young people who experience suicidal ideation will not go on to take their lives, however any report of suicidal ideation should be taken seriously as suicidal ideation has been found to be associated with clinically significant symptoms of depression (Evans et al., 2005). Furthermore, young people experiencing persistent, severe suicidal ideation are at increased risk of attempting suicide (Fergusson and Lynskey, 1998).

Turecki and Brent (2016) argue that suicide in young people is rarely caused by one thing; it usually follows a combination of previous vulnerability and recent events. The stresses identified before suicide are common in young people; most come through them without serious harm.

Young people experiencing suicidal ideation in the absence of other risk factors are at a relatively low-risk, whereas those experiencing suicidal ideation in addition to exposure to multiple risk factors such as mental disorders, previous suicide attempts, specific personality characteristics, family factors, exposure to inspiring models and availability of means of committing suicide are at high-risk (Bilson, 2018).

Table 2.1 A checklist of signs that a young person may be contemplating suicide

Key Signs	Your Observations
Threatening to hurt themselves or suicide	
Looking for ways to suicide e.g. seeking access to pills, weapons, or other means	
Deliberately hurting themselves i.e. by scratching, cutting, or burning	
Talking or writing about death, dying or suicide	
When students express hopelessness	
When they express excessive rage, anger, and a desire to seeking revenge	
Acting recklessly or engaging in risky activities, seemingly without thinking	
Students say they are feeling trapped in which there is nowhere to go	
Increasing alcohol or drug use	
Withdrawing from friends, family or society	
When Students complain of feeling anxious, or agitated and having problems sleeping or eating	
When you perceive dramatic changes in mood	
Students tell you they see no reason for living, no sense of purpose in life	

Adapted from Mental Health First Aid (2008) Suicidal Thoughts and Behaviours: First Aid Guidelines.

Figure 2.13   Helping activity

Encourage your student to create their own Hope box. It should be personal to them and contain items that either distract them or feel better about themselves. It can be helpful to have a mixture of items, that use all five senses. It can be filled with anything including the following:

- *Favourite CD or USB with music you like*
- *A puzzle or colouring book*
- *Reminders of positive experiences such as trips parties*
- *A copy of a crisis plan (if there is one)*
- *Photographs of people they love and who make you happy*
- *Favourite sweets or chocolates*
- *Bottle of favourite perfume or after shave*

It can be helpful to have a mixture of items that use all five senses.

References

Bailey, D., and Wright, N. (2017). Self-harm in young people: a challenge for general practice *British Journal of General Practice*, 67: 542–543.

Baker, H. J., Hollywood, A., and Waite, P. (2022). Adolescents' lived experience of panic disorder: An interpretative phenomenological analysis. *BMC Psychology*, 10: 143. doi:10.1186/s40359-022-00849-x

Baker, T. B., and Lewis, Stephen P. (2013). Responses to online photographs of non-suicidal self-injury: A thematic analysis, *Archives of Suicide Research*, 17(3): 223–35. doi:10.1080/13811118.2013.805642

Basu, A., Boland, A., Witt, K., Robinson, J. (2022). Suicidal behaviour, including ideation and self-harm, in young migrants: A systematic review. *International Journal of Environmental Research and Public Health*, 19(14): 8329. doi:10.3390/ijerph19148329

Beesdo-Baum, K., and Knappe, S. (2012). Developmental epidemiology of anxiety disorders. *Child and Adolescent Psychiatric Clinics of North America*, 21(3): 457–78. doi:10.1016/j.chc.2012.05.001

Bhardwaj, Anita. (2001). Growing up young, Asian and female in Britain: A report on self-harm and suicide. *Feminist Review*, no. 68: 52–67. JSTOR, http://www.jstor.org/stable/1395744. Accessed 29 July 2023.

Bilsen, J. (2018). Suicide and youth: Risk factors. *Frontiers in Psychiatry*, 30(9): 540. doi:10.3389/fpsyt.2018.00540

Breslau, N., Davis, G. C., Peterson, E. L., and Schultz, L. R. (2000). A second look at comorbidity in victims of trauma: The posttraumatic stress disorder-major depression connection. *Biological Psychiatry*, 48(9): 902–9. doi:10.1016/s0006-3223(00)00933-1

Buchanan, D., and Warwick, I. (2020). Supporting adults with mental health problems through further education. *Health Education Journal*, 79(8): 863–874. doi:10.1177/0017896920929739

Cackovic, C., Nazir, S., and Marwaha, R. (2022). Panic Disorder. In: *StatPearls* [Internet]. Treasure Island (FL): StatPearls Publishing. PMID: 28613692.

Compas, B. E., Jaser, S. S., Bettis, A. H., Watson, K. H., Gruhn, M. A., Dunbar, J. P., Williams, E., and Thigpen, J. C. (2017). Coping, emotion regulation, and psychopathology in childhood and adolescence: A meta-analysis and narrative review. *Psychological Bulletin*, 143(9): 939–91. doi:10.1037/bul0000110

Cooper, J., Husain, N., Webb, R., Waheed, W., Kapur, N., Guthrie, E., and Appleby, L. (2006). Self-harm in the UK: Differences between South Asians and Whites in rates, characteristics, provision of service and repetition. *Social Psychiatry and Psychiatric Epidemiology*, 41(10): 782–8. doi:10.1007/s00127-006-0099-2. Erratum in: (2008). Social Psychiatry and Psychiatric Epidemiology, 43(12): 1024.

Coyle, L. D., and Vera, E. M. (2013). Uncontrollable stress, coping, and subjective well-being in urban adolescents. *Journal of Youth Studies*, 16(3): 391–403. doi:10.1080/13676261.2012.756975

Daly, M., Sutin, A. R., and Robinson, E. (2022). Longitudinal changes in mental health and the COVID-19 pandemic: Evidence from the UK Household Longitudinal Study. *Psychological Medicine*, 52(13): 2549–58. doi:10.1017/S0033291720004432

de Lijster, Jasmijn M., Dieleman, Gwen C., Utens, Elisabeth M.W.J., Dierckx, Bram, Wierenga, Milou, Verhulst, Frank C., and Legerstee, Jeroen S. (2018). Social and academic functioning in adolescents with anxiety disorders: A systematic review. *Journal of Affective Disorders*, 230: 108–17. ISSN 0165-0327. (https://www.sciencedirect.com/science/article/pii/S0165032717311606).

Diagnostic and Statistical Manual of Mental Disorders. (2023). 5th edn, Text Revision (DSM-5-TR). American Psychiatric Association (APA).

Dursun, P., Alyagut, P., and Yılmaz, I. (2022). Meaning in life, psychological hardiness and death anxiety: Individuals with or without generalized anxiety disorder (GAD). *Current Psychology*, 41(6): 3299–317. doi:10.1007/s12144-021-02695-3

Emerson, E., and Hatton, C. (2007). *The Mental Health of Children and Adolescents with Learning Disabilities in England*. Lancaster: University of Lancaster.

Etheridge, B., and Spantig, L. (2022). The gender gap in mental well-being at the onset of the Covid-19 pandemic: Evidence from the UK. *European Economic Review*, 145: 104114. doi:10.1016/j.euroecorev.2022.104114

Evans, D. L., et al. (2005). Mood disorders in the medically ill: Scientific review and recommendations. *Biological Psychiatry*, 58: 175–89. http://www.ncbi.nlm.nih.gov/pubmed/16084838 doi:10.1016/j.biopsych.2005.05.001

Fancourt, D., Steptoe, A., and Bradbury, A. (2022). *Tracking the Psychological and Social Consequences of the COVID-19 Pandemic across the UK Population: Findings, Impact, and Recommendations from the COVID-19 Social Study (March 2020–April 2022)*. London: UCL.

Farooq, S., Tunmore, J., Wajid Ali, M., and Ayub, M. (2021). Suicide, self-harm and suicidal ideation during COVID-19: A systematic review. *Psychiatry Research*, 306: 114228. doi:10.1016/j.psychres.2021.114228

Fergusson, D. M., and Lynskey, M. T. (1998). Conduct problems in childhood and psychosocial outcomes in young adulthood: A prospective study. *Journal of Emotional and Behavioral Disorders*, 6(1): 2–18. doi:10.1177/106342669800600101

Fox, Claudine, and Hawton, Keith. (2004). *Deliberate Self-Harm in Adolescence*. Child and Adolescent Mental Health Series. London: Jessica Kingsley. ISBN 9781843102373

Galmiche, Marie, Déchelotte, Pierre, Lambert, Gregory, and Tavolacci, Marie-Pierre. (2019). Prevalence of eating disorders over the 2000–2018 period: A systematic literature review. *The American Journal of Clinical Nutrition*, 109: 1402–13. doi:10.1093/ajcn/nqy342

Hatchel, T., Ingram, Katherine M., Huang, Yuanhong, and Espelage, Dorothy L. (2020). Homophobic bullying victimization trajectories: The roles of perpetration, sex assigned at birth, and sexuality. *Aggressive Behaviour*, 46(5): 370–79

Hay, P., Aouad, P., Le, A., et al. (2023). Epidemiology of eating disorders: population, prevalence, disease burden and quality of life informing public policy in Australia—A rapid review. *Journal of Eating Disorders*, 11: 23. doi:10.1186/s40337-023-00738-7

Hetrick, S. E., Subasinghe, A., Anglin, K., Hart, L., Morgan, A., and Robinson, J. (2020). Understanding the needs of young people who engage in self-harm: A qualitative investigation. *Frontiers in Psychology*, 10(10): 2916. doi:10.3389/fpsyg.2019.02916

Holmes, E. A., Ghaderi, Ata, Harmer, Catherine J, Ramchandani, Paul G., Cuijpers, Pim, Morrison, Anthony P., Roiser, Jonathan P., Bockting, Claudi L. H., O'Connor, Rory C., Shafran, Roz, Moulds, Michelle L., and Craske, Michelle G. (2018). The Lancet Psychiatry Commission on psychological treatments research in tomorrow's science. *The Lancet Psychiatry*, 5(3): 237–86. ISSN 2215-0366. doi:10.1016/S2215-0366(17)30513-8

Huryk, K. M., Drury, C. R., and Loeb, K. L. (2021). Diseases of affluence? A systematic review of the literature on socioeconomic diversity in eating disorders. *Eating Behaviors*, 43: 425–457.

Hudson, J. I., Hiripi, E., Pope, H. G. Jr, and Kessler, R. C. (2007). The prevalence and correlates of eating disorders in the National Comorbidity Survey Replication. *Biological Psychiatry*, 61(3), 348–58.

Jefferies, P., and Ungar, M. (2020). Social anxiety in young people: A prevalence study in seven countries. *PLoS One*, 15(9): e0239133. doi:10.1371/journal.pone.0239133

Joiner, T. (2005). *Why People Die by Suicide*, 276. Available online at: https://psycnet.apa.org/fulltext/2006-06716-000.pdf (accessed July, 26th 2023)

Kessler, R. C., McLaughlin, K. A., Green, J. G., Gruber, M. J., Sampson, N. A., Zaslavsky, A. M., Aguilar-Gaxiola, S., Alhamzawi, A. O., Alonso, J., Angermeyer, M., Benjet, C., Bromet, E., Chatterji, S., de Girolamo, G., Demyttenaere, K., Fayyad, J., Florescu, S., Gal, G., Gureje, O., Haro, J. M., Hu, C. Y., Karam, E. G., Kawakami, N., Lee, S., Lépine, J. P., Ormel, J., Posada-Villa, J., Sagar, R., Tsang, A., Üstün, T. B., Vassilev, S., Viana, M. C., and Williams, D. R. (2010). Childhood adversities and adult psychopathology in the WHO World Mental Health Surveys. *The British Journal of Psychiatry*, 197(5): 378–85. doi:10.1192/bjp.bp.110.080499

Kim, B. H., Kim, M. K., Jo, H. J., et al. (2022). Predicting social anxiety in young adults with machine learning of resting-state brain functional radiomic features. *Scientific Reports*, 12: 13932 doi:10.1038/s41598-022-17769-w

Laye-Gindhu, Aviva, and Schonert-Reichl, Kimberly. (2005). Nonsuicidal self-harm among community adolescents: Understanding the "whats" and "whys" of self-harm. *Journal of Youth and Adolescence*, 34: 447–57. doi:10.1007/s10964-005-7262-z

Lewis, S. J., Arseneault, Louise, Caspi, Avshalom, Fisher, Helen L., Matthews, Timothy, Moffitt, Terrie E., Odgers, Candice L., Stahl, Daniel, Teng, Jia Ying, and Danese, Andrea. (2018). The epidemiology of trauma and post-traumatic stress disorder in a representative cohort of young people in England and Wales. *The Lancet*, 6(3): 247–56. doi:10.1016/S2215-0366(19)30031-8

Lewis, S. P., and Baker, T. G. (2011). The possible risks of self-injury web sites: A content analysis. *Archives of Suicide Research*, 15(4): 390–6.

Licence, L., Oliver, C., Moss, J., and Richards, C. (2020). Prevalence and risk-markers of self-harm in autistic children and adults. *Journal of Autism and Developmental Disorders*, 50(10): 3561–74. doi:10.1007/s10803-019-04260-1

Liu, R. T., and Mustanski, B. (2012). Suicidal ideation and self-harm in lesbian, gay, bisexual, and transgender youth. *American Journal of Preventive Medicine*, 42(3): 221–8. doi:10.1016/j.amepre.2011.10.023

Madge, N., Hewitt, A., Hawton, K., de Wilde, E. J., Corcoran, P., Fekete, S., van Heeringen, K., De Leo, D., and Ystgaard, M. (2008). Deliberate self-harm within an international community sample of young people: Comparative findings from the Child & Adolescent Self-harm in Europe (CASE) Study. *Journal of Child Psychology and Psychiatry*, 49(6): 667–77. doi:10.1111/j.1469-7610.2008.01879.x

Marmot, M., Allen, J., Boyce, T., Goldblatt, P., and Morrison, J. (2020). Health equity in England: The Marmot review 10 years on. *Institute for Health Equity*. https://www.health.org.uk/sites/default/files/upload/publications/2020/Health%20Equity%20in%20England_The%20Marmot%20Review%2010%20Years%20On_full%20report.pdf

Mars, B., Heron, J., Crane, C., Hawton, K., Kidger, J., Lewis, G., Macleod, J., Tilling, K., and Gunnell, D. (2014). Differences in risk factors for self-harm with and without suicidal intent: Findings from the ALSPAC cohort. *Journal of Affective Disorders*, 168: 407–14. doi:10.1016/j.jad.2014.07.009

Mason, T. B., and Heron, K. E. (2016). Do depressive symptoms explain associations between binge eating symptoms and later psychosocial adjustment in young adulthood? *Eating Behaviors*, 23: 126–30. doi:10.1016/j.eatbeh.2016.09.003

Mental Health Foundation (MHF). (2019). Tackling social inequalities to reduce mental health problems: How everyone can flourish equally. https://www.mentalhealth.org.uk/sites/default/files/2022-04/MHF-tackling-inequalities-report.pdf

Milne, J. M., Garrison, C. Z., Addy, C. L., McKeowen, R. E., et al. (1995). Frequency of phobic disorder in a community sample of young adolescents. *Journal of the American Academy of Child and Adolescent Psychiatry*, 34: 1202–1211.

Mondin, T. C., Konradt, C. E., de Cardoso, T. A., de Quevedo, L. A., Jansen, K., Mattos, L. D., de Pinheiro, R. T., and da Silva, R. A. (2013). Anxiety disorders in young people: A population-based study. *Brazilian Journal of Psychiatry*, 35(4). doi:10.1590/1516-4446-2013-1155

Munir, S., and Takov, V. (2023). Generalized anxiety disorder. In: *StatPearls [Internet]*. Treasure Island (FL): StatPearls Publishing. Available at: https://www.ncbi.nlm.nih.gov/books/NBK441870/

National Autistic Society (NAS). (2021). School Report. Available at: https://www.autism.org.uk/what-we-do/news/school-report-2021

National Health Service (NHS) Mental Health of Children and Young People in England. 2020. Wave 1 follow up to the 2017 survey. 2020. Official statistics, Survey. https://digital.nhs.uk/data-and-information/publications/statistical/mental-health-of-children-and-young-people-in-england/2020-wave-1-follow-up

National Health Service (NHS) Mental Health of Children and Young People in England. 2022. Wave3 follow up to the 2017 survey. 2020. Official statistics, Survey. https://digital.nhs.uk/data-and-information/publications/statistical/mental-health-of-children-and-young-people-in-england/2022-follow-up-to-the-2017-survey

Niermann, Hannah C.M., Voss, Catharina, Pieper, Lars, Venz, John, Ollmann, Theresa M., and Beesdo-Baum, Katja. (2021). Anxiety disorders among adolescents and young adults: Prevalence and mental health care service utilization in a regional epidemiological study in Germany. *Journal of Anxiety Disorders*, 83: 102453. ISSN 0887-6185. doi:10.1016/j.janxdis.2021.102453

Norholm, S. D., Ressler, K. J. (2009). Genetics of anxiety and trauma-related disorders. *Neuroscience*, 164(1), 272–87.

Office of National Statistics (ONS) Cost of living and depression in adults, Great Britain. 29 September to 23 October 2022 Analysis into the prevalence of depression among adults in Great Britain in autumn 2022. Exploring this in the context of the rising cost of living. https://www.ons.gov.uk/peoplepopulationandcommunity/healthandsocialcare/mentalhealth/articles/costoflivinganddepressioninadultsgreatbritain/29septemberto23october2022

Office of National statistics (ONS). (2021a). Suicides in England and Wales: 2021 registrations. Registered deaths in England and Wales from suicide analysed by sex, age, area of usual residence of the deceased, and suicide method.

Office of National Statistics (ONS) Young people's well-being in the UK. 2021b. (https://www.ons.gov.uk/peoplepopulationandcommunity/wellbeing/bulletins/youngpeopleswellbeingintheuk/previousReleases

Ollendick, T. H., Raishevich, N., Davis, T. E. 3rd, Sirbu, C., and Ost, L. G. (2010). Specific phobia in youth: Phenomenology and psychological characteristics. *Behavior Therapy*, 41(1): 133–41. doi:10.1016/j.beth.2009.02.002

Overseas Economic Corporation Development (OECD). (2021). Young people's concerns during COVID-19: Results from risks that matter. https://www.oecd.org/coronavirus/policy-responses/young-people-s-concerns-during-covid-19-results-from-risks-that-matter-2020-64b51763/

Perry-Parrish, C., Copeland-Linder, N., Webb, L., and Sibinga, E. M. (2016). Mindfulness-based approaches for children and youth. *Current Problems in Pediatric and Adolescent Health Care*, 46(6): 172–8. doi:10.1016/j.cppeds.2015.12.006

Plener, P. L., Schumacher, T. S., Munz, L. M., and Groschwitz, R. C. (2015). The longitudinal course of non-suicidal self-injury and deliberate self-harm: A systematic review of the literature. *Borderline Personality Disorder and Emotion Dysregulation*, 30(2): 2. doi:10.1186/s40479-014-0024-3

Pope, L. (2018). *Self-Harm by Adult Men in Prison: A Rapid Evidence Assessment (REA)*. HMPPS. https://assets.publishing.service.gov.uk/media/5b977f3d40f0b67896977b55/self-harm-adult-men-prison-2018.pdf

Potterton, R., Richards, K., Allen, K., and Schmidt, U. (2020). Eating disorders during emerging adulthood: A systematic scoping review. *Frontiers in Psychology*, 31(10): 3062. doi:10.3389/fpsyg.2019.03062

Racine, N., McArthur, B. A., Cooke, J. E., Eirich, R., Zhu, J., and Madigan, S. (2021). Global prevalence of depressive and anxiety symptoms in children and adolescents during COVID-19: A meta-analysis. *JAMA Pediatrics*, 175(11): 1142–1150. doi:10.1001/jamapediatrics.2021.2482

Radez, J., Reardon, T., Creswell, C., et al. (2022). Adolescents' perceived barriers and facilitators to seeking and accessing professional help for anxiety and depressive disorders: A qualitative interview study. *European Child Adolescent Psychiatry*, 31: 891–907. doi:10.1007/s00787-020-01707-0

Raleigh, Veena. (1996). Suicide patterns and trends in people in Indian subcontinent and Caribbean origin in England & Wales. *Ethnicity & Health*, 1: 55–63. doi:10.1080/13557858.1996.9961770

Robinson, J. (2017). Repeated self-harm in young people: A review. *Australasian Psychiatry*, 25(2): 105–107. doi:10.1177/1039856216679542

Rouski, C., Knowles, S. F., Sellwood, W., and Hodge, S. (2021). The quest for genuine care: A qualitative study of the experiences of young people who self-harm in residential care. *Clinical Child Psychology and Psychiatry*, 26(2): 418–29. doi:10.1177/1359104520980037

Royal College of Paediatrics and Child Health (RCPCH). (2020). *State of Child Health*. London: RCPCH. https://stateofchildhealth.rcpch.ac.uk/

Sabbagh, H. J., Abdelaziz, W., Alghamdi, W., Quritum, M., AlKhateeb, N. A., Abourdan, J., Qureshi, N., Qureshi, S., Hamoud, A. H. N., Mahmoud, N., Odeh, R., Al-Khanati, N. M., Jaber, R., Balkhoyor, A. L., Shabi, M., Folayan, M. O., Alade, O., Gomaa, N., Alnahdi, R., Mahmoud, N. A., El Wazziki, H., Alnaas, M., Samodien, B., Mahmoud, R. A., Abu Assab, N., Saad, S., Alhachim, S. G., and El Tantawi, M. (2022). Anxiety among adolescents and young adults during COVID-19 pandemic: A multi-country survey. *International Journal of Environmental Research and Public Health*, 19(17): 10538. doi:10.3390/ijerph191710538

Schneier, F. R., Liebowitz, M. R., Abi-Dargham, A., Zea-Ponce, Y., Lin, S. H., and Laruelle, M. (2000). Low dopamine D(2) receptor binding potential in social phobia. *The American Journal of Psychiatry*, 157(3): 457–9. doi:10.1176/appi.ajp.157.3.457

Slade, T., and Watson, D. (2006). The structure of common DSM-IV and ICD-10 mental disorders in the Australian general population. *Psychological Medicine*, 36(11): 1593–600. doi:10.1017/S0033291706008452

Taylor, S., Paluszek, M. M., Rachor, G. S., McKay, D., and Asmundson, G. J. G. (2021). Substance use and abuse, COVID-19-related distress, and disregard for social distancing: A network analysis. *Addictive Behaviors*, 114: 106754. doi:10.1016/j.addbeh.2020.106754

Thapar, A., Eyre, O., Patel, V., and Brent, D. (2022). Depression in young people. *Lancet*, 400(10352): 617–31. doi:10.1016/S0140-6736(22)01012-1

Turecki, G., and Brent, D. (2016). Suicide and suicidal behaviour. *Lancet*, 387: 1227–39. doi:10.1016/S0140-6736(15)00234-2

Vitagliano, J. A., Jhe, G., Milliren, C. E., Lin, J. A., Spigel, R., Freizinger, M., Woods, E. R., Forman, S. F., and Richmond, T. K. (2021). COVID-19 and eating disorder and mental health concerns in patients with eating disorders. *Journal of Eating Disorders*, 9(1): 80. doi:10.1186/s40337-021-00437-1

World Health Organisation (WHO) (2021). Mental health of adolescents. https://www.who.int/news-room/fact-sheets/detail/adolescent-mental-health

Williams, T., and Shafran, R. (2015). Obsessive–compulsive disorder in young people. *BJPsych Advances*, 21(3): 196–205. doi:10.1192/apt.bp.113.011759

3 Approaches to effective college wellbeing systems

Principles that underpin effective mental health policy

There are several main principles to promoting a whole school and college approach to mental health and wellbeing (Rainer and Abdinasir, 2021),

- Leadership and management that support and champions efforts to promote emotional health and wellbeing is placed at the centre and the commitment is referenced within improvement plans and policies such as safeguarding and confidentiality
  This core principle is supported by the following principles:
- Curriculum teaching and learning to promote resilience and support social and emotional learning by embedding these principles into teaching to give them practical application and relevance
- Student voice should be utilised to influence decisions and to help students feel they have some control over their lives building their knowledge and skills to make healthy choices and developing their independence
- Demonstrate a commitment to staff health and wellbeing by working within the DFE education wellbeing charter by providing opportunities for assessing the mental health and wellbeing needs of staff, and providing support to enable staff to reflect on and to take actions to enhance their own wellbeing and by promoting a work-life balance for staff by driving down an unnecessary workload (DFE, 2020)
- Working with parents and carers
- Targeted support and appropriate referral
- An ethos and environment that promotes respect and values diversity

> **Figure 3.1 Self-reflection task**
>
> *Here are two self-reflection tasks for developing a whole college approach to mental health and wellbeing in schools and colleges in the UK:*
>
> 1. *Reflect on the current mental health and wellbeing support in your school/college. What are the strengths and weaknesses of the current approach? Are there any gaps or areas for improvement? Consider factors such as accessibility, diversity and inclusivity, cultural sensitivity, and student/staff feedback. Based on this reflection, brainstorm potential strategies or initiatives that could be implemented to create a more comprehensive and effective whole college approach to mental health and wellbeing*
> 2. *Reflect on your own role and responsibilities in promoting mental health and wellbeing in your school/college. How can you use your position and influence to create a positive and supportive environment for students and staff? Consider ways to raise awareness and reduce stigma around mental health, build relationships and foster a sense of community, promote self-care and resilience, and identify and respond to mental health concerns. Think about how you can collaborate with other staff members and departments to create a coordinated and integrated approach to mental health and wellbeing*

Comments from the frontline

> *Lots of young people are leading double or even triple lives. They are dealing with family breakdowns, working in the evenings, caring for a parent or sibling as well as coming to college. My role as a tutor has to adapt to meet all their different needs.*

Central to this is measuring mental health and wellbeing in the institution. There are three main ways in which this can be done, although there is often overlapping between them (Hewett, 2019):

- A survey snapshot of student mental wellbeing can inform planning evidence and prevention work for Ofsted and whole college or school practice. This approach serves as a sort of 'temperature check' of wellbeing within the school and college. Schools and colleges in the UK tend to use young person self-report instruments which tend to focus on a limited number of domains such as individual, family, community or learning environment

Table 3.1 Example of an identification survey (based on the The Warwick-Edinburgh Mental Wellbeing Scales – WEMWBS)

Student feelings	Rating score
I've been feeling optimistic about the future	
I've been feeling useful*	
I've been feeling relaxed*	
I've been feeling interested in other people	
I've had energy to spare	
I've been dealing with problems well	
I've been thinking clearly	
I've been feeling good about myself	
I've been feeling close to other people	
I've been able to make up my own mind about things	
I've been feeling loved	
I've been feeling cheerfu	
I've been interested in new things	
Response Optionse 1 = None of the time 2 = Rarely 3 = Some of the time 4 = Often 5 = All of the time	

- Identification. Individual students who might benefit from early support need to be identified quickly using instruments than measure mental health issues. A range of approaches can be considered to help identify and target students who may benefit from more targeted support from people such as teachers, pastoral staff and learning mentors. The DFE (2021) suggests that a targeted approach should be based on a cyclical strategy centring on continuous analysis and monitoring of data and effective pastoral or tutorial systems based on support and feedback. This method is also applied using surveys, online and off-line (see below for an example)

Evaluation will ensure that those students who are receiving targeted support through interventions are benefiting from it and that the impact of it is measurable and using measurement to evaluate a system gives: an indication of its effectiveness; signposts for improvement; shows the ability of the institution to reflect on its systems; and ensures that good services continue to be funded (PHE, 2020)

MH college policies and procedures

According to research promoting students' mental health and emotional wellbeing has been linked to greater educational engagement, improved behaviour and attendance and help rising attainment (Maxwell et al., 2008; DFE, 2021). 75% of colleges state that they had dedicated mental health policies for both staff and learners, and 94% of colleges regularly report to College Corporations on this matter.

According to research by Maxwell and Warwick (2008) a strong whole college policy and the effective promotion of positive mental health and emotional wellbeing was linked to a holistic, multi-layered system of support for students. This could include:

- Personal tutor systems
- Learning support programmes (learning assistants, extra tuition)
- Mentors
- Counselling service
- Health drop-ins (sexual health clinic with a nurse, drugs support drop-in)
- Health awareness events (stop smoking initiatives, anti-bullying campaigns)
- Group work (on, for example, anger management, relationship violence)
- Information about both college and external sources of support (in college diaries for instance)
- An active student union (organising social events, outings, representing student views to senior management)
- A range of places to spend free time (quiet spaces, student cafés, student common rooms)

One of the case studies used in their research illustrated the importance of a commitment to young people with mental health difficulties laid out in the college's strategic plan which included core funding for specialist posts to include a student services manager, mental health manager and equality, diversity and inclusion coordinator (2008).

Another of the case studies showed how a partnership between Connexions, the Child and Adolescent Mental Health Service (CAMHS) and a variety externally-funded posts in place, such as a substance misuse adviser, a Connexions intensive support personal adviser and a local young adults' mental health adviser, and the college could meet the range of mental health problems students were presenting with, and created an ethos of support, trust and inclusiveness within the setting (PHE, 2020).

Senior Mental Health Lead (SMHL)

The Senior Mental Health Lead (SHML) has a mental health strategic implementation and planning role. They are responsible for creating a whole-school and college approach to supporting mental health and wellbeing and a culture in which staff and students can discuss their mental health and wellbeing openly. Other aspects of the role include:

- Discussing mental health and wellbeing issues with students
- Training staff to identify signs and symptoms of emerging mental health needs in students
- Facilitating a clear process in which staff can report concerns and how they can be managed

- Developing systems and policies for students to seek help if they need it and to support students through referrals to specialists
- Develop links with national and local support outside colleges and schools

Training for the post is funded by the Department for Education which forms part of their commitment to have SMHLs in every school and college by 2025. According to the Academy of Learning (AoL) survey 87% of colleges stated that they have a mental health lead in the college. In Spring 2023 the Department for Education announced the commissioning of the curation of a Senior Mental Health Lead Hub and Toolkit for Schools and Colleges in addition to the training grants for SMHL.

Tonks (2022) suggested that there were several barriers to the effective performance of the role. For example, the Ofsted systems, suggesting that standardised assessments and inspections prevented the schools they worked in from caring for a child holistically. They also commented on the lack of time given to them for the role and the lack of emotional and psychological support they received.

The researcher also highlighted issues with lack of co-ordination between the SMHL role and other roles within the school, including staff in the development and the implementation of mental health and wellbeing initiatives, targeting the mental health of parents when required and finding novel ways of getting support from external agencies, such as consultancy (Tonks, 2022).

The effective deployment of student services in colleges

There has been a significant amount of research conducted on the mental health support functions of student services in UK colleges. Many studies have highlighted the importance of providing mental health support to students, particularly given the high levels of stress and anxiety that students often experience during their time at college (Morgan, 2012; PHE, 2020; Hughes and Bowers-Brown, 2021; Campbell et al., 2022.

Some of the key findings from this research include:

- Many studies have found that early intervention is crucial for improving mental health outcomes for college students# (Hughes and Bowers-Brown, 2021; Campbell et al., 2022). This includes providing timely access to counselling services and other forms of support
- Research has highlighted the importance of providing a range of support services to students, including counselling, peer support, and online resources (Hubble and Bolton, 2019). This allows students to choose the type of support that works best for them
- Many studies have emphasised the importance of a whole institution approach which requires collaboration between different departments within colleges to provide effective mental health support (Warwick et al., 2008; Garside et al., 2021; Fazel et al., 2023). This includes collaboration

between counselling services, academic departments, and other student support services
- Research has also highlighted the role that stigma can play in preventing students from seeking help for mental health issues (Ahmedani, 2011; Corrigan et al., 2014; Stewart, 2016). To address this, many colleges have implemented campaigns to reduce stigma and promote mental health awareness
- The importance of integrating mental health support into the wider college environment and the need for a multi-disciplinary approach
- The need to develop a mental health strategy which is clear and comprehensive strategy that outlines how the institution will support students' mental health and wellbeing. This should include training for staff and students, policies and procedures, and access to mental health services (DFE, 2020)
- The importance of fostering a positive and inclusive culture. A culture that is open, supportive, and non-stigmatising when it comes to mental health. This includes providing opportunities for students to connect with others and building positive relationships with staff (Lauchlan and Susan, 2015)
- The significance of increased awareness and understanding and the raising of awareness of mental health issues and the provision of information on how to recognize and respond to mental health concerns. This can be done through training, workshops, and information resources (Yamaguchi, et al., 2011; Livingstone et al., 2013)
- The importance of timely support to ensure that students have access to timely and appropriate mental health support. This includes offering a range of services, such as counselling, peer support, and self-help resources

The need to foster resilience and coping skills via the development of coping skills and resilience-building strategies. This can be done through workshops, support groups, and other programs that focus on self-care, stress management, and problem-solving (Cho et al., 2021)

The need to address systemic issues that may contribute to poor mental health outcomes, such as discrimination, inequality, and poverty. This may involve working with community organisations, advocacy groups, and policymakers to address these issues. (Knifton and Inglis, 2020)

Here are some suggestions for how student services can be effectively deployed to support student mental health in the UK:

- Colleges should ensure that mental health services are easily accessible to all students. This can be done by having a dedicated mental health support team on campus or by partnering with local mental health services
- All staff, including academic and non-academic staff, should receive training on how to identify students who may be struggling with mental health issues and how to provide support.

- Peer support programs can be an effective way to help students who may feel more comfortable talking to someone their own age. Peer support programs can be set up by the college or by student-led organisations
- Create a supportive campus environment. Institutions should work to create a supportive campus environment where students feel safe and comfortable. This can be done by promoting mental health awareness campaigns and providing resources such as stress management workshops
- Counselling services can provide students with a safe and confidential space to talk about their mental health concerns. Colleges should ensure that counselling services are adequately staffed and offer flexible hours to accommodate students' schedules
- Use technology to enhance mental health support for example, colleges can use chatbots or mobile apps to provide students with quick access to mental health resources
- Colleges should regularly evaluate their mental health services to ensure that they are effective and meeting the needs of students. Feedback from students should be considered to continually improve services
- Student services should provide a range of easily accessible support services that cater to the diverse needs of students. This can include face-to-face counselling, telephone support, and online resources
- Student services should work to increase awareness of mental health issues among students, faculty, and staff. which can involve running awareness campaigns, providing mental health education programs, and creating safe spaces for students to talk about their mental health
- Targeted support for individual students needs to be matched by college wide wellbeing programmes. Nearly all colleges were running wellbeing activities for students, with 99% of colleges having a mental wellbeing focus in tutorials in 2023 and there were also programmes including AoC Sport, which highlighted the links between physical and mental wellbeing (AoC, 2023)
- Student services can work to foster a supportive campus environment that promotes positive mental health. This can involve creating support networks, providing opportunities for social engagement, and promoting physical activity and healthy lifestyle choices
- Student services should develop partnerships with external agencies such as local mental health providers and community organisations. This can help to ensure that students receive the appropriate support when needed
- Student services should provide appropriate training and support to staff members who work directly with students. This can include training in mental health first aid, counselling, and crisis intervention

Findings from a DFE (2021) survey showed that a range of forms of support was being provided to students. Out of the 56 colleges responding, most had staff members with specific responsibility for mental health, college counselling services, information to students about how to access internal and external support services learning mentors and support assistants, a personal tutor system and provided special examination arrangements for students with mental health difficulties (2021).

Figure 3.2 Self-reflection tasks

1. *Conduct a survey:* Design and distribute a survey to your students who have accessed mental health services at the college. The survey should include questions about their satisfaction with the services, whether the services met their needs, and if they felt supported throughout the process. Additionally, the survey should include open-ended questions to allow students to provide more detailed feedback. Analyse the survey results to identify areas of improvement and areas of strength
2. *Review policies and procedures:* Review the college's policies and procedures related to mental health services. This could include reviewing the intake process, counselling sessions, and the referral process for more specialized mental health care. Analyse these policies and procedures to identify any gaps or inconsistencies that may be affecting the quality of mental health services. Additionally, review any relevant literature or best practices to identify potential changes or improvements to the policies and procedures

---

Counselling services

The average college now provides 40 hours of counselling for their students, with over two-thirds of colleges employing their own counselling staff. Investment in college-run support services and staff development is evidenced by 68% of colleges now employing their own counsellors, which on average equates to two part-time counsellors and one full time counsellor per college. A further 36% of colleges buy in counselling support from external organisations (and some colleges will do both). Although 68% of colleges now employ their own counsellors, this is much lower than the provision within universities.

The roles of student counsellors

In the United Kingdom, student counsellors play a crucial role in supporting the emotional and mental wellbeing of students in colleges and schools. These professionals provide a safe and confidential environment where students can talk about their personal, social, and academic issues. Student counsellors are trained to help students identify and overcome their problems so that they can achieve their full potential.

The roles of student counsellors in colleges and schools in the UK are varied and complex. They work with students who are facing a range of issues, including anxiety, depression, stress, relationship problems, academic difficulties, and personal crises. The following are some of the primary roles and responsibilities of student counsellors:

- Student counsellors can use various techniques to assess and diagnose mental health problems. They use standardised psychological tests, interviews, and observations to understand the student's problems and make a diagnosis
- Once the student's problems have been identified, student counsellors can develop a treatment plan. The plan may include individual counselling, group therapy, or referral to other professionals or services
- Student counsellors provide individual counselling to students who are experiencing emotional or mental health problems. They use various therapeutic techniques, such as cognitive-behavioural therapy (CBT), psychoanalytic therapy, and humanistic therapy to help students manage their problems
- Student counsellors can offer to facilitate group therapy sessions for students who share similar issues. Group therapy can be particularly effective for students who feel isolated or alone
- Student counsellors are able to refer students to other professionals or services when necessary for example, to psychiatrists, psychologists, or social workers for more specialised care (Pearce et al., 2017)
- Student counsellors are trained to intervene in crisis situations, such as suicide attempts or severe mental health crises. They provide immediate support and referral to appropriate services
- Student counsellors provide education and training to students, staff, and parents about mental health issues. They promote mental health awareness and provide information about self-care, stress management, and healthy coping mechanisms (Stafford et al., 2018)
- Student counsellors advocate for the needs of students with mental health problems. They work with school administrators, teachers, and parents to create a supportive and inclusive environment for students (Cooper, 2013)
- In addition to these roles, student counsellors in colleges and schools in the UK also play a crucial role in promoting student retention and academic success. They work closely with teachers, staff, and parents to identify and address academic difficulties and provide support to students who are struggling with their studies (Cooper et al., 2020). Student counsellors may provide study skills training, time management support, and academic coaching to help students improve their academic performance

Student counsellors also play a vital role in promoting diversity, equality, and inclusion in colleges and schools in the UK. They work with students from diverse backgrounds, including students from different ethnic, cultural, and religious backgrounds, students with disabilities, and students from disadvantaged backgrounds and provide support and advocacy for these students, ensuring that they have access to the resources and services they need to succeed (Cooper, 2013).

A study by a University of Roehampton team found school-based humanistic counselling led to significant reductions in pupils' psychological distress over the long-term, compared to pupils who only received pastoral care and that pupils who were offered counselling experienced significantly improved self-esteem, as well as large increases in their achievement of personal goals. The central obstacle to counselling provision in every institution continues to be costly, however, and the study calculates that the cost per student ranges between £300 and £400 (Cooper et al., 2020).

However, there are some challenges associated with providing mental health support in schools and colleges, and student counsellors may face some barriers to providing effective support. In some cases, student counsellors may also face challenges in balancing the demands of their role with other responsibilities, such as administrative tasks and meeting with parents and teachers. Additionally, there may be stigma associated with seeking mental health support, which can make it more difficult for students to access the services they need (Caldwell et al., 2019).

Figure 3.3 Self-reflection case studies

Case Study Scenario 1: A student counsellor is appointed in your college to help students with academic and personal problems. The counsellor is trained and experienced, but students are hesitant to approach them.

Self-reflection Exercise:

Reflect on the following questions:

1. *What measures can you take to make students more comfortable approaching the counsellor?*
2. *How can you help the counsellor promote their services to students and create awareness?*
3. *How can you help to overcome any systemic barriers that might be discouraging students from seeking counselling?*

Case Study Scenario 2: A new counsellor is well trained, but there is a lack of communication between the counsellor and teachers.
  Self-reflection Exercise:
  How can communication between the counsellor and teachers be improved?

1. *Could you suggest any policies or procedures that need to be established to ensure better communication between the counsellor and teachers?*
2. *What training or professional development can be provided to teachers to enable them to better support the counsellor and their services?*

Mental Health awareness training

On top of direct counselling provision, 86% of colleges also provided general mental health awareness training for all staff, complimented with focused mental health training for pastoral staff (90%) and teaching staff (69%). This was backed up further by a large majority of colleges now training all staff in mental health awareness and 90% of pastoral staff receiving training on specific issues such as suicide awareness, holding difficult conversations and other mental health related issues (AoC, 2023).

Mental Health First Aid (MHFA)

One highly recommended form of mental health training in schools and colleges in the UK is Mental Health First Aid training (Hadlaczky et al. (2014). The role of a Mental Health First Aider is to provide initial support for people experiencing signs or symptoms of mental health issues and refer them to more appropriate care if necessary. They also help to open the lines of communication between the employer and staff and to reduce stigma in the workplace.

Mental Health First Aid (MHFA) courses are short introductions which aim to enable the individual to be able to recognise the signs and symptoms of common workplace mental health issues and know how to effectively guide a person towards the right mental health support. The course aims to provide:

- An in depth understanding of mental health and the factors that can affect wellbeing and knowledge on how to implement reasonable mental health adjustments when an individual returns to work and to create a positive mental health culture in the workplace
- The practical skills to spot the triggers and signs of mental illness which include an understanding of how to perform some physical first aid as part of their response to mental illness (SJA online)

According to research by Hadlaczky et al. (2014) MHFA training had several positive impacts on staff who had undertaken training on it. These included:

- Increasing knowledge regarding mental health problems
- Decreasing negative attitudes toward individuals suffering from mental health problem
- Increasing help-providing behaviour

Overall, researchers suggest that it has impacts on the general population of schools and colleges as it increases mental health literacy, improves self-recognition, into own and others emotional wellbeing, enhances mental health-related vocabulary, and increases coping skills.

77% of colleges stated they had staff trained in MHFA in 2017, which rose to 95% in 2023 and 96% of colleges reported to have trained Mental Health First Aiders (AoC, 2023).

Suicide training

Since the COVID-19 lockdowns colleges in the UK have been experiencing far higher numbers of learners presenting with low mood, suicidal ideation, and self-harming behaviours. Research by the AoC in 2023 reported that 70% of colleges in their survey reported and increase in attempted suicide As part of their staff development programmes, 61% of colleges are providing Suicide First Aid training (AoC, 2023).

Suicide First Aid training courses are short courses designed to provide basic knowledge in identifying the warning signs of suicide, enhanced skills on how to communicate with persons-at-risk or may be having suicidal thoughts and motivate them to seek help (Hadlaczky et al., 2014).

Research into the training of Suicide first Aid programmes suggested that the pilot training raised awareness and improved participants' knowledge on how to assist a suicidal person, including warning signs. It also contributed to a positive change in attitude or beliefs towards suicide and helped them to develop skills how to communicate with persons-at-risk and motivate them to seek help, while keeping the person safe (Hadlaczky et al., 2014).

Specialist Mental Health Mentors (SMHMs)

SMHMs support students across a range of issues including managing the impact of mental health conditions such as anxiety, depression personality disorders. Suicidal thoughts, self-harm and using drugs and alcohol (Hubble and Bolton, 2019). In addition, they can also help with dealing with stressful situations such as leaving home and living independently, transition to/from Higher Education, arranging clinical support, transition between years, reconnecting after a period of absence, examinations and assessments and coursework deadlines and self-care (UMO, 2020).

Specialist Mental Health Mentors also provide support with timetabling, goal setting, workload prioritisation, and managing expectations about appropriate levels of study. They will work with the student on short- and long-term targets, providing them with the tools and the mindset to achieve personal academic goals.

Recent research has shown that Specialist Mental Health Mentoring positively impacts on three key areas for individuals: functioning, performance, and experience. Students consistently report improved course engagement and attainment, better participation in student life, increased ability to take responsibility for their own mental health, improved relationships with peers, academic staff and family, and better preparedness for work after graduation. These outcomes are not only beneficial to the individual student but benefit the institution and wider society by ensuring successful completion of studies and entry into the workforce (UMO, 2020). The Specialist Mentor role is normally funded by Disabled Students Allowances (DSAs).

Specialist Mentors either have specific mental health professional qualifications or significant equivalent experience in the field of Mental Health. The qualifications required are set by the Department of Education in consultation with relevant professional bodies and consider the need for mentors to understand and respond to a student's mental health condition as it manifests within the duration of their course (DFE, 2021). Although a Mentor should not be directly responsible for crisis support and intervention, they need an ability to assess risk and safety within the context of their role, in order to ensure that students are correctly signposted.

Figure 3.4 Teaching exercises

Here are two self-help exercises that could be useful to one of your students who is finding it difficult to focus on their work because of mental health barriers.

1 Visualisation Exercise: Take a moment to imagine yourself completing the assignment. Close your eyes and breathe deeply. Imagine yourself sitting at your desk or table with your materials spread out in front of you. Visualise the process of completing the assignment step by step, from beginning to end. See yourself writing, researching, and editing. Imagine the satisfaction and relief you feel as you finish each section. See yourself submitting the completed assignment on time. Finally, visualise the sense of accomplishment and pride you feel when you receive a good grade. Hold onto this positive image as you begin working on the assignment

2 Goal-Setting Exercise: Start by setting a specific, achievable goal for completing the assignment. Break the assignment down into manageable chunks and set a goal for completing each section. Write down your goals on a piece of paper or in a planner. Use a timer to help you stay on track and work in short, focused bursts. Celebrate your progress along the way by taking short breaks or rewarding yourself with a small treat. When you reach your goal, take a moment to reflect on your accomplishment and set a new goal for the next section. By breaking the assignment down into smaller, more achievable goals, you can reduce feelings of overwhelm and increase your sense of control over the process

---

Peer support and mental health

According to Coleman et al. (2017) peer support involves developing the knowledge, skills and experience of young people and children to develop their understanding and skills to enable them to support the confidence and self-awareness of other children and young people

The backbone of modern peer support is based upon a 'disposition to kindness' characterised by empathy, normalising of experiences, sharing of coping strategies and the building of a support community, which are just some of the reported benefits (Cate, 2022).

There are different types of peer support, but they all involve both giving and receiving support. This could be sharing knowledge or providing emotional support, social interaction or practical help. Everyone's experiences are treated as equally important, and no one is more of an expert than anyone else.

Research shows that peer support can improve people's wellbeing, meaning they have fewer hospital stays, larger support networks, and better self-esteem, confidence, and social skills (Theodosiou and Glick, 2020). Peer-led programmes focusing on mental health have demonstrated positive outcomes regarding increasing knowledge, reducing stigma and an increase in perception of self-efficacy and autonomy, which relate strongly to the idea of resilience (Bartoli et al. (2018).

School-based peer support provision in the UK has gained in popularity especially over recent years. Houlston and Smith (2010) estimate that the figure is over half of schools. There are no official figures for post compulsory education, but its use appears to have increased since the COVID-19 lockdown.

Peer Support is an umbrella term to encompass an array of interventions and approaches that may be offered across different settings. These might include peer tutoring, peer coaching, peer listening, peer mentoring, peer mediation, peer counselling, befriending, and buddying. (DFE, 2017). Although approaches to peer support can be quite distinctive and varied, they offer three common features that include:

- Children and young people helping and supporting each other
- Support being offered in a planned and structured way
- Supporters that are trained to fulfil their role (Cowie and James, 2016)

There are many different types of peer support. Some examples include:

- Support groups or self-help groups. These are run by trained peers and focus on emotional support, sharing experiences, education, and practical activities
- One-to-one support sometimes called mentoring or befriending. Students meet in person and discuss individual problems, Many school-based peer support projects are based on one-to-one delivery, for example with peer supporters who undergo training 'matched' with or assigned to particular targeted individuals, or offering ad hoc support on a drop-in or appointment basis to anyone in need
- Online forums. Peer support can take many forms. It may be for particular groups of people (with a specific health condition or from a certain ethnic

group, for instance). It could be provided face-to-face, on the phone or online. It may be weekly, monthly, ongoing or for a limited time.
- Peer support is often targeted at the following groups in education who can be seen as vulnerable Young people (Mental Health Foundation, 2020). These include.
- Young people with parents with mental health difficulties (Wasserstein and La Greca, 1996)
- Who offend or join gangs
- Who are in care
- With a parent in prison
- Who are young carers
- Who are at risk from being excluded from education
- Who are migrants and refugees –
- With a long-term illness/disability
- Who are experiencing family conflict and domestic violence
- In the lowest socio-economic group
- Members of the LGBTQ community and concerns/question about Gender Identity

Peer support programmes can help with various issues, including:

- Addiction
- Anxiety
- Depression
- Bereavement
- Relationship problems
- Other mental health conditions

According to DFE (2017) there are five core principles to a successful peer mentoring strategy:

- Work where young people are at and be creative in how you engage young people
- Involve the right people by thinking carefully about mentor and mentee recruitment
- Focus on relationships to build trust to create space for change
- Encourage young people's ownership through collaboration, co-design, and co-production with young people
- Be safe and work within boundaries by ensuring that mentors are adequately trained and supervised

According to research by Coleman et al. (2017) peer support is generally effective and most popular with females and there is some evidence to show that some forms of peer mentoring programmes in UK schools can potentially result in a range of positive outcomes for young people. Such as increased happiness and wellbeing, improved self-esteem, confidence, and emotional resilience, improved social skills and relationships and have a positive impact on the school environment.

Some of the risks of peer mentoring that have been identified by researchers include the fear young people may not give constructive help and may in fact cause more harm than good which may be especially significant for mental health, as it is perceived as a complex topic (Anna Freud Centre (2019). There is also a secondary concern over 'tip sharing', whereby support groups for certain problems such as anorexia can lead to information sharing about hiding problems or avoiding scrutiny. These fears have been countered by Theodosiou and Glick (2020) who suggest that "given that children are turning to their peers most, it is hoped that peer support will improve the effectiveness of a resource children and young people are already using".

A study by Butler et al. (2022) into determining whether different sources of social support, including family adult support, school adult support, and school peer support, are associated with mental wellbeing in children and adolescents suggested that the different forms of support had variable impacts on the mental health of children and young people in the UK.

They suggested that firstly, all three sources, family, school and peer support working together was the most effective type of support. Secondly that having access to an adult both at home and in school provided a greater protective effect against mental health issues than either one alone. Thirdly, that schools provide a crucial context in fostering positive peer relationships and supportive teacher–student relationships to promote mental health and resilience for all children, including both those with and without supportive home environments was highlighted. Finally, the study indicated that peer support might be the most important protective factor against low mental wellbeing (2022).

Figure 3.5 Self-reflection exercise

1 *Think about your experiences with supporting students with mental health issues*
2 *Consider the ways in which peer support has been effective in helping these students*
3 *Reflect on the specific instances in which peer support has made a significant impact on a student's mental health*
4 *Ask yourself: what aspects of peer support seem to be most helpful to students? Is it the shared experience of struggling with mental health, the opportunity to connect with someone who can relate to their experience, or something else entirely?*
5 *Finally, consider ways in which you can promote and enhance peer support programs at your institution. How can you better engage students in peer support opportunities, and how can you ensure that these programs are meeting the needs of students with mental health challenges?*

> **Figure 3.6 Self-reflection exercise**
>
> 1 Reflect on your own experiences with mental health challenges
> 2 Think about the support systems you have had in place throughout your journey with mental health
> 3 Consider whether or not you have ever sought out peer support as a means of coping with your mental health issues
> 4 Ask yourself: what impact has peer support had on your own mental health? Has it been a positive or negative experience?
> 5 Finally, think about how your own experiences with peer support can inform your approach to supporting students with mental health challenges. How can you use your own insights to better connect with students and help them find the support they need?

Intelligent student referral systems

Schools and colleges are often the first point of contact for young people seeking support. By providing an intelligent mental health referral system, schools and colleges can ensure that young people can access appropriate and timely support. By providing an intelligent mental health referral system, schools and colleges can help to mitigate these negative effects of mental health such as poor attendance, decreased motivation, and reduced academic achievement and ensuring that young people can access the support they need to manage their mental health.

It can help to reduce the stigma associated with mental health issues among young people. Many young people may be reluctant to seek help for mental health problems due to the fear of being stigmatised or ostracised by their peers (Ahmedani, 2011). By providing a discreet and confidential referral system, schools and colleges can ensure that young people feel comfortable seeking help and can receive support without fear of judgement.

It could help to improve the overall mental health of young people in schools and colleges. Early intervention and support, schools and colleges can help young people to develop coping mechanisms and build resilience to manage their mental health (Cho et al., 2021). This can have long-term benefits for their wellbeing and may even prevent more serious mental health problems from developing in the future.

It can also help to reduce the workload of school and college staff who may otherwise be responsible for providing mental health support to young people. Teachers and other staff members may not have the training or expertise to provide the appropriate support for mental health issues, and an intelligent referral system can ensure that young people receive the support they need from trained professionals (Faisal et al., 2023).

An intelligent mental health referral system in schools and colleges in the UK would ideally have the following features:

- Automated screening and assessment. The system should have the ability to screen and assess students for mental health issues through online assessments or surveys. This would help to identify students who may be struggling with mental health issues
- Personalisation. It should be able to provide personalised recommendations and referrals based on the specific needs and preferences of each student. This could include recommendations for mental health services, self-help resources, or peer support groups
- Accessibility. The system should be accessible to all students, regardless of their location or background. This could include providing online resources or referrals to local mental health services
- Confidentiality and privacy. The system should prioritise confidentiality and privacy in all interactions with students, ensuring that their personal information and mental health status are protected and have the ability to track and analyse data on student mental health referrals and outcomes to continuously improve and optimise its recommendations and services
- Integration with existing school and college systems. It should be integrated with existing school and college systems to ensure seamless communication and collaboration between teachers, counsellors, and mental health professionals and work in collaboration with mental health professionals to ensure that students receive appropriate and timely support (Hayes et al., 2023). This could involve providing referrals to mental health professionals or incorporating mental health professionals into the system's recommendations

Research into Mental Health Services and Schools Link Expanded Programme by Campbell-Jack (2020) provided the following conclusions as to the effectiveness of referral and inter agency collaboration:

- Overall, the expanded programme resulted in measurable improvements to some aspects of communication and joint working between schools and NHS Children and Young People's Mental Health Services
- Workshop participants in the new training programmes reported in surveys greater awareness and knowledge of risk factors and mental health issues relating to children and young people and a clearer understanding of referral pathways across different professionals and evidence-based practice

Figure 3.7   Self-reflection activities

Self-reflection Case Study Activity 1:Evaluating Mental Health Referral Systems in Schools

Step 1:   Begin by taking a moment to reflect on your own experiences with mental health referral systems in schools. Ask yourself the following questions:

- Have you ever needed to access mental health support at school? If so, what was your experience like?
- Did you feel that the referral system was easy to navigate? Were there any barriers to accessing support?
- Did you feel that your privacy and confidentiality were respected during the referral process?
- Were you satisfied with the quality of the mental health support that you received?
- What improvements would you suggest to the mental health referral system in your school?

Step 2:   Research the mental health referral system in your school or college. Look for information about:

- The process for accessing mental health support
- The types of support available (e.g., counselling, therapy, group support)
- The qualifications and training of mental health professionals providing support
- The policies and procedures in place to protect student privacy and confidentiality

Step 3:   Compare your personal experiences with the information you have gathered about the mental health referral system in your school or college. Consider the following questions:

- Does the information you have gathered align with your personal experiences? If not, how do they differ?
- Are there any gaps or inconsistencies in the information provided by your school or college?
- What improvements would you suggest to the mental health referral system in your school based on your personal experiences and the information you have gathered?

Self-reflection Case Study Activity 2: Evaluating Mental Health Referral Systems in Colleges

Step 1: Begin by taking a moment to reflect on your own experiences with mental health referral systems in college. Ask yourself the following questions:

- Have you ever needed to access mental health support at college? If so, what was your experience like?
- Did you feel that the referral system was easy to navigate? Were there any barriers to accessing support?
- Did you feel that your privacy and confidentiality were respected during the referral process?
- Were you satisfied with the quality of the mental health support that you received?
- What improvements would you suggest to the mental health referral system in your college?

Step 2: Research the mental health referral system in your college. Look for information about:

- The process for accessing mental health support
- The types of support available (e.g., counselling, therapy, group support)
- The qualifications and training of mental health professionals providing support
- The policies and procedures in place to protect student privacy and confidentiality

Step 3: Compare your personal experiences with the information you have gathered about the mental health referral system in your college. Consider the following questions:

- Does the information you have gathered align with your personal experiences? If not, how do they differ?
- Are there any gaps or inconsistencies in the information provided by your college?
- What improvements would you suggest to the mental health referral system in your college based on your personal experiences and the information you have gathered?

Partnerships with NHS MH providers

According to the Association of Colleges 2023 survey 80% of colleges reported working with other local and national mental health providers and charities to try to meet the demand from learners working within a range of systems, including Public Health services run by local authorities, NHS Children and Adolescent services, Integrated Care Partnerships, and other voluntary and community providers.

The level of collaboration and integration with local mental health services also varied and according to the AoC survey, 72% of colleges reported that they do not have joined up mental health provision with their local NHS system, and 47% colleges were not aware of local mental health support teams. Of the 53% of colleges who reported knowing about their local mental health support team, over a quarter were not yet linked up with them.

According to a study by Stem 4 (2022) long waiting lists for learners who sought access to Community and Mental Health Services (CAMHS) also put added pressure on colleges when students could not receive help from elsewhere. Additionally, FE providers noted that the lack of data sharing with local authorities meant that colleges had no data about pre-existing mental health issues or previous support accessed. This data vacuum caused delays in students being identified for support and getting the help they need, both from the college and wider mental health services (AoC, 2023).

Social prescribing can also be used effectively by colleges and other institutions which can help to improve mental health by connecting people to community services, reducing pressure on GPs and overprescribing. It connects people to non-medical support to address these issues and other unmet needs. It can be effective when young people are representing anxiety and loneliness, emotional difficulties, being socially isolated or at risk of social isolation, general mental health difficulties, and young mothers who were classified as vulnerable and lacking in self-esteem (Hayes et al., 2023). In 2022 £3.6m was awarded by the government to the National Association for Social Prescribing to support its services.

Unfortunately, the level of integration of local services, transition data from schools and engagement with local Mental Health Support Teams varied significantly depending on location as only 28% of colleges reported they had joined up mental health provision with their local NHS system, and only 43% of colleges were aware of local mental health support teams in 2023 (AoC, 2023).

The role of Mental Health Support Teams (MHSTs)

In 2017, the Government published its Green Paper. Transforming Children and Young People's Mental Health Provision, which detailed proposals for expanding access to mental health care for children and young people, building on the national NHS transformation programme. The proposals were focused on providing additional support through schools and colleges and reducing waiting times for treatment. As a result of the proposals the government established Mental Health Support Teams to act as links with children and young people's mental health (CYPMH) services and be supervised by NHS staff (DFE, 2018).

Since 2023 287 MHSTs have become operational, covering over 4,700 schools and colleges. The government estimates that there will be 500 teams up and running in the next few years (DFE, 2018). MHSTs have three main functions: delivering evidence-based mental health interventions, supporting the senior mental health lead on a whole school or college approach to mental health and providing advice to school and college staff and liaising with external specialist services.

They are made up of a range of different health professionals, including a new role educational mental health practitioner (EMHPs) and trained to deliver evidence-based mental health interventions in schools and colleges, supporting those with mild to moderate mental health needs including providing low intensity, direct support, whole-school or college evidence-based interventions for teachers and students and supporting parents and carers with workshops. They are area dependent and in partnership with local stakeholders including the local authority, NHS England, and local education partners.

They can provide one-to-one tailored support programmes for problems such as for anxiety or stress or worries and also organise a variety of workshops and groups throughout the year on a range topics.

A pilot program for MHSTs was launched in 2018, and a recent evaluation of the pilot found that MHSTs were associated with improvements in mental health outcomes for young people. Specifically, the evaluation found that young people who received support from MHSTs had significant reductions in anxiety, depression, and behavioural difficulties, as well as improvements in self-esteem and emotional wellbeing (DFE, 2020). Additionally, MHSTs have been found to be particularly effective in identifying and supporting young people with mild to moderate mental health difficulties. By providing early intervention and support, MHSTs may help prevent mental health problems from becoming more severe and long-term (2020).

While MHSTs are still a relatively new initiative, some research evidence suggests that they may be effective in providing mental health support to young people. A report published by the Education Policy Institute in 2020 found that MHSTs can improve access to mental health services, reduce waiting times, and provide early intervention for young people with mental health needs (Crenna-Jennings and Hutchinson, 2020).

Barnardo's research (2022) into their effectiveness suggested that:

- MHSTs are effective at supporting children and young people with mild to moderate mental health problems. They improve outcomes for those with access to them
- MHSTs are cost effective, saving the government £1.90 for every £1 invested. The analysis also suggests that the cost to the state of failing to roll-out MHSTs to 6.5 million children and young people is an estimated £1.3 billion
- High demand and long waiting lists for Children and Adolescent Mental Health Services (CAMHS), as well as a lack of other support options, places pressure on MHSTs which are set up only for mild to moderate mental health issues
- Three quarters of children and young people want more support in schools (76%) and 73% of parents would like to see more funding available for mental health in schools

Figure 3.8 Self-refection exercises

1 *Reflection on Communication Strategies:* Think about the current communication strategies your institution has in place with external agencies that support students' mental health. Reflect on whether these strategies are effective or not. Ask yourself:

- How do we currently communicate with external agencies?
- Are there any barriers to effective communication?
- How can we improve our communication strategies with external agencies?
- Do we have a designated point person responsible for liaising with external agencies?
- Are there any particular agencies that we need to reach out to that we are not currently in contact with?

2 *Reflection on Collaboration:* Think about how your institution collaborates with external agencies to support students' mental health. Reflect on whether these collaborations are effective or not. Ask yourself:

- What is our current level of collaboration with external agencies?
- Are we effectively utilising their services and resources?
- Are we incorporating external agencies' recommendations and feedback into our mental health programs and services?
- Are we collaborating with external agencies in a way that is mutually beneficial?
- Are there any particular areas of collaboration that we need to improve upon?

3 *Reflection on Student Feedback:* Think about the feedback you have received from students about the mental health support services and resources provided by your institution. Reflect on whether these services and resources are meeting students' needs and if external agencies could provide additional support. Ask yourself:

- What feedback have we received from students about our mental health services and resources?
- Are there any areas of concern or improvement highlighted in the feedback?
- Are there any gaps in the services and resources we provide that external agencies could fill?
- How can we better incorporate student feedback into our collaborations with external agencies?

> **Figure 3.9   Teaching activities**
>
> *In tutorials I find it useful to explain to students what external systems are in place to support their mental health issues. I like to use activities to keep it engaging for them. Here are two that I have used over the past years to teach them about MHSTs.*
>
> *1 Role-Playing Scenarios: I divide the students into small groups and give each group a different scenario in which a student is experiencing mental health issues. Each group should take turns acting out the role of a Mental Health Support Team member and providing support and guidance to the student. After each scenario, have the groups debrief and discuss how they handled the situation and what they could have done differently*
>
> *2 Panel Discussion: When there is time, I invite Mental Health Support Team members to speak to the students in a panel format. The panellists can share their experiences, roles, and responsibilities in providing mental health support to students. After the panel discussion, encourage the students to ask questions and engage in a dialogue with the panellists. This can help the students gain a better understanding of how Mental Health Support Teams work and how they can collaborate with them to provide the best support for their clients*

Supporting parents

According to research by the Department for Education (2017) schools and colleges in their survey worked hard to engage parents and families in issues around mental health through various communication approaches. Parents were also encouraged to support their child to access more tailored interventions aimed at improving mental health. In some settings, parents themselves were provided with support for their own mental health needs, including signposting to organisations that provide help and counselling.

Schools and colleges in the UK can support parents of students with mental health issues by taking a proactive approach to communication, providing access to resources and support, and by partnering with mental health professionals (DFE, 2017). This can include:

- Proactive Communication. Schools and colleges should establish open lines of communication with parents, including regular updates on student progress and opportunities for parents to share concerns. Educators should be trained to recognise signs of mental health issues and provide parents with guidance on how to seek help

- Access to Resources and Support. Schools and colleges should provide parents with resources and support services to help them better understand mental health issues and how to support their children. This could include training sessions, informational handouts, and access to support groups
- Partnership with Mental Health Professionals. Schools and colleges should partner with mental health professionals to provide parents with the necessary resources and support. This could involve offering access to mental health professionals who can provide counselling and support or working with local mental health clinics to provide referrals for families in need

Pastoral staff saw engaging parents as one of their prime roles and used three key facilitators in this process; a variety of communication approaches, which included newsletters, portals apps and face to face events such as parent evenings or coffee mornings, positive and non-judgemental dialogue and dedicated staffing/space for families (DFE, 2017).

The benefits of this collaboration with parents included:

- Improved communication pathways between families and schools/colleges
- Designated and accessible staff members, who parents had met and with whom they had developed positive relationships, led to more honesty from parents about their circumstances
- Schools and colleges could support the whole family more appropriately and refer to other relevant support (both internal and external to the school)
- Schools to intervene early and more effectively tackle issues which may be impacting upon children's education. This holistic support was felt to be more likely to sustain lasting impact and increase positive long-term outcomes for both children and their families (Butler et al., 2022)

Some of the central barriers to developing a supporting relationship with parents included the following areas:

- Type of provision. It was suggested that primary schools tended to have a stronger infrastructure to build these relationships than secondary schools or colleges.
- Parents' views of the school. If parents had a negative view of school based on their own experience or past communication from the school around their child's behaviour, they tended to be hostile or indifferent to closer relationships
- Stigma. Some parents are loath to label their children with potential mental health problems, which could make it hard to gain their permission to put in place specialist support or referrals
- Confidentiality. Some staff had struggled with being upfront with parents because of the conflict with confidentiality which could be frustrating for parents where there had previously been an open dialogue (DFE, 2021)

Parental mental health issues

Many parents with mental health problems are able to manage their condition and minimise its impact on their children, particularly if they are able to access appropriate support. But sometimes it does affect their ability to cope with family life. Parental mental health problems may affect children differently according to the severity and type of mental health condition, the child's age and stage of development, and the child's personality (Cleaver et al., 2011; Gatsou et al., 2017; Grove et al., 2015; Hogg, 2013; Wolpert et al., 2015).

Figure 3.10 Self-reflection exercises

Context: You have been liaising with the parents of a college student who has mental health issues. The student has been struggling with depression and anxiety and has been seeing a therapist on campus. The parents have been expressing their concerns about their child's well-being and have been seeking updates on their progress.

1. What biases and assumptions did you bring to the liaison with the parents? How did they affect your communication with them?
2. How did you manage the confidentiality of the student's mental health information while also addressing the parents' concerns?
3. How did you balance the needs and perspectives of the student and their parents in your liaison with them?
4. What strategies did you use to maintain a supportive and non-judgmental stance towards the parents while also advocating for the student's autonomy and agency?

Self-reflection case study activity 2:

Context: You have been liaising with the parents of a college student who has mental health issues. The student has been struggling with severe anxiety and has been hospitalised twice in the past year. The parents have been expressing their concerns about their child's safety and have been asking for updates on their treatment plan.

1. How did you address the parents' concerns about their child's safety without breaching the student's privacy or violating their autonomy?
2. What ethical considerations did you need to consider while liaising with the parents, given the student's mental health issues and hospitalisations?
3. How did you navigate any potential conflicts between the student's preferences and their parents' desires for their care and treatment?
4. What strategies did you use to communicate with the parents in a way that was compassionate, empathetic, and supportive, while also being clear and transparent about the limitations of what you could share with them?

Supporting Transitions to further study and employment

Transitions, such as moving from school to college or from college to employment, can be particularly challenging for students with mental health issues. Educational institutions should provide additional support during these transitions to ensure that students can continue to progress in their studies and careers. Here are some ways in which this can be done:

Prepare students from an early stage for practical, social, and cultural changes. Preparing students as early as possible, and well in advance of their move, is important. Some universities and colleges do this by holding student taster days and parent sessions. It can be vital for these sessions to focus on issues like identity, resisting peer pressure, resilience in the face of adversity, maintaining good mental health and seeking help when needed. Teachers also need to discuss with them about maintaining good mental health and the importance of seeking help when needed

- Offer transition support programs to students. Schools and colleges can provide students with additional resources and guidance during these periods of change. By providing these additional resources and support, educational institutions can help students with mental health issues navigate these transitions successfully (Cate, 2022)
- Provide a range of student led therapies. The introduction of student-led therapies such as peer support, identified by students themselves as a first choice intervention (Byrom, 2018), and digital support tools, used alongside early intervention, can provide opportunities for students take responsibility for their own mental wellbeing, but also to free up resources for those students who are experiencing more critical problems (Batchelor et al., 2019)
- Develop strategies of self-care. Students could be familiarised with some of the main challenges and given the tools to self-manage and by signposting students to the relevant support services upon entry to college or university during this transitional period they can develop self-care, resilience, and self-regulation (Cate, 2022). These can also be facilitated by some of the following strategies: encouraging self-care by spending time with friends and family, providing vocational support through career counselling, job placement services and addressing stigma (Conley et al., 2020)

Transitions to employment

Employment can be a significant source of stress for people with mental health issues. Educational institutions should work with local employers to create inclusive and supportive workplaces that accommodate the needs of employees with mental health issues. Employers should be encouraged to provide mental health resources, such as counselling services and mental health awareness training, to their employees. Additionally, educational institutions can provide career guidance and job placement services that help students with mental health issues find employment opportunities that are suited to their needs (Conley et al., 2020).

Schools and colleges should continue to provide support for students with mental health issues even after they have completed their education or entered employment. This could include alumni networks, continued access to mental health services, or information on how to access mental health support in the community. Continued support can help ensure students are able to manage their mental health effectively throughout their lives and reduce the risk of relapse or other issues (Cage et al., 2021).

Figure 3.11 Supporting exercises

If you are supporting students who are undergoing transitions to education. You might want to give them these self-reflection exercises to work upon,

1 *Self-Reflection on Coping Strategies*
    For this exercise, students can reflect on coping strategies that have helped them manage their mental health challenges in the past, and consider how they can apply these strategies in the context of their transition to work or education. They can ask themselves questions such as:

- *What coping strategies have worked for me in the past when I've faced difficult situations related to my mental health?*
- *How can I apply these coping strategies in the context of my transition to work or education?*
- *Are there any new coping strategies that I can learn or adopt that might be helpful for me during this transition?*

    Students can use a journal or online platform to document their reflections and develop a plan for incorporating coping strategies into their transition.

2 *Self-Reflection on Support Systems*
    For this exercise, students can reflect on the support systems that have been helpful for them in managing their mental health challenges and consider how they can build or maintain these support systems during their transition to work or education. They can ask themselves questions such as:

- *Who are the people in my life who have been supportive of me in managing my mental health challenges?*
- *How can I maintain these relationships during my transition to work or education?*
- *Are there any new support systems that I can build or access to help me during this transition?*

    Students can use a journal or online platform to document their reflections and develop a plan for building or maintaining support systems during their transition. This can include identifying individuals or organisations they can reach out to for help, as well as strategies for maintaining connections with friends and family.

References

Ahmedani, B. K. (2011). Mental health stigma: Society, individuals, and the profession. *Journal of Social Work Values and Ethics*, 8(2): 4-1–4-16.

Anna Freud Centre. (2019). Peer support for children and young people's mental health and emotional wellbeing programme facilitator toolkit [Online]. Available from: https://www.annafreud.org/media/10015/new-toolkit_afc-3-003.pdf [Accessed 12 March 2023].

Association of Colleges Mental Health Survey Report. (2023). https://feweek.co.uk/wp-content/uploads/2023/03/AoC-Mental-Health-Survey-Report-2023.pdf

Barnardo's (2022) 'It's hard to talk'; expanding Mental Health Support Teams in education. Accessed from: https://www.barnardos.org.uk/sites/default/files/2023-01/hardtotalk-expandingmentalhealthsupportteamsschools-MHSTs-report-jan2022-v2.pdf

Bartoli, A., Cock, N., Booker, E., and Kaji, S. (2018). *An Evaluation of a Peer-Led Intervention to Build Resilience and Mental Well-Being in Young People*. Goldsmiths: University of London.

Batchelor, R., Pitman, E., Sharpington, A., Stock, M., and Cage, E. (2019). Student perspectives on mental health support and services in the UK. *Journal of Further and Higher Education*: 1–15. doi:10.1080/0309877X.2019.1579896

Butler, N., Quigg, Z., Bates, R., et al. (2022). The contributing role of family, school, and peer supportive relationships in protecting the mental wellbeing of children and adolescents. *School Mental Health*, 14: 776–88. doi:10.1007/s12310-022-09502-9

Byrom, N. (2018). An evaluation of a peer support intervention for student mental health. *Journal of Mental Health*, 27(3): 240–6. doi:10.1080/09638237.2018.1437605

Cage, E., Jones, Emma, Ryan, Gemma, Hughes, Gareth, and Spanner, Leigh. (2021). Student mental health and transitions into, through and out of university: Student and staff perspectives. *Journal of Further and Higher Education*, 45(8): 1076–89. doi:10.1080/0309877X.2021.1875203

Caldwell, D. M., Davies, S. R., Hetrick, S. E., et al. (2019). School-based interventions to prevent anxiety and depression in children and young people: A systematic review and network meta-analysis. *Lancet Psychiatry*, 6: 1011–20.

Campbell, F., Blank, L., Cantrell, A., et al. (2022). Factors that influence mental health of university and college students in the UK: A systematic review. *BMC Public Health*, 22: 1778. doi:10.1186/s12889-022-13943-x

Campbell-Jack, D. (2020). Laurie Day, and Natasha Burnley – Evaluation of the Mental Health Services and Schools Link Expanded Programme. Final Report. Department for Education.

Cate, N. (2022). *The Importance of Supporting Student Wellbeing During Transition into Higher Education*. Lincoln, UK: Lincoln Higher Education Research Institute.

Cho, I. K., Lee, Jihoon, Kim, Kyumin, Lee, Joohee, Lee, Sangha, Yoo, Soyoung, Suh, Sooyeon, and Chung, Seockhoon. (2021). Schoolteachers' resilience does but self-efficacy does not mediate the influence of stress and anxiety due to the COVID-19 pandemic on depression and subjective well-being. Social psychiatry and psychiatric rehabilitation. 12. doi:10.3389/fpsyt.2021.756195

Cleaver, H., Unell, I., and Aldgate, J. (2011). *Children's Needs: Parenting Capacity: Child Abuse: Parental Mental Illness, Learning Disability, Substance Misuse, and Domestic Violence (PDF)*. London: The Stationery Office (TSO).

Coleman, N., Sykes, Wendy, and Groom, Carola. (2017). Independent social research (ISR) peer support and children and young people's mental health. *Research Review*. Department for Education. https://assets.publishing.service.gov.uk/media/5a820b3d40f0b62305b922c5/Children_and_young_people_s_mental_health_peer_support.pdf

Conley, C. S., Shapiro, J. B., Huguenel, B. M., and Kirsch, A. C. (2020). Navigating the college years: Developmental trajectories and gender differences in psychological functioning, cognitive-affective strategies, and social well-being. *Emerging Adulthood*, 8(2): 103–117. doi:10.1177/2167696818791603

Cooper, M. (2013). *School-Based Counselling in UK Secondary Schools: A Review and Critical Evaluation*. Lutterworth: British Association for Counselling and Psychotherapy and Counselling MindEd.

Cooper, M., Stafford, M. R., Saxon, D., et al. (9 more authors). (2020). Humanistic counselling plus pastoral care as usual versus pastoral care as usual for the treatment of psychological distress in adolescents in UK state schools (ETHOS): A randomised controlled trial. *The Lancet Child & Adolescent Health*, 5(3): 178–89. ISSN 2352-4642.

Corrigan, P. W., Druss, Benjamin G., and Perlick, Deborah A. (2014). The impact of mental illness stigma on seeking and participating in Mental Health Care. *Psychological Science in the Public Interest*, 15(2): 37–70.

Cowie, H., and James, A. I. (2016). Peer support in England, Japan and South Korea. In: P. K. Smith, K. Kwak, and Y. Toda (eds.), *School Bullying in Different Cultures – Eastern and Western Perspectives*. Cambridge, UK: Cambridge University Press.

Crenna-Jennings, W., and Hutchinson, J. (2020). *Access to Child and Adolescent Mental Health Services in 2019*. Education Policy Institute. https://epi.org.uk/publications-and-research/access-to-child-and-adolescent-mental-health-services-in-2019/

Department for Education. (2017). Peer support and children and young people's mental health [Online]. https://assets.publishing.service.gov.uk/government/uploads/system/uploads/attachment_data/file/603107/Children_and_young_people_s_mental_health_peer_support.pdf [Accessed 12 May 2023].

Department for Education. (2018). *Government Response to the Consultation on Transforming Children and Young People's Mental Health Provision: A Green Paper and Next Steps*. London: HMSO.

Department for Education. (2020). Evaluation of the peer support for mental health and wellbeing pilots [Online]. Available from: https://assets.publishing.service.gov.uk/government/uploads/system/uploads/attachment_data/file/863560/Evaluation_of_the_peer_support_pilots_-_Main_report.pdf [Accessed 12 March 2020].

Department for Education. (2021). Promoting and supporting mental health and wellbeing in schools and colleges. Guidance. Find out what help you can get to develop a whole school or college approach to mental health and wellbeing. Available from: https://www.gov.uk/guidance/mental-health-and-wellbeing-support-in-schools-and-colleges

Fazel, M., Soneson, E., Sellars, E., Butler, G., and Stein, A. (2023). Partnerships at the interface of education and mental health services: The utilisation and acceptability of the provision of specialist liaison and teacher skills training. *International Journal of Environmental Research and Public Health*, 20(5): 4066. doi:10.3390/ijerph20054066

Garside, M., Wright, B., Nekooi, R., and Allgar, V. (2021). Mental health provision in UK secondary schools. *International Journal of Environmental Research and Public Health*, 18: 12222. doi:10.3390/ijerph182212222

Gatsou, L., et al. (2017). The challenges presented by parental mental illness and the potential of a whole-family intervention to improve outcomes for families. *Child & Family Social Work*, 22(1): 388–97

Grove, C., Reupert, A., and Maybery, D. (2015). Gaining knowledge about parental mental illness: How does it empower children? *Child & Family Social Work*, 20(4): 377–86.

Hadlaczky, Gergö, Hökby, Sebastian, Mkrtchian, Anahit, Carli, Vladimir, and Wasserman, Danuta. (2014). Mental Health First Aid is an effective public health intervention for improving knowledge, attitudes, and behavior. A meta-analysis. *International Review of Psychiatry*, 26. doi:10.3109/09540261.2014.924910

Hayes, D., Jarvis-Beesley, P., Mitchell, D., Polley M., Husk K., [On behalf of the NASP Academic Partners Collaborative]. (2023). *The Impact of Social Prescribing on Children and Young People's Mental Health and Wellbeing*. London: National Academy for Social Prescribing.

Hewett, R. (2019). *Measuring Well-Being in Higher Education*. Higher Education Policy Institute. https://www.hepi.ac.uk/2019/05/09/measuring-well-being-in-higher-education/

Hogg, S. (2013). *Prevention in Mind: All Babies Count: Spotlight on Perinatal Mental Health*. London: NSPCC.

Houlston, N. and Smith, C. 2010. The impact of a peer counselling scheme to address bullying in an all-girl London secondary school: A short-term longitudinal study. *British Journal of Educational Psychology*, 79(1): 69–86.

Hubble, S., and Bolton, P. (2019). Support for students with mental health issues in higher education in England, Briefing Paper, House of Commons Library (accessed 04/23).

Hughes, G., and Bowers-Brown, T. (2021). Student services, personal tutors, and student mental health: A case study. In: H. Huijser, M. Kek, and F. F. Padró (eds.), *Student Support Services*. Singapore: University Development and Administration. Springer. doi:10.1007/978-981-13-3364-4_23-2

Knifton, L., and Inglis, G. (2020). Poverty and mental health: Policy, practice and research implications. *BJPsych Bulletin*, 44(5): 193–96. doi:10.1192/bjb.2020.78

Lauchlan, Fraser, and Greig Susan. (2015). Educational inclusion in England: Origins, perspectives, and current directions: Inclusive Education in England. *Support for Learning*, 30. doi:10.1111/1467-9604.12075

Livingston, J. D., Tugwell, A., Korf-Uzan, K., et al. (2013). Evaluation of a campaign to improve awareness and attitudes of young people towards mental health issues. *Social Psychiatry and Psychiatric Epidemiology*, 48: 965–73. doi:10.1007/s00127-012-0617-3

Maxwell, C., Aggleton, Peter, Warwick, Ian, Yankah, Ekua, Hill, Vivian, and Mehmedbegovic-Smith, Dina. (2008). Supporting children's emotional wellbeing and mental health in England: A review. *Health Education*, 108: 272–86. doi:10.1108/09654280810884160

Mental Health Foundation. (2020). Peer Support [Online]. Available from: https://www.mentalhealth.org.uk/a-to-z/p/peer-support [Accessed 12 March 2020].

Morgan, M. (2012). The evolution of student services in the UK. *Perspectives: Policy and Practice in Higher Education*, 16(3): 77–84. doi:10.1080/13603108.2011.652990

Pearce, P., Sewell, R., Cooper, M., Osman, S., Fugard, A. J. B., and Pybis, J. (2017). Effectiveness of school-based humanistic counselling for psychological distress in young people: Pilot randomized controlled trial with follow-up in an ethnically diverse sample. *Psychology and Psychotherapy*, 90: 138–55.

Public Health England. (2020). Measuring and monitoring children and young people's mental wellbeing: A toolkit for schools and colleges. *Evidence Based Practice Unit* https://assets.publishing.service.gov.uk/media/5c2f66daed915d731281fdc2/Measuring_mental_wellbeing_in_children_and_young_people.pdf

Rainer, C., and Abdinasir, K. (2021). The state of mental health support for babies, children and young people. Members Report. The Children and Young People's Mental Health Coalition.

Stafford, M. R., Cooper, M., Barkham, M., et al. (2018). Effectiveness and cost-effectiveness of humanistic counselling in schools for young people with emotional distress (ETHOS): Study protocol for a randomised controlled trial. *Trials*, 19: 175.

STEM 4. (2022). "A service in crisis" Survey reveals GPs concerns about mental health services for children and young people. Available from: https://stem4.org.uk/

wp-content/uploads/2022/04/A-service-in-crisis-Survey-reveals-GPs-concerns-about-mental-health-services-for-CYP-Apr-22.pdf

Stewart, H. (2016). Policy and systems review Reducing the stigma of mental illness. *Global Mental Health*, 3: e17, page 1 of 14. doi:10.1017/gmh.2016.11

Theodosiou, L., and Glick, Oliver. (2020). Peer support models for children and young people with mental health problems. Children and Young People's Mental Health Coalition. https://voicesunique.org/ws/media-library/d9500dca865b4e298aa19d35b6bdda7d/peer-support-models-for-children-and-young-people-with-mental-health-problems-by-children--young-peoples-mental-health-coalition-and-centre-for-mental-health.pdf

Tonks, A. (2022). Exploring primary school Senior Mental Health Leads' experiences of supporting mental health across a school and wider community: An interpretative phenomenological analysis. Unpublished doctoral thesis for the University of Essex.

University Mentoring Organization (UMO). (2020). *The role and impact of specialist mental health mentoring on students in UK Higher Education institutes*. London: UMO.

Warwick, Ian, Maxwell, Claire, Statham, June, Aggleton, Peter, and Simon, Antonia. (2008). Supporting Mental Health and Emotional Well-Being Among Younger Students in Further Education. *Journal of Further and Higher Education*, 32: 1–13. doi:10.1080/03098770701560331

Wasserstein, S. B., and La Greca, A. M. (1996). Can peer support buffer against behavioral consequences of parental discord. *Journal of Clinical Child Psychology*, 25(2): 177–82.

Wolpert, M., et al. (2015). An exploration of the experience of attending the Kids time programme for children with parents with enduring mental health issues: Parents' and young people's views. *Clinical Child Psychology and Psychiatry*, 20(3): 406–18.

Yamaguchi, S., Mino, Yoshio, and Uddin, Shahir. (2011). Strategies and future attempts to reduce stigmatization and increase awareness of mental health problems among young people: A narrative review of educational interventions. *Psychiatry and Clinical Neurosciences*, 65(5): 405–15.

4 The relationships between social and emotional wellbeing and learning and attainment

Wellbeing and learning

Physical wellbeing and learning

Numerous studies have demonstrated the impact of physical wellbeing on student learning and performance. Sleep, hydration, exercise, and diet have all been shown to have clear effects on how students feel, learn and perform (Scullin, 2019). Having reserves of energy, concentration and stamina can help to ensure students are able to learn at their optimum level and perform in stretching academic assessments. Regular physical rest and breaks have been shown to positively impact on cognitive function making learning, problem solving and creative activity more possible (Raspberry et al., 2011).

Social wellbeing and learning

Social belonging, interaction and connection have been shown to be beneficial for student learning. Researchers such as Tinto (1992) have long argued that student sense of belonging to their college plays a significant role in determining student persistence and success. Bandura (1992), has suggested that learning is often socially situated and therefore students are more likely to learn well in classrooms in which they have a sense of connection, support and psychological safety in which the social learning environment is a safe place in which to experiment, make mistakes and correct misconceptions (Craig, and Zinkiewicz, 2010) This has implications for inclusion, as students who are marginalised by in class experiences or by curriculum content, are likely to feel a reduced sense of belonging and lower levels of psychological safety (Cacioppo et al., 2000).

Psychological wellbeing and learning

International research has indicated that students who experience mental illness are more likely to drop out of colleges and universities and underperform academically (Sutherland, 2018; Hjorth et al., 2016; Del Savio et al., 2022).

Students' ability to handle emotional stress during their studies was also found to be an important factor in preventing academic delay and dropout (Storrie et al., 2010). Heinrich and Gullone (2006) reported that loneliness, also commonly linked to depression, was an independent risk factor for low study progress. High levels of negative emotional arousal (anxiety, fear, low mood etc.) can reduce cognitive functioning, making it more difficult to learn, concentrate and problem solve (Robinson et al., 2013).

According to research by Schulte-Körne (2016) stress factors at college and school such as unempathetic and unsupportive teacher-student relationships and a poor classroom or school climate can also increase the risk for children and adolescents of developing mental health problems. They also suggested that students who reported symptoms of severe mental health problems were twice as likely to report delayed study progress compared with those who reported few and moderate problems (2016). Good wellbeing, however, has been associated with enhanced creativity and the ability to enter into a 'flow' state of learning and thus good psychological wellbeing can support good learning (Ryff, 2014).

Impact of learning on wellbeing

Research also suggests that how students engage with learning, how they are taught and how they are assessed can influence their wellbeing and therefore there is a transactional relationship between wellbeing and effective learning (Postareff et al., 2017). Deci and Ryan's (1985) research suggested that students who engage in deep learning, driven by intrinsic motivation and who gain meaning from their learning by a desire to understand and interrogate knowledge are more likely to have better wellbeing than those who engage in surface learning, driven by extrinsic motivation and learning for assignments or tests, as this can impact on stress, anxiety and a sense of overwhelm (Postareff et al., 2017).

Impact of mental health issues and wellbeing on engagement

The impact of mental health and wellbeing on engagement in teaching, learning and assessment can be broadly placed in the following categories (Lereya et al., 2019):

Lack of involvement in studies

Students with mental health challenges may seem less interested in their course, and their attendance overall may decline. Students facing anxiety or depression may feel unable to go into classes or unable to face the social interaction that comes with daily school and college life. These signs of withdrawal are typical indicators of a student facing mental health risks.

Lack of engagement in class

They may also struggle with their concentration in classes. They may be distracted by other challenges in life or maybe feeling the strain of their mental health. This may mean students are unable to contribute to sessions in their usual way, take longer to understand concepts or are simply not able to focus on the task in hand. There may be signs that a student is distracted or unfocussed.

Attainment issues

Students facing mental health challenges may see a decline in their results or prove unable to respond effectively to the high-pressure expectations of exams and assignments. Often expectations around attainment and results can compound mental health issues and become the focus for anxiety, stress, or depression (Dalsgaard et al., 2020).

Progression

Whether it be progression through the course or looking towards long-term career goals and future employment, mental health risks can often block this long-term thinking. Students may be unable to think beyond the day they are facing or their immediate problems (Tregaskis et al., 2020).

Energy and enthusiasm

Not all the effects of mental health are directed towards the academic experience. The character and personality of a student may be impacted upon by mental health challenges. This can mean that a student has less energy, they may seem less enthusiastic about college life and as a result may not engage with extra-curricular activities and social occasions. This lack of enthusiasm can often become a cycle in which they become more isolated and less able to engage with their peers and studies (Clayborne et al., 2019).

Sociability and relationships

Students facing mental health risks can often very quickly become less sociable or less interested in making new friends or building relationships. Those around the student may notice they become withdrawn and unwilling to take part in social activities (Halpern-Manners et al., 2016). Many students facing mental health risks need a support network and friends around them to help them and the change in these relationships can be a key warning sign.

Mental health and behaviour in classrooms

Young people who struggle with their mental health can be prone to irritability, emotional outbursts, aggressive behaviours, or boredom that leads to disobedience and disruption. Those exhibiting these behavioural issues are often punished to reduce the risk of disrupting other students. Behavioural problems caused by mental health challenges also make it difficult for students to form relationships with their classmates (Rainer et al., 2023).

Anxiety and learning

According to Grotan et al. (2019) students in Sweden who reported symptoms of severe mental health problems had about four times the risk of experiencing low academic self-efficacy compared with those who reported few and moderate symptoms of mental health problems. They suggested that anxiety may contribute to excessive worrying, restlessness, unfounded fear of not accomplishing things which combined with procrastination and avoidance behaviour, may contribute to students developing problems in learning participation in class. This could in turn contribute to avoidance, isolation and loneliness, leading to poorer academic- and social inclusion with both fellow students and staff at the educational institution (Byrd and McKinney, 2012; Salzer, 2012).

High levels of stress and anxiety can also reduce cognitive functioning at a neurological level. This reduces students' ability to engage in complex thinking, to access old memories or make new, complex memories, to problem solve and to maintain concentration. In other words, anxiety reduces the capacity for learning and academic performance at a biological level (Vogel and Schwabe, 2016).

Figure 4.1   Learners Self-reflection task

This can used as a checklist and given to learners to reflect on their feelings after a summative assessment:

1 Was I appropriately prepared and did I understand what I had to do and how to do it?
2 Did I recognise my own skills and resources?
3 Did I have the necessary skills to undertake the task or was I able to develop them as a result of completing the task?
4 Did I have the necessary and appropriate support from staff?
5 Did I have the necessary and appropriate support from other students?
6 Did I have the resources I needed – including time?
7 Did I feel intrinsically motivated and focussed on the aspects of the task that were meaningful to me?
8 Was I in an environment that felt psychologically safe?

Wellbeing and the curriculum

The curriculum is one of the few guaranteed points of contact between student and school and college. Curriculum therefore plays a central role in the student experience and any school or college approach to mental health and wellbeing. Students must interact with their curriculum if they are to progress and remain a student. While learning and academic achievement are the primary foci of the curriculum, it can only succeed in maximising both outcomes if the curriculum is also conducive to wellbeing (Houghton and Anderson, 2017).

Recent work in this area has suggested that the design and delivery of curriculum can have both positive and negative impacts on student wellbeing and on student learning (Upsher et al., 2022; Lister et al., 2023). Research has shown that changes to the structure of the curriculum, to curriculum content, to modes and methods of assessment, to grading and to the social environment within the classroom (online and in person) and in group learning activities, have the potential to improve both student wellbeing and learning (Brooker and McKague, 2019). There are many ways in which the curriculum could undermine the mental health and wellbeing of students and include the following:

According to research (Aubrecht, 2019) it can exclude students, through hidden curricula, undermining sense of identity and belonging and can undermine students' sense of autonomy if it is overly prescriptive or if students do not have clarity on why they are being asked to engage in particular learning and assessment tasks.

- It can undermine students' sense of competence, self-confidence, and achievement if it is not appropriately stretching, if feedback is overly critical or absent, and if students are not supported to develop their ability to self-reflect on their own growth and develop self-efficacy (Silveira et al., 2019).
- It can undermine autonomous motivation if learning is confused, improperly sequenced, lacks personal meaning and assumes the existence of pre-knowledge which students do not have (Kickert et al., 2022).
- The curriculum can create stress if deadline pile-up results in students having to complete significant amounts of work at the same time, potentially competing with other responsibilities leading to exhaustion and the adoption of surface learning strategies (Rubin, 2010).
- It can impact on levels of anxiety in students when the learning environment feels hostile or potentially threatening. For example, if it lacks psychological safety or peers are characterised as the competition rather than collaborative learners or when it encourages students to adopt unhealthy study behaviours such as going without sleep, or working long hours without breaks (Baik et al., 2017).

A curriculum that supports student wellbeing could be characterised as one in which:

- Learning provides meaning, purpose, and a sense of fulfilment within a learning environment is inclusive, supportive, health promoting and psychologically safe (Aubrecht, 2019). It supports sustainable personal growth in knowledge, understanding, skills and confidence and which engages student voice and teaching, learning and assessment are modified in response to student learning, experience, and insight (Kickert et al., 2022).
- It should take a holistic approach to education, which means it should focus on the physical, emotional, social, and mental well-being of the students and also to promote physical activity and should encourage physical activity and provide opportunities for students to engage in sports and other forms of physical exercise (Silveira et al., 2019).
- It should provide mental health support and resources, such as counselling services and workshops on stress management and mindfulness and in addition, the curriculum should be flexible and allow students to have some control over their learning. This can include options for personalised learning plans, self-directed study, and a variety of learning experiences (Baik et al., 2017).

Assessment and wellbeing

Assessment strategy is a central aspect of the curriculum and with high stakes summative assessment there is a significant price to pay for failure. Students will be focussed mainly or solely on what they need to do to succeed which can create unhelpful stress, anxiety, self-doubt, and fatigue in students (Jones et al., 2021).

Assessment for Learning (AFL), however, places a priority on promoting student learning and can support a performance focussed culture that is beneficial for learning and wellbeing as it can provide a supportive and flexible approach to assessing students' progress and learning and therefore be beneficial for students with mental health needs (Hattie and Timperley, 2007). Here are some specific ways in which AfL strategies can support UK college students with mental health needs:

Providing regular feedback

Regular feedback can be helpful for students with mental health needs who may struggle with self-esteem and self-doubt. Providing regular feedback on their progress can help students to build confidence and recognise their strengths (Hattie and Timperley, 2007).

Using a variety of assessment methods

A variety of assessment methods, such as quizzes, essays, and presentations, can help to accommodate different learning styles and allow students to demonstrate their knowledge and skills in different ways and build confidence and self-belief

Encouraging self-reflection

Reflecting on their learning can help students to develop self-awareness and self-regulation skills, which can be particularly beneficial for them. This can be done through self-assessment, peer assessment, or reflection exercises.

Creating a supportive learning environment

> This can help to reduce stress and anxiety. This can include providing clear instructions and expectations, offering opportunities for collaboration and social support, and providing resources for mental health support if needed (Howard, 2020).

Setting achievable goals

These can help to provide a sense of structure and purpose for students who may struggle with motivation and focus. They can be tailored to the individual student's needs and abilities and can be adjusted as needed (Mulliner and Tucker, 2015)

Figure 4.2 Self-Reflection task

Take a few moments to reflect on your current approach to setting goals for struggling students. Consider the following questions and jot down your responses:

1 How do you currently determine goals for struggling students? Is there a systematic process in place?
2 Are the goals you set realistic and attainable for each student's unique needs and abilities?
3 Do you involve struggling students in the goal-setting process? If yes, how? If not, why?
4 Do you track progress regularly to assess if the goals set are being achieved or if adjustments are needed?
5 How do you provide support and guidance to help struggling students work towards their goals?
6 How do you celebrate or acknowledge their progress and success along the way?

After reflecting on your current practices, write a brief paragraph summarising what you believe are the strengths and weaknesses of your approach to setting achievable goals for struggling students.

Identify the areas where you feel confident and effective in your goal-setting practices and acknowledge any weaknesses or challenges you may have encountered in this area.

Based on your reflection, brainstorm strategies and techniques that you could implement or improve upon to enhance your ability to set achievable goals for struggling students. Consider the following prompts:

1 How can you involve struggling students more actively in the goal-setting process?
2 Are there specific tools or resources that you can utilise to help students set realistic and attainable goals?
3 What strategies can you implement to track progress more effectively and make necessary adjustments?
4 How can you provide ongoing support and guidance to help students stay motivated and focused on their goals?
5 What methods can you use to celebrate and acknowledge student progress and success in a meaningful way?

Choose at least two strategies from your brainstorming session and develop an action plan for implementing them in your teaching practice. Outline specific steps you will take and a timeline for each step.

Reflect on how this self-reflection activity has influenced your understanding of setting achievable goals for struggling students. Identify any changes or adjustments you plan to make and how you anticipate these changes will positively impact your students' learning journey.

Optional: Share your reflections and action plan with a colleague or mentor for feedback and support.

Empowerment through self-declaration

According to the World Health Organisation the empowerment of people with mental health problems within institutions including schools and colleges involves the following external conditions and internal qualities: hope and respect, reclaiming one's life, feeling connected, understanding that people have rights, learning skills that the individual defines as important, moving from secrecy to transparency and growth and change that are never ending and self-initiated (2010).

Although according to research by Lewis and Bolton (2023) the percentage of students who have disclosed a mental health condition to their institution has increased rapidly since 2010 and was over 5% in 2020/21, these figures could be underestimates. 57% of student respondents self-reported a mental health issue and 27% said they had a diagnosed mental health condition in a survey conducted by Student Minds in 2022. They suggest that these types of figures are underestimates for a variety of reasons:

- Firstly, a stigma remains around mental ill health and students may feel uncomfortable or worry about being discriminated against if they declare a mental health issue. A 2019 Unite Students survey showed that, of students with such a mental health condition who responded, only 53% had declared it to their university (2019)
- Secondly, disability information (including whether a student has a mental health condition) is recorded by universities and colleges at the student's point of entry and therefore if a student develops a mental health issue during the course of their study it is uncertain whether their original record will have been updated.
- Thirdly, of students who self-report a disability and are full-time (or apprenticeship) undergraduate students, 15.8% declare 'multiple disabilities and it is uncertain whether these include issues with mental health or not' (Lewis and Bolton 2023)
- Finally, students who come from lower socioeconomic backgrounds, those from minority ethnic backgrounds and those who are lesbian, gay, bisexual, transgender or of other minority sexualities and sexual identities (LGBT+) are more likely to experience mental ill health and least likely to report it (Unite Students, 2019).

Consent and disclosure of mental health or wellbeing issues

In the UK, there are several key principles behind seeking consent from a student to share their mental health disclosures (DHSC, 2021). These principles include:

Confidentiality

Students have a right to expect that their mental health information will be kept confidential. Before sharing any information, it is important to obtain the student's explicit consent and explain how their information will be used.

Informed consent

This means that the student is fully aware of what they are consenting to. This includes understanding what information will be shared, who it will be shared with, and how it will be used (Vallance, 2016). Students should not be offered levels of confidentiality that cannot be kept. It is the teacher's responsibility to explain to pupils clearly and periodically exactly what this means in practice. They should be assured that the best decisions regarding confidentiality would be made in the interest of safeguarding and promoting students' welfare, preferably with their knowledge and consent (McGinnis and Jenkins, 2008).

Capacity to consent

Before seeking consent, it is important to assess the student's capacity to understand the information they are being given and make an informed decision. If the student does not have the capacity to consent, alternative arrangements may need to be made (Dhai and Payne-James, 2013).

Respect for autonomy

Students have the right to make their own decisions about their mental health information. This includes the right to refuse consent or to withdraw consent at any time. Developing autonomy and individuation from one's parents is particularly critical in adolescence (Erikson, 1968). While the majority of the counselling is kept confidential in colleges, there may be some sharing of information and liaison with parents and college staff, with the student's knowledge and consent, about their situation and their reason for referral. (DHSC 2021).

Duty of care

As professionals, there is a duty of care to ensure that students receive appropriate care and support for their mental health needs. This includes sharing relevant information with other professionals or services when it is necessary to ensure the student's safety and wellbeing (DFE, 2023, Erikson, 1968).

Figure 4.3 Self-reflection exercise

I am a pastoral tutor in a college. I received a request from a fellow staff member for information about a student's mental health status. The staff member was concerned about the student's erratic behaviour and thought that the student might pose a risk to themselves or others. However, they did not have a legitimate reason for requesting the student's confidential mental health information.

What would you do in this situation?

> **Figure 4.4 Self-reflection exercise**
>
> *Here are some comments made about confidentiality issues by teachers and students. How would you address these points?*
>
> *There are things that I have passed on then I have thought have I done the right thing because is it breaching that kind of trust? (Female Teacher)*
>
> *I had a student once ... I was concerned because she had all these cuts and I didn't know whether her parents should be informed or you know what to do so you know I think training on that would be good. (Male Teacher)*
>
> *I think the college could be supportive if they knew about it. I have the feeling it will not always be totally confidential, I just don't know whether something will be written somewhere and that person will have access to that file and that this will follow me around in my career as a Social Worker when I leave the course (Tamara, final year Social Work student).*

Some problematic issues regarding confidentiality

The duty of confidentiality to young persons is not an absolute one. It may be appropriate to share confidential information if any of the following apply:

- When the disclosure of personal information is justified in the public interest. This would apply where the benefits to a child or young person as a result of sharing the information will outweigh both the individual's right to confidentiality and that of society as a whole. For example, a suspected risk of abuse, neglect or suffering – in which case the teacher should normally inform an appropriate agency without unnecessary delay such as the police or the local authority children's or social work services, unless the disclosure of the information could in itself place the child at risk of harm (Snelling and Quick, 2022).

It will also be necessary to explain to students the institution's commitment to confidentiality and to outline the following issues:

- There can be a need to discuss issues raised by students with your immediate colleagues as appropriate in order to be able to support them. But this would usually be discussed with them first. The exceptions to this would include when a teacher believes that a student poses a serious risk of harm to themselves, or someone else, is made aware of terrorist activities or is made aware of a student who is being abused or is at risk of abuse (DFE, 2023)

- While institutions have a duty of care for all students, there are some legal restrictions on the confidentiality that can be offered by them. In the UK the following laws limit the extent which confidentiality can be maintained:
  - The Prevention of Terrorism Act 2005
  - The Proceeds of Crime Act 2002
  - The Children Act 2004.

Personal information and the Data Protection Act

- All information provided to the institution will be considered sensitive under the Data Protection Act 1998 and will remain strictly confidential. The only exceptions to this are detailed above
- During tutorial sessions, notes may be taken and kept securely in accordance with the General Data Protection Regulation (GDPR).and in the UK, the Data Protection Act 1998. These will only be accessed when there is a clinical or administrative need to do so. Students have the right to view any personal information that is stored and can request to view it privately (DFE, 2023)

Figure 4.5 Some case studies

Case study (1)
Zoe, a 16 year-old girl, comes to you asking your advice about contraception. She explains that she is in a steady relationship with her 33 year-old boyfriend and that they are thinking of having sex for the first time.
What should you do?

Case study (2)
Adele is a 17 year-old girl has a depressive disorder. In an individual tutorial session, she reports self-harming by cutting regularly for several weeks. She also has occasional suicidal ideation, although has never had any firm intent or plan. She begs her doctor not to tell her family. She is concerned that if they found out, they would just get angry.
What would you do?

Some considerations:
You need to decide whether Adele's cutting and suicidal ideation, without suicidal intent, would constitute a risk of serious harm. On one hand, superficial cutting may arguably constitute a low risk of serious harm. Furthermore, given the lack of suicidal intent, and considering that about 30% of adolescents report having had suicidal ideation (the overwhelming majority of whom do not attempt suicide) (Evans et al. 2005), again the risk of serious harm here does not appear high.

> **Figure 4.6 A. Mini Multiple-Choice Test**
>
> 1 Research shows that:
>
>   a Young person's belief that information will invariably be shared with parents does not affect the likelihood that they will disclose risky behaviours or attend healthcare services
>   b Parents generally believe that they do not have a right to know about risks relating to their adolescent children
>   c **Aspects of confidentiality are rarely discussed with adolescent patients and their families in primary care**
>   d When deciding whether to breach confidentiality, clinicians prioritise the risk of patient disengagement more than the seriousness, frequency, intensity, and duration of the risky behaviour
>   e Ethnic and religious factors rarely influence parents' attitudes towards their child's right to confidentiality
>
> 2 Which factor does not support the protection of confidentiality in a competent young person?
>
>   a Confidentiality may increase the likelihood of the young person disclosing information that helps guide treatment
>   b The individual has a right to autonomy, the development of which constitutes an important part of adolescence
>   c Confidentiality may help to protect or enhance the therapeutic relationship and service engagement
>   d Society has an interest in maintaining trust between doctor and patient, and so confidential medical care is recognised in law as being in the public interest
>   e **Parental rights to know information in order to help safeguard their child**
>
> *Answers*
> 1 c 2 e

Student self-disclosure

Disclosure is not a black and white choice. Self-care is a complex experience. People need to decide which parts of this experience to disclose. (Mayer et al., 2022).

Corrigan et al. discuss two levels of disclosure: selective and indiscriminate disclosure. Selective disclosure refers to choosing who specifically to tell about one's mental illness and when to tell. Indiscriminate disclosure requires a change of attitude by the person who no longer conceals a mental illness in general (2004).

There can be costs involved in these disclosure which can include disapproval of the mental illness or the disclosure by friends or family, including the risks of social ostracism and gossip, or having increased anxiety due to perceptions that people are thinking about them or pitying them. There are also fears about being discriminated against in employment, housing, and other opportunities, thinking that future relapses may be more stressful because others will be "watching "(Pahwa et al., 2017).

Self-disclosure in a public setting

This can be both advantageous and problematic for the teacher and the class when students decide to self-disclose and relate to mental health problems during discussions or presentations in classes such psychology, sociology, counselling, health and social care or tutorials. According to research by Wood et al. (2014) this could have the following positive and negative impacts in a class:

- Increase student understanding of the lived experiences of mental health problems making them more sympathetic. They could use the information to examine their own mental health and have a deeper knowledge of how to react to someone living with a disorder
- Help students relate to one another more clearly and bond as a group. They could develop new-found respect for the individual because of the way they manage their mental health concerns and feel protective of the person disclosing
- Prompt other students to feel that it is safe for them to self -disclose and thus develop a more caring and open learning environment and therefore trigger interest so that students want to hear about real-life examples of an issue
- Promote discomfort and embarrassment amongst students who find these issues difficult to handle or shocking for a variety of reasons, including stigma, and indifference. Or make some feel fearful that they might be attacked by the person with a mental health issue

Encouraging students' self-disclosure

Staples-Bradley et al. (2019) argue that for effective support to take place for appropriate student self-disclosure, teachers must establish a positive supervisory alliance, communicate to the student that a particular self-disclosure will not result in negative evaluation, clarify the purpose of this specific self-disclosure to the student, and reinforce appropriate disclosure to address remaining fears of future repercussions for self-disclosure.

Teachers can also use the following methods in tutorial sessions:

- Outline the parameters for using the method and provide examples of the types of issues they can raise, and how and where to seek help early or in an emergency
- Model the language to use which could include how to express their feelings, for example, 'I feel scared, worried, angry because...' 'I think I need 'x' to happen/talk to' etc. They may want to mention frequency of the event, intensity of their response e.g. 'I feel 8 out 10 anxious most days,' etc
- Describe what they can expect teachers to do once they've shared their worry e.g. when will they be contacted, by whom, who will be told, what might happen next and emphasise that they can keep asking for support until they feel that the issue is resolved / manageable
- Confirm that they can tell someone else their worry if they are not getting the support they need
- Explain that if they have special or additional needs there are alternative methods that they can use
- Emphasise that they can approach any teacher in the college that they feel comfortable with. It doesn't have to be their class teacher, tutor, etc

If and when a student decides to disclose, they will need to decide how specific to be about the disability and how much additional information they will provide to the teacher. They might be very general and:

- Refer to a medical condition or an illness
- Be a little more specific: indicate a biochemical imbalance, a neurological problem, a brain disorder, or difficulty with stress
- Mention mental illness specifically: mental illness, a psychiatric disorder, or a mental disability
- Give an exact diagnosis: For example, clinical depression, panic disorder, obsessive compulsive disorder, and other conditions (Hyman, 2008)

Teacher self-disclosure

Teacher-student interaction inherently involves some amount of self-disclosure by both parties. Teacher self-disclosure is defined as "teacher statements in the classroom about self that may or may not be related to subject content but reveal information about the teacher that students are unlikely to learn from other sources" (Sorensen, 1989, p 260). It is becoming increasingly used as a pedagogical tool (Safaei and Shahrokhi, 2019).

Researchers argue that there are three main dimensions to the issue:

- Amount, which is the extent to which revealing information is incorporated in the interaction context by one of the parties engaged

- Relevance, is a student's perception of whether or not the teacher's self-disclosure content can meet his/her personal needs, personal goals, or career goals
- Positiveness is the extent to which the content of self-disclosure is characterised by. or displaying certainty, acceptance, or affirmation (Safaei and Shahrokhi, 2019).

It has been suggested that if used effectively by working within the previous three dimensions it can have the following positive impacts on learners:

- Establish positive teacher-student relationships
- Create a constructive environment
- Helps students understand their teachers better and participate more enthusiastically in their studies
- Students often see beyond the personal stories teachers tell, interpreting their self-disclosures as attempts to be honest and open about themselves, to make personal connections
- Encourage students to open up and explain their own problems in more depth (Henry and Thorsen, 2020)

Some issues related to teacher self-disclosure:

- Once a teacher self-discloses, the student may naturally be inclined to ask questions seeking additional personal information about them and therefore the teacher needs to be mindful of the point at which to draw the line
- It can also divert the focus of discussion away from the student to the teacher
- It can also reinforce a power relationship between the teacher and the student or blur the boundaries between teacher and students
- It can create issues with boundaries if the teacher is working with the student in a wider classroom context
- It could also develop issues around student dependency
- It may impact on a student's value system or on the trust in the teacher as an appropriate source of help (Zur, 2010)

Figure 4.7 Teacher Self-reflection

Before you decided to self-disclose during a helping situation you might want to ponder on the three questions:

1 Will it provide new information to the student?
2 Will it shift my relationship with them, perhaps making me more available?
3 Could it help create a positive and healthy sense of shared vulnerability?

Figure 4.8 Case study

A student is delivering a presentation on Safeguarding for an Early Years class. She gives some s examples of recent safeguarding issues and mentions, Female Genital Mutilation (FGM). She casually adds that when she was a child aged eight she was sent by her parents back to Ghana to have it done to her. And then moves onto another subject.

What would you do in this situation?

Roles and boundaries

When carrying out support the teacher will become closely associated with students' emotional and overall wellbeing which can expose them to some of the dangers of getting 'too close' to the issues and by implication, at times, to the students themselves (Shavard, 2022). Being mindful of roles and boundaries become critical in this situation and support needs to be provided by the institution (Tinklin et al., 2005; Robotham and Julian, 2006; Jordá, 2013; Hughes et al., 2018).

Clear boundaries apply to both teachers and to students themselves. In other words, an understanding and articulation of boundaries is absolutely necessary for the benefit and protection of both the student and the tutor (Luck, 2010; Hughes et al., 2022). On the student side, recognising boundaries can avoid over-dependency. From a tutor's perspective, boundaries can help them to achieve a healthy balance and ensure self-care and the compartmentalisation of personal and professional responsibilities (McFarlane, 2016).

Figure 4.9 Self-reflection task

- *Here is a list of ideas to illustrate the importance of professional boundaries in colleges and colleges. Place them in your own order of importance.*
- *The importance of boundaries*
- *Boundaries will help you in supporting students in various ways. They will help you:*
- *Provide structure around what is expected between staff and their managers*
- *Avoid over promising and under delivering*

- *Provide clarity about what is expected of you, your colleagues, your staff and your leaders*
- *With workload management and keeping excessive stress at bay*
- *Manage priorities to ensure objectives are delivered and commitments met*
- *Keep you healthy and grounded*
- *Better navigate relationships with colleagues at all levels*
- *Protect yourself, specifically your role, your career and your responsibilities (in and out of college)*
- *Be more productive*
- *Preserve your mental health and emotional energy*
- *Uphold your own standards and values*

Some boundary issues

There are many different types of boundaries including:

Expertise and referral

Tutors may lack certain levels of expertise or training and so may not feel comfortable in providing specific types of information, advice, guidance and support. At the same time, colleagues elsewhere in the institution may be employed specifically for these purposes (Hughes et al., 2018). Issues like Self-harm, (sexual) abuse, (domestic) violence, suicidal tendencies, would benefit from professional mental health support (Luck, 2010; Hughes et al., 2018).

Time

Time is a major determinant in how the personal tutor role is undertaken and how effective it will be (Gidman et al., 2000, p 406). Tutors have limited time to support struggling students due to competing or even conflicting demands (Rhodes and Jinks, 2005; Gubby and McNab, 2013).

Independence and engagement

If students become overly dependent on teachers support, the relationship can become damaging and the consequences severe (Luck, 2010; Hughes et al., 2022). Students generally accept the idea of independent learning but require support to learn autonomously and reflect upon this learning (Dobinson-Harrington, 2006;).

Maintaining professional boundaries

Duty of care

The Education Act 2002 imposes clear duties to provide acceptable levels of care and to protect children and young people from all reasonably foreseeable risk of harm or injury. Duty of Care refers to the responsibility of those staff members, employed within a position of trust, to provide students with adequate levels of protection against harm and to safeguard their welfare at all times (Hughes et al., 2022).

Shared and agreed boundaries

Appropriate language

Teachers need to be mindful about the language they might be using. Examples to avoid include:

- The use of inappropriate names or terms of endearment and names such as buddy, mate, pal, friend
- Inappropriate conversation, gestures and language or enquiries of a sexual nature and, jokes or innuendo (Bull et al., 2023)
- Inappropriate comments about a student's appearance, including excessive flattering or personal criticism
- Disrespectful or discriminatory opinion either related or unrelated to the student (Cooper, 2012)

Information sharing

Avoid sharing offline and online personal information. Examples to avoid include personal lifestyle details of self, other staff or students, correspondence of a personal nature via any medium (phone, text, letters, email etc) that is unrelated to the staff member's role and different forms of unrelated media content, such as still or moving or audio images (Hughes et al., 2022).

Work and home

It is important not to blur the boundary between home life and work life. Things to avoid should include:

- Inviting, allowing, or encouraging students to attend a teacher's home or theirs and their social gatherings
- Allowing students access to a staff member's personal internet locations and personal devices (e.g. social networking sites)
- Transporting a pupil unaccompanied without prior permission
- Giving personal gifts or special favours
- Colluding with students

> **Figure 4.10 Self-reflection exercise**
>
> *Firstly, think of yourself as a student and take a few moments to reflect on the following questions:*
>
> - How have you experienced the misuse of power when you have been a student?
> - What was your response to this?
> - Why do you think you responded in this way?
> *Now think of yourself as a teacher:*
> - When and how might you have misused your power?
> - What may have caused you to do that?
> - How do you own and/or deny your own power?
> *Now think about the following questions:*
> - Who and what do you think has had an influence on the way you respond to power issues as a teacher and as a student?
> - What do you consider to be some of the legitimate ways teachers can exercise their power and authority?
> - How might your exploration of these questions inform your own practice as a teacher?

Cultural boundaries

Self-disclosure can also be construed as a vehicle for cultural sharing. When providing mental health support to students from other countries, teachers in the UK may face several cultural boundaries that need to be considered (Aultman et al., 2009). Some of these cultural boundaries include:

Language barriers

One of the biggest challenges that teachers may face is the language barrier. Students from different countries may speak a different language or have a different dialect, which may make it difficult for teachers to understand their needs and provide effective mental health support (Webb, 1997).

Stigma around mental health

The stigma around mental health may vary across different cultures. Some cultures may view mental health issues as a sign of weakness or shame, which may prevent students from seeking help. Teachers may need to address this stigma and provide reassurance that seeking help is a sign of strength (Cooper, 2012).

Different cultural beliefs

Different cultures have different beliefs about mental health and how it should be treated. Teachers may need to be aware of these cultural beliefs and adapt their approach accordingly. For example, western cultures often view mental illness as a medical condition that requires diagnosis and treatment from mental health professionals such as psychologists or psychiatrists. However, some other cultures may view mental health issues as a spiritual or moral issue. In these cultures, traditional healers or religious leaders may be consulted for treatment rather than medical professionals (Pethe-Kulkani, 2017).

In many Asian cultures, there may be a reluctance to openly discuss mental health issues due to a stigma attached to mental illness. The focus may be on maintaining harmony within the family or community rather than seeking individual treatment. Family members may be expected to provide support to the individual struggling with mental illness, and it may be seen as a sign of weakness to seek help outside of the family unit (Kramer et al., 2002).

In some African cultures, mental illness may be viewed as a result of supernatural forces or witchcraft (Aina, 2004). Traditional healers or spiritual leaders may be consulted for treatment, which may involve rituals or herbal remedies. There may be a belief that mental illness is a sign of a spiritual calling or that it is caused by ancestors seeking attention or intervention (2004).

Different attitudes towards education

Students from different cultures may have different attitudes towards education and may not place the same emphasis on mental health support in schools. Teachers may need to educate students and their families about the relationships between effective mental health support and academic success (Aultman et al., 2009).

Different communication styles

Communication styles may differ across different cultures. For example, some cultures may use indirect language or nonverbal cues to express themselves, which may be misinterpreted by teachers as problems with mental health and wellbeing (Link and Phelan, 2001). Teachers may need to be aware of these communication styles and adapt their approach accordingly.

Figure 4.11 A checklist

These are some of the strictly no go areas that teachers need to be mindful of when supporting students with mental health and wellbeing needs (although they obviously apply to all students too!):

- *Sexual contact with a student*
- *Causing physical harm or injury to individuals*
- *Making aggressive or insulting comments, gestures or suggestions*
- *Seeking information on personal history where it is neither necessary nor relevant*
- *Sharing your own private or intimate information where it is unnecessary*
- *Inappropriate touching, hugging or caressing*
- *Concealing information about individuals from colleagues, for example, not reporting incidents and concerns, safeguarding issues, not completing records, colluding with criminal acts*
- *Acceptance of gifts and hospitality in return for better support*
- *Spreading rumours or hearsay about an individual or others close to them*
- *Misusing an individual's money or property*
- *Encouraging individuals to become dependent or reliant for the teachers own gain*
- *Giving special privileges to 'favourite' individuals, for example spending excessive time with someone, becoming over-involved, or using influence to benefit one individual more than others*
- *Providing specialist advice or counselling where the teacher is not qualified to do this*
- *Failing to provide and support for or rejecting a student, for example, due to negative feelings about an individual*
- *Trying to impose own religious, moral or political beliefs on an individual*

Figure 4.12 Self-reflection task

Ashe is a teenager who is a student at your institution. She has recently asked one of the teachers, Clover, to be her friend on Facebook. Ashe has opened up to Clover about her feelings since the death of her friend and says that Clover really listens to her. They both share a passion for music and Rebecca would like to share their interest in music through Facebook, which she thinks will help her recovery from the death of her friend. She also suggests exchanging mobile phone numbers: if she has a problem with her

> assignment work she thinks that Clover will sort it out quicker than anyone else. This is the first time she has shown any real interest in getting on with life since her friend's death. What are the risks in this situation? What are the potential benefits? How could you apply the principles outlined in the previous sections? What advice would you give to Clover? What action would you take?

Reducing stigma and discrimination

Many people with mental illness experience shame, ostracism, and marginalisation due to their diagnosis, and often describe the consequences of mental health stigma as worse than those of the condition itself (Mayer, et.al 2022). Stigma becomes even more problematic for individuals with multiple complex needs, such as those with personality disorders, homelessness, addiction, or criminal convictions (The Lancet, 2016).

Researchers identify different types of stigma:

- Public stigma involves the negative or discriminatory attitudes that others have about mental illness
- Self-stigma refers to the negative attitudes, including internalised shame that people with mental illness have about their own condition.
- Institutional stigma, is more systemic, involving policies of government and private organisations that intentionally or unintentionally limit opportunities for people with mental illness

Stigma not only directly affects individuals with mental illness but also the loved ones who support them, often including their family members. "Courtesy" stigma can occur (Goffman, 1963) when families, friends and others become objects of prejudice and discrimination because of their association with the person with mental illness. Like people with mental illness, they may also may be affected by public and by self-stigma (Phelan, Bromet, and Link, 1998; Link et al., 2001; Van der Sanden et al., 2013). Stigma and discrimination can contribute to worsening symptoms and reduced likelihood of getting treatment. An extensive review of research found that self-stigma leads to negative effects on recovery among people diagnosed with severe mental illnesses (Yanos et al., 2020).

Impact of mental health stigma on students

Mental health stigma can have significant and detrimental impacts on students (Link and Phelan, 2001). Here are some of the key effects:

Reduced help-seeking behaviour

Stigma surrounding mental health can make students reluctant to seek help or support when they are experiencing mental health challenges. They may fear judgment, discrimination, or social isolation if they disclose their struggles, leading to delays in seeking appropriate assistance (Henderson et al., 2013).

Academic performance

Mental health issues, if left unaddressed, can significantly impact a student's ability to concentrate, focus, and perform well academically. The stigma around mental health may prevent students from accessing necessary resources further hindering their academic progress (Eleftheriades et al., 2020).

Social isolation

Stigma can lead to social exclusion and isolation, as students may feel ashamed or embarrassed to talk about their mental health issues with their peers. This isolation can exacerbate their mental health problems and create a sense of loneliness (Corrigan, and Watson, 2002).

Emotional distress

The fear of being judged or misunderstood due to mental health stigma can cause emotional distress and internal conflict. This distress may lead to anxiety, depression, or other mental health conditions, making it difficult for students to cope with their daily challenges (Rössler, 2015).

Underreporting of mental health issues

Stigma can lead to underreporting of mental health problems. Some students may deny or downplay their struggles to avoid being labelled as weak or unstable, which can prevent them from receiving appropriate support and treatment (Chatmon, 2020).

Impact on relationships

Mental health stigma can affect interpersonal relationships among students. Friends or classmates may distance themselves from someone struggling with mental health issues due to lack of understanding or fear, further increasing feelings of isolation (Ng et al., 2023).

Substance abuse

In some cases, students facing mental health stigma may turn to substance abuse as a way to cope with their emotions or mask their difficulties. This can lead to a cycle of further mental health deterioration and dependency issues (Wogen and Restrepo, 2020).

Delayed treatment

This can create barriers to accessing mental health services and treatment. Students may avoid seeking professional help until their conditions have worsened, making recovery more challenging (Wood, 2014).

Suicide risk

In severe cases, the combination of untreated mental health issues and the stigma surrounding them can increase the risk of suicidal ideation and suicide attempts among students (Carpiniello & Pinna, 2017).

Figure 4.13   Self-reflection task

Here are three self-reflection tasks you can use to evaluate your own prejudices towards mental health:

1. *Reflect on Your Past Experiences: Take some time to reflect on your past experiences with mental health, either your own or those of someone close to you. Consider how you reacted to these situations and whether you had any prejudices or biases towards mental health at the time. Ask yourself whether you treated the person with the respect and understanding they deserved or if you let your own biases get in the way*
2. *Challenge Your Assumptions: Identify any assumptions or stereotypes you hold about people with mental health conditions. Ask yourself where these assumptions come from and whether they are based on facts or prejudices. Challenge these assumptions by seeking out new information or talking to someone with a mental health condition to gain a better understanding of their experiences*
3. *Examine Your Language: Pay attention to the language you use when talking about mental health. Do you use stigmatising language or perpetuate stereotypes? Make a conscious effort to use respectful language and avoid stigmatizing or offensive terms. You can also examine the language used by others around you and challenge them when necessary.*

References

Aina, O. F. (2004). Mental illness and cultural issues in West African films: Implications for orthodox psychiatric practice. *Medical Humanities*, 30: 23–26.

Aubrecht, K. (2019). The 'nothing but': University student mental health and the hidden curriculum of academic success. *CJDS*, 8: 4.

Aultman, L. P., Williams-Johnson, Meca R., and Schutz, Paul A. (2009). Boundary dilemmas in teacher–student relationships: Struggling with "the line". *Teaching and Teacher Education*, 25: 636–646.

Baik, C., Larcombe, Wendy, Brooker, Abi, Wyn, Johanna, Allen, Lee, Brett, Matthew, Field, Rachael, and Jame, Richard. (2017). Enhancing student mental wellbeing. *A Handbook for Academic Educators*. Available from: https://melbourne-cshe.unimelb.edu.au/__data/assets/pdf_file/0006/2408604/MCSHE-Student-Wellbeing-Handbook-FINAL.pdf

Bandura, A. (1992). Exercise of personal agency through the self-efficacy mechanism. In R. Schwarzer (Ed.), *Self-efficacy: Thought control of action* (pp. 3–38). Hemisphere Publishing Corp.

Brooker, A. M., and McKague, Lisa Phillips. (2019). Implementing a whole-of-curriculum approach to student wellbeing. *Student Success*, 10(3). Available from: https://studentsuccessjournal.org/article/view/1417

Bull, A., Bradley, Alexander, Kanyeredzi, Ava, Page, Tiffany, Shi, Chi Chi, and Wilson, Joanne. (2023). Professional boundaries between faculty/staff and students in UK higher education: Students' levels of comfort with personal and sexualised interactions. *Journal of Further and Higher Education*, 47: 6: 711–26. 10.1080/0309877X.2023.2226612

Byrd, D. R., and McKinney, K. J. (2012). Individual, interpersonal, and institutional level factors associated with the mental health of college students. *Journal of American College Health*, 60: 185–93. 10.1080/07448481.2011.584334

Cacioppo, J. T., Ernst, J. M., Burleson, M. H., McClintock, M. K., Malarkey, W. B., Hawkley, L. C., Kowalewski, R. B., Paulsen, A., Hobson, J. A., Hugdahl, K., Spiegel, D., and Berntson, G. G. (2000). Lonely traits and concomitant physiological processes: The MacArthur social neuroscience studies. *International Journal of Psychophysiology*, 35(2–3): 143–54. 10.1016/s0167-8760(99)00049-5

Carpiniello, B., and Pinna, F. (2017). The reciprocal relationship between suicidality and stigma. *Frontiers in Psychiatry*, 8(8): 35. 10.3389/fpsyt.2017.00035

Chatmon, B. N. (2020). Males and mental health stigma. *American Journal of Men's Health*, 14(4). 10.1177/1557988320949322

Clayborne, Z. M., Varin, M., and Colman, I. (2019). Systematic review and meta-analysis: adolescent depression and long-term psychosocial outcomes. *Journal of the American Academy of Child and Adolescent Psychiatry*, 58: 72–9. doi:10.1016/j.jaac.2018.07.896

Cooper, F. 2012. *Professional Boundaries in Social Work and Social Care: A Practical Guide to Understanding, Maintaining and Managing Your Professional Boundaries*. London: Jessica Kingsley Publishers.

Corrigan, P. W., Druss, Benjamin G., and Perlick, Deborah A. (2014). The impact of mental illness stigma on seeking and participating in mental health care. *Psychological Science in the Public Interest*, 15(2): 37–70. doi:10.1177/1529100614531398pspi.sagepub.com

Corrigan, P. W., and Miller, F. E. (2004). Shame, blame, and contamination: A review of the impact of mental illness stigma on family members. *Journal of Mental Health*, 13(6): 537–548. doi:10.1080/09638230400017004

Corrigan, P. W., and Watson, A. C. (2002). Understanding the impact of stigma on people with mental illness. *World Psychiatry*, 1(1): 16–20.

Craig, N., and Zinkiewicz, Lucy. (2010). Inclusive practice within psychology. Higher Education Academy. https://www.advance-he.ac.uk/knowledge-hub/inclusive-practice-within-psychology-higher-education

Dalsgaard, S., McGrath, J., Østergaard, S. D., et al. (2020). Association of mental disorder in childhood and adolescence with subsequent educational achievement. *JAMA Psychiatry*, 77: 797–805. doi:10.1001/jamapsychiatry.2020.0217

Deci, E. L., and Ryan, R. M. (1985). *Intrinsic Motivation and Self-Determination in Human Behavior*. New York: Plenum Publishing Co.

Del Savio, A. A., Galantini, K., and Pachas, A. (2022). Exploring the relationship between mental health-related problems and undergraduate student dropout: A case study within a civil engineering program. *Heliyon*, 8(5): e09504. doi:10.1016/j.heliyon.2022.e09504

Department for Education (DFE). (2023). Keeping children safe in education 2023 Statutory guidance for schools and colleges. https://assets.publishing.service.gov.uk/media/64f0a68ea78c5f000dc6f3b2/Keeping_children_safe_in_education_2023.pdf

Department of Health and Social Care. (2021). SHARE. End the silence end suicide consent, confidentiality & information sharing in mental healthcare & suicide prevention. https://www.gov.uk/government/publications/share-consent-confidentiality-and-information-sharing-in-mental-healthcare-and-suicide-prevention/share-consent-confidentiality-and-information-sharing-in-mental-healthcare-and-suicide-prevention

Dhai, A., and Payne-James, J. (2013). Problems of capacity, consent and confidentiality. *Best Practice & Research. Clinical Obstetrics & Gynaecology*, 27(1): 59–75. doi:10.1016/j.bpobgyn.2012.08.007

Dobinson-Harrington, A. (2006). Personal tutor encounters: understanding the experience. *Nursing Standard*: 23–29; 20(50): 35–42. doi:10.7748/ns2006.08.20.50.35.c4485

Eleftheriades, R., Fiala, C., and Pasic, M. D. (2020). The challenges and mental health issues of academic trainees. *F1000Res*, 11(9): 104. doi:10.12688/f1000research.21066.1

Erikson, E. (1968). *Identity: Youth and crisis*. New York: W. W. Norton & Company.

Evans, E., Hawton, K., Rodham, K., and Deeks, J. (2005). The prevalence of suicidal phenomena in adolescents: a systematic review of population-based studies. *Suicide Life Threatening Behavior*, 35(3): 239–50. doi:10.1521/suli.2005.35.3.239

Gidman, J., Humphreys, Amanda, and Andrews, Margaret. (2000). The role of the personal tutor in the academic context. *Nurse Education Today*, 20(5): 401–407.

Goffman, E. (1963). *Stigma. Notes on the Management of Spoiled Identity*. London: Penguin Books.

Grøtan, K., Sund, E. R., and Bjerkeset, O. (2019). Mental health, academic self-efficacy and study progress among college students – The SHoT study, Norway. *Frontiers in Psychology*, 10: 45. doi:10.3389/fpsyg.2019.00045

Gubby, Laura, and McNab, Nicole. 2013. Personal tutoring from the perspective of the tutor. *Capture*, 4: 7–16.

Halpern-Manners, A. and others. (2016). The relationship between education and mental health: New evidence from a discordant twin study. *Social Forces*, 95(1): 107–131, doi:10.1093/sf/sow035

Hattie, J. and Timperley, H. (2007). The power of feedback. *Review of Educational Research*, 77(1): 81–112. doi:10.3102/003465430298487

Heinrich, L. M., and Gullone, E. (2006). The clinical significance of loneliness: a literature review. *Clinical Psychology Review*, 26(6): 695–718. doi:10.1016/j.cpr.2006.04.002

Henderson, C., Evans-Lacko, S., and Thornicroft, G. (2013). Mental illness stigma, help seeking, and public health programs. *American Journal of Public Health*, 103(5): 777–80. doi:10.2105/AJPH.2012.301056

Henry, A., and Thorsen, C. (2020). Disaffection and agentic engagement: 'Redesigning' activities to enable authentic self-expression. *Language Teaching Research*, 24(4): 456–475.

Hjorth, C.F., Bilgrav, L., Frandsen, L.S., et al. (2016). Mental health and school dropout across educational levels and genders: A 4.8-year follow-up study. *BMC Public Health*, 16: 976. doi:10.1186/s12889-016-3622-8

Houghton, A. M., and Anderson, Jill (2017). Embedding mental wellbeing in the curriculum: Maximising success in higher education/Higher Education Academy. https://www.advance-he.ac.uk/knowledge-hub/embedding-mental-wellbeing-curriculum-maximising-success-higher-education

Howard, E. (2020). A review of the literature concerning anxiety for educational assessments [Internet]. Coventry. Ofqual. Available from: https://assets.publishing.service.gov.uk/government/uploads/system/uploads/attachment_data/file/865832/A_review_of_the_literature_concerning_anxiety_for_educational_assessment.pdf

Hughes, G., Panjwani, Mehr, Tulcidas, Priya, and Byrom, Nicola. (2018). *Student Mental Health: The Role and Experiences of Academics*. Derby, UK: University of Derby.

Hughes, G., Upsher, R., Nobili, A., Kirkman, A., Wilson, C., BowersBrown, T., Foster, J., Bradley, S., and Byrom, N. (2022). *Education for Mental Health*. Online: Advance HE. https://kclpure.kcl.ac.uk/ws/portalfiles/portal/196347302/AdvHE_Education_for_mental_health_online_1644243779.pdf

Hyman, I. (2008). *Self-Disclosure and Its Impact on Individuals Who Receive. Mental Health Services*. Rockville, MD. Center for Mental Health Services, Substance Abuse and Mental Health Services Administration. HHS Pub. No. (SMA)-08-4337.

Jones, E., Priestley, M., Brewster, L., Wilbraham, S. J., Hughes, G., and Spanner, L. (2021). Student wellbeing and assessment in higher education: the balancing act. *Assessment & Evaluation in Higher Education*, 46(3): 438–50. doi:10.1080/02602938.2020.1782344

Jordá, J. M. M. (2013). The academic tutoring at the university level: development and promotion methodology through project work. *Procedia - Social and Behavioral Sciences*, 106: 2594–601.

Kickert, R., Meeuwisse, M., Stegers-Jager, K. M., et al. (2022). Curricular fit perspective on motivation in higher education. *Higher Education*, 83, 729–45. doi:10.1007/s10734-021-00699-3

Kramer, E. J., Kwong, K., Lee, E., and Chung, H. (2002). Cultural factors influencing the mental health of Asian Americans. *The Western Journal of Medicine*, 176(4): 227–31.

Lereya, S. T., Patel, M., Dos Santos, J. P. G. A., and Deighton, J. (2019). Mental health difficulties, attainment and attendance: A cross-sectional study. *European Child & Adolescent Psychiatry*, 28(8): 1147–52. doi:10.1007/s00787-018-01273-6

Lewis, J., and Bolton, Paul (2023). *Student Mental Health in England: Statistics, Policy, and Guidance*. Department for Education.

Link, B. G., and Phelan, J. C. (2001). Conceptualizing stigma. *Annual Review of Sociology*, 27: 363–385. doi:10.1146/annurev.soc.27.1.363

Link, B. G., Struening, E. L., Neese-Todd, S., Asmussen, S., and Phelan, J. C. (2001). Stigma as a barrier to recovery: The consequences of stigma for the self-esteem of people with mental illnesses. *Psychiatric Services*, 52(12): 1621–6. doi:10.1176/appi.ps.52.12.1621

Lister, Kate, Andrews, Kyle, Buxton, Jo, Douce, Chris, and Seale, Jane. (2023). Assessment, life circumstances, curriculum and skills: Barriers and enablers to student mental wellbeing in distance learning. *Frontiers in Psychology*, 14: 1076985. doi:10.3389/fpsyg.2023.1076985

Luck, C. (2010). Challenges faced by tutors in higher education. *Psychodynamic Practice*, 16(3): 273–87. doi:10.1080/14753634.2010.489386

Mayer, L., Corrigan, P. W., Eisheuer, D., Oexle, N., and Rüsch, N. (2022). Attitues towards disclosing a mental illness: impact on quality of life and recovery. *Social Psychiatry and Psychiatric Epidemiology*, 57(2): 363–74. doi:10.1007/s00127-021-02081-1

McFarlane, K. J. (2016). Tutoring the tutors: Supporting effective personal tutoring. *Active Learning in Higher Education*, 17(1), 77–88. doi:10.1177/1469787415616720

McGinnis, S., and Jenkins, P. (2008). *Good Practice Guidance for Counselling in Schools*, (4th edn). BACP.

Mulliner, E., and Tucker, M. (2015). Feedback on feedback practice: perceptions of students and academics. *Assessment & Evaluation in Higher Education*, 42(2): 266–88.

Ng, S., Reidy, H., Wong, P. W., and Zayts-Spence, O. (2023). The relationship between personal and interpersonal mental health experiences and stigma-related outcomes in Hong Kong. *BJPsych Open*, 9(3): e72. doi:10.1192/bjo.2023.39

Pahwa, R., Fulginiti, A., Brekke, J. S., and Rice, E. (2017). Mental illness disclosure decision making. *American Journal of Orthopsychiatry*, 87(5): 575–584. doi:10.1037/ort0000250

Pethe-Kulkani, A. (2017). Culture and ethnicity in psychological practice: A thematic study. An unpublished thesis submitted in partial fulfilment of the requirements of the University of East London for the Professional Doctorate in Clinical Psychology

Phelan, J. C., Bromet, E. J., and Link, B. G. (1998). Psychiatric illness and family stigma. *Schizophrenia Bulletin*, 24(1): 115–26. doi:10.1093/oxfordjournals.schbul.a033304

Postareff, L., Mattsson, M., Lindblom-Ylanne, S., & Hailikari, T. (2017). The complex relationship between emotions, approaches to learning, study success and study progress during the transition to university. *Higher Education*, 73(3), 441–457. doi:10.1007/s10734-016-0096-7

Rainer, C., Le, Huong, and Abdinasir, Kadra. (2023). *Behaviour and Mental Health in schools*. Children and Young People's Mental Health Coalition. https://cypmhc.org.uk/wp-content/uploads/2023/06/Behaviour-and-Mental-Health-in-Schools-Full-Report.pdf

Raspberry, C. N., Lee, S. M., Robin, L., Laris, B. A., Russell, L. A., Coyle, K. K., Nihiser, A. J. (2011). The association between school-based physical activity, including physical education, and academic performance: A systematic review of the literature. *Preventive Medicine*, 52(Suppl 1): S10–20. doi:10.1016/j.ypmed.2011.01.027

Rhodes, S., and Jinks, A. (2005). Personal tutors' views of their role with preregistration nursing students: An exploratory study. *Nurse Education Today*, 25: 390–97.

Robinson, O. J., Vytal, K., Cornwell, B. R., and Grillon, C. (2013). The impact of anxiety upon cognition: Perspectives from human threat of shock studies. *Frontiers in Human Neuroscience*, 17(7): 203. doi:10.3389/fnhum.2013.00203

Robotham, D. and Julian, C. (2006). Stress and the higher education student: A critical review of the literature. *Journal of Further and Higher Education*, 30(2): 107–17. doi:10.1080/03098770600617513

Rubin, E. (2010). Curricular stress. *Journal of Legal Education*, 60(1): 110–121. http://www.jstor.org/stable/42894156

Rössler, W. (2015). The stigma of mental disorders: A millennia-long history of social exclusion and prejudices. *EMBO Reports*, 17(9), 1250–3.

Ryff, C. D. (2014). Psychological well-being revisited: Advances in the science and practice of eudaimonia. *Psychotherapy and Psychosomatics*, 83(1): 10–28. doi:10.1159/000353263

Safaei, N., and Shahrokhi, Mohsen. (2019). Relationship between teacher self-disclosure and teaching style: Perception of EFL teachers. *Cogent Education*, 6. doi:10.1080/2331186X.2019.1678231

Salzer, M. (2012). A comparative study of campus experiences of college students with mental illnesses versus a general college sample. *Journal of American College Health*, 60: 1–7. doi:10.1080/07448481.2011.552537

Schulte-Körne, G. (2016). Mental health problems in a school setting in children and adolescents. *Deutsches Ärzteblatt International*, 113: 183–90. doi:10.3238/arztebl.2016.0183

Scullin, M. K. (2019). The eight hour sleep challenge during final exams week. *Teaching of Psychology*, 46(1): 55–63. doi:10.1177/0098628318816142

Shavard, G. (2022). Teachers' collaborative work at the boundaries of professional responsibility for student wellbeing. *Scandinavian Journal of Educational Research*. doi:10.1080/00313831.2022.2042851

Silveira, G. S., Campos, Lia K. S., Schweller, Marcelo, Turato, Egberto R., Helmich, Esther, de Carvalho-Filho, Marco Antonio. (2019). "Speed up"! The Influences of the Hidden Curriculum on the Professional Identity Development of Medical Students. *Health Professions Education*, 5(3): 198–209.

Snelling, P., and Quick, O. (2022). Confidentiality and public interest disclosure: A framework to evaluate UK healthcare professional regulatory guidance. *Medical Law International*, 22(1): 3–32.

Sorensen, G. (1989). The relationships among teachers' self-disclosive statements, students' perceptions, and affective learning. *Communication Education*, 38: 259–76. doi:10.1080/03634528909378762

Staples-Bradley, L. K., Duda, B., and Gettens, K. (2019). Student self-disclosure in clinical supervision. *Training and Education in Professional Psychology*, 13(3): 216–221. doi:10.1037/tep0000242

Storrie, K., Ahern, K., and Tuckett, A. (2010). A systematic review: Students with mental health problems – A growing problem. *International Journal of Nursing Practice*, 16(1): 1–6. doi:10.1111/j.1440-172X.2009.01813.x

Sutherland, Patricia Lea. (2018). The impact of mental health issues on academic achievement in high school students. Electronic Theses, Projects, and Dissertations. 660. https://scholarworks.lib.csusb.edu/etd/660

The Lancet. (2016). Editorial the health crisis of mental health stigma. 387. www.thelancet.com

Tinklin, T., Riddell, S., and Wilson, A. (2005). Support for students with mental health difficulties in higher education: The students' perspective. *British Journal of Guidance and Counselling*, 33(4): 495–512. doi:10.1080/03069880500327496

Tinto, V. (1992). Collaborative Learning: A Sourcebook for Higher Education (with A. Goodsell and M. Maher), National Center on Postsecondary Teaching, Learning, and Assessment, Pennsylvania State University. https://files.eric.ed.gov/fulltext/ED357705.pdf

Tregaskis, O., Nandi, A., and Watson, D. (2020). An examination of the relationship between adolescent mental health and educational outcomes in early adulthood: secondary analysis of understanding Society data wave 1 to wave 8. https://whatworkswellbeing.org/wp-content/uploads/2020/02/Summary-Report-gender-wellbeing-learning.pdf

Unite students. (2019). The new realists Unite Students Insight Report. Higher Education Policy Initiative.

Upsher, R., Percy, Z., Cappiello, L., et al. (2022). Understanding how the university curriculum impacts student wellbeing: A qualitative study. *Higher Education*. doi:10.1007/s10734-022-00969-8

Vallance, A. K. (2016). Shhh! Please don't tell...' Confidentiality in child and adolescent mental health. *BJPsych Advances*, 22: 25–35. doi:10.1192/apt.bp.114.013854

Van der Sanden, R. L., Bos, A. E., Stutterheim, S. E., Pryor, J. B., and Kok, G. (2013). Experiences of stigma by association among family members of people with mental illness. *Rehabilitation Psychology*, 58(1): 73–80. doi:10.1037/a0031752

Vogel, S., and Schwabe, L. (2016). Learning and memory under stress: Implications for the classroom. *npj Science of Learning*, 1: 16011. doi:10.1038/npjscilearn.2016.11

Webb, Susan B. (1997). Training for maintaining appropriate boundaries in counselling. *British Journal of Guidance and Counselling*, 25(2): 175–88. doi:10.1080/03069889708253800

Wogen, J., and Restrepo, M. T. (2020). Human rights, stigma, and substance use. *Health and Human Rights*, 22(1): 51–60.
Wood, B. T., Bolner, Olivia, and Gauthier, Phillip. (2014). Student mental health self-disclosures in classrooms: Perceptions and implications. *Psychology Learning and Teaching*, 13(2). www.wwwords.co.uk/PLAT
World Health Organisation. (2010). User empowerment in mental health – A statement by the WHO regional office for Europe. https://iris.who.int/handle/10665/107275
Yanos, P. T. Joseph, DeLuca, S., Roe, David, and Lysaker, Paul H. (2020). The impact of illness identity on recovery from severe mental illness: A review of the evidence. *Psychiatry Research*, 288: 112950. ISSN 0165-1781.
Zur, O. (2010). Self-disclosure. In: I. B. Weiner and W. E. Craighead (eds.), *Corsini Encyclopedia of Psychology*, (4th edn), 1532–34. Hoboken, NJ: John Wiley & Sons Inc.

5 Approaches to pastoral care when supporting social wellbeing and emotional health issues in Further Education

Models of the tutorial systems in further education

According to Chandler (2001) based on models provided by the Further Education Development Agency (FEDA, 1995), there are four main models of tutorial provision. These are the action planning, the learning development model, academic learning coach and personal tutor model. Each of these models is different in terms of the underlying principles and each varies in their appropriateness for use according to the demographics and needs of the student population.

The action planning model

This is a model which is most commonly found in vocational education in FE and is predominantly aimed at full-time learners. The role of the tutor is that of a learning manager whose responsibility is to record and to monitor individual progress and achievement. The approach to tutorials is defined, planned, structured, and evaluated across the institution and thus the tutor 'works as part of a professional team to produce data which can be codified and fed into wider information systems such as the college Standardised Assessment Report (SAR)' (Chandler, 2001, 27).

The learning development model

This is a model based on the idea of a learning partnership as tutor and tutee work together as collaborators to develop learning aims and outcomes. The tutor's role is to guide and support the tutee in order for them to become an autonomous, self-directed, self-motivated independent learner. The tutorial process is characterised by 'negotiation of individual programmes with the learners, co-ordination between the activities of learning and those of guidance and support' (Chandler, 2001, p28).

The academic learning coach model

During the past 20 years there has emerged a model of tutoring which combines some of the approaches of the traditional models in order to develop a model of tutoring which fits into the more instrumental philosophy of post-new-managerialist FE. This model which can be found in many FE institutions and increasingly in private sector providers for full-time learners can be termed the professional model or the academic learning manager model (Crosling and Webb, 2002).

This model can be seen as a fusion of the action planning and the learning development model. The tutor is normally employed full-time to support learners across the curriculum. These professionals have no teaching responsibilities, and their role is solely to support the academic development of the learners within their 'caseload'. They are positioned to be independent of day-to-day classroom teaching and hence it is argued they can take a more objective and independent approach to tutorial supervision than classroom teachers who have a more complicated set of relationships with their learners.

The personal tutoring role

This is mainly a personal pastoral/parental 'enrichment' model concerned solely with the development of general academic, social, and cultural skills. It is said to be found more commonly in school sixth forms, sixth form colleges and universities. According to Chandler (2001) the key to an effective personal tutorial system lies in the quality and commitment of the individual tutors and the nature of the relationship with their students.

With this approach, a specific member of staff is allocated to each student and provides both pastoral support and academic guidance. When pastoral models are adopted, it is usual for all learners to be allocated a single specific personal tutor. Pastoral tutoring is often unstructured and reactive to situations and learners approach tutors for assistance as and when needed (Best et al., 1985). This has been noted to carry some weaknesses. As they point out, some students 'fall through the net' due to a lack of confidence to approach the tutor or the tutor being unavailable at times when needed. This latter issue is seen as especially problematic for marginalised learners such as disaffected learners, those with learning difficulties, ESOL learners, and young female learners. The model also relies on parity in quality of provision and not all tutors are as suited to this role as might be desired.

The personal tutoring role provides an opportunity for one-to-one time with learners, either face to face or remotely. The purpose of this is to create a sense of value and wellbeing for the learner as an individual and as a member of the learning Community, regardless of the type of learning environment. These one-to-one learning conversations can be referred to in a number of ways.

Depending on the organisation the teacher works for they could be called personal tutorials, progress reviews or one-to-one reviews. Personal tutoring enables learners to explore their aspirations, plan their individual learning experience, reflect on their progress, identify barriers to learning and explore potential areas for support (Wooton, 2013).

It has been found that effective tutoring contributes to improved mental health, retention, achievement, and successful progression. It has also been recognised that poor tutoring can be detrimental to learners' potential to succeed and, in some cases, to their confidence, self-esteem and overall self-worth (Chandler, 2001).

Best et al. (1985) define the work of a tutor as having four dimensions, disciplinary/order, welfare, pastoral and academic/curriculum which can inevitably lead to conflict between the disciplinary and welfare functions and impact on boundaries during sensitive mental health issue situations (King, 1999).

Although a teacher/tutor can never be a counsellor not only because of training and qualifications but also because the type of relationships are different and the aims of counselling and the boundaries are very different, a teacher can play a key role in supporting the mental health needs of their students as a helper using a range of counselling skills (King, 1999).

Key roles and responsibilities of a tutor

According to Neville (2007) the principal roles and responsibilities of a tutor in FE, subject to variation in context and programme, can be summarised as follows:

- Directed Learning. This is subject specialist teaching given either individually or in small groups. It is normally based on supplementing support for classroom teaching
- Planning and overseeing the completion of planning. This involves the establishing and reviewing of learning contracts and the development of individual learning plans. This can be placed in the context of the action planning model.
- Academic Supervision. This is similar to directed learning but is based more on advice and academic guidance, such as reviewing assignment work, rather than teaching. It could be placed within the approaches found in the learning development model.
- Vocational Guidance. This may be a part of a component within a formal tutorial system. It may be an aspect of the role of the course tutor or the personal/pastoral tutor. The tutor also has a liaison role to play with careers guidance services, prospective employers, and vocational stakeholders. Their role is especially crucial on vocational programmes, which have a work experience requirement (2007, 39).
- Pastoral Care. The tutor has general welfare duties which can involve dealing with personal/interpersonal issues.

According to Best et.al (1985) there are five primary pastoral tasks:

1. Reactive pastoral casework which is undertaken on a one-to-one basis in response to the needs of children with personal problems
2. Proactive, preventive pastoral care aimed at pre-empting the need for reactive casework

3. Developmental pastoral curricula which can take the form of programmes like PHSE, structured tutorial work and cross-curricular activities
4. The management and administration of pastoral care through the planning, motivating, resourcing, monitoring, supporting, evaluating, encouraging, and facilitating all of the above pastoral tasks (2000:34)
5. Informal support. This can take place on an ad hoc basis whereby a subject teacher provides informal or occasional academic or personal support for a learner. This mode of support can often be found where there are not distinct tutorial systems in place such as in Adult Education Institutes or can be supplementary to formal tutorial systems.

(Neville, 2007)

Teachers and school and college counsellors

The roles of a teacher and a counsellor in supporting a student's mental health and wellbeing can be quite different, and therefore the relationship between a student and each of these professionals may differ as well.

A teacher's primary focus is on delivering academic instruction and assessing student learning. However, teachers can still play a vital role in supporting a student's mental health and wellbeing by creating a positive classroom environment, promoting social-emotional learning, and identifying and referring students who may need additional support to the school's counselling services (Padmore, 2016).

A counsellor, on the other hand, is specifically trained to provide support for a student's mental health and wellbeing. The relationship between a student and their counsellor may involve more personal and in-depth conversations about the student's emotional state and personal experiences and use various techniques such as talk therapy, cognitive-behavioural therapy, and mindfulness to help students manage their emotions, develop coping strategies, and promote their overall wellbeing (Padmore, 2016).

Additionally, counsellors may work closely with other professionals, such as teachers, parents, and healthcare providers, to ensure that a student's mental health needs are met both in and out of college or school (Crosling and Webb, 2002).

Teachers and counselling skills

Research suggests that teachers who have a basic toolbox of counselling skills can be more effective in their pastoral roles and supportive roles than those who lack knowledge of these (King, 1999). Counselling skills rest loosely within the British Association of Counsellors and Psychotherapists Ethical Framework for the Counselling Professions (EFfCP), and also according to them, there are many roles that could benefit from counselling skills across diverse professions, settings and specialisms and covering a wide range of responsibility, knowledge, skills and ability. (BACP, 2020b).

The BACP suggest that if teachers and other people in helping capacities use counselling skills competently it will help them to recognise when someone needs to talk, respond using appropriate skills to facilitate a safe listening space and refer by sensitively signposting or referring when someone needs further help or assistance (2020a).

There are several main suggested requirements and skills related to the framework. (BACP, 2020a) which include:

- Professional context. The primary role is to be enhanced by embedding counselling skills, but not changed and the role of the BACP framework will be to support the primary ethical frameworks and codes of practice
- Empathy. Good teaching support requires the empathy to see and understand the world from another's perspective and from a variety of diverse backgrounds and to respond to empathic opportunities. Teachers also need to be mindful of the importance of knowing when to stay with the primary remit of their teaching professional role and when to offer a listening space
- Skills and techniques. There are a number of skills which are important to support learners' wellbeing needs, such as active listening skills, communication skills and responding skills. These include Carl Rogers' three core conditions from person centred theory which are: empathy, Unconditional Positive Regard (a nonjudgmental approach) and congruence (genuineness- see below for further discussion) (Rogers, 1957)
- Working alliance. The teacher needs to keep the focus on the student's wants, needs and abilities, within a respectful, safe and ethical working alliance and to collaborate with the student and also if required with external agencies
- Personal qualities. The BACP suggest that these skills need to be underpinned by personal qualities which included self-awareness, self-efficacy, self-care and commitment to personal development

---

Figure 5.1   Self-reflection

Complete this self-evaluation activity based on some of the key areas of the BACP's five counselling skills competencies:

Active Listening Skills

  a *Take a recording device or use your phone and record a conversation or an interview that you had with someone, it can be a friend, family member or even a stranger*
  b *Listen to the recording and evaluate your own active listening skills. Were you able to focus on the speaker and avoid interruptions? Did you demonstrate empathy and understanding? Did you use verbal and non-verbal cues to show that you were actively listening?*
  c *Identify areas where you could improve and design an action plan to work on those areas*

Empathy Skills

a Think about a recent conversation where someone shared a personal struggle or challenge with you

b Reflect on how you responded. Did you demonstrate empathy by acknowledging their feelings and showing understanding? Or did you offer unsolicited advice or try to "fix" their problem?

c Identify one or two strategies you could use in the future to improve your empathy skills

Rapport Building Skills

a Choose a recent interaction with someone you didn't know well, such as a cashier or a colleague from a different department

b Evaluate how you built rapport with them. Did you make eye contact and use open body language? Did you ask questions and actively listen to their responses?

c Identify one or two strategies you could use in the future to improve your rapport-building skills

Working with Difference and Diversity

a Think about a recent conversation where you interacted with someone from a different cultural background or with different beliefs than your own

b Evaluate how you worked with difference and diversity. Did you demonstrate respect and curiosity for their perspective? Did you avoid assumptions or stereotypes?

c Identify one or two strategies you could use in the future to improve your ability to work with difference and diversity

Self-Awareness and Self-Reflection

a Take some time to reflect on your own biases, assumptions, and limitations as a counsellor or a helper

b Write down any areas where you feel you need to improve and why you think that is

c Identify one or two strategies you could use in the future to increase your self-awareness and self-reflection

After completing each of these activities, take some time to reflect on what you learned about yourself and how you can apply these skills in your personal and professional life. Remember to be kind to yourself and to celebrate your successes, as well as to acknowledge areas where you need to improve.

Counselling skills models

According to McLeod and McLeod (2011) There are two broad approaches to understanding counselling skills:

- The micro skills model associated with Ivey (1971)
- A variety of three-stage models, developed by Hill, Egan, and others

The micro skills model

This has been in existence since the 1960s and has become more multi-dimensional over the decades. In this model there are core attending skills such as eye contact, a warm and interested tone of voice, 'verbal tracking' (willingness to stick with the client's story rather than changing the subject) and appropriate body language. These are also known as the three V + B, Visuals, Vocals, Verbals, and Body Language. These are integrated together to form the interview (Ivey, 1971).

A session using this model will tend to have the following structure: developing a relationship which will involve initiating the session, offering structure, and establishing rapport, gathering data about the person's story, and their concerns and issues, identifying what the client wants to happen, their goals, restorying.ie exploring alternatives and confronting incongruities in the story, and finally, action, acting on new stories and understandings and ending the session (Ivey, 1971).

The core skills can also be supplemented by advanced skills which could include: identifying contradictions and mixed messages in the client's story; challenging the client in a supportive manner; clarifying issues; looking at the issue from multiple perspectives; reframing or reinterpreting the client's experience; and working with the immediate, here-and-now responses of the client (McLeod and McLeod, 2011).

Three stage models

The Helping Skills Model (Hill, 2004) consists of three stages: exploration, insight, and action:

- Exploration (which is influenced by the person-centred theories of Carl Rogers, 1957). In this stage, the teacher would be encouraging students to tell their stories, to share their thoughts and feelings, providing encouragement and open up emotionally and learning about the client's own perspective on their problem. The teacher would use skills such as using open questions, listening, restating, and reflecting feelings and developing a therapeutic relationship
- Insight (influenced by the psychodynamic theories of Freud and others (King, 1999)).

During this stage the teacher would be working with students to construct new insights, encouraging students to determine their role in their thoughts, feelings and actions and working with students to address issues in their relationships (e.g., misunderstandings). The teacher would use skills such as using challenges and interpretation
- Action (influenced by Cognitive Behavioural Therapy (CBT) developed by Beck and Ellis (King, 1999)). As part of this stage the teacher would be encouraging students to explore possible new behaviours, decide on actions, support skills development for change, feedback and evaluation on change and encourage, inspire and modify action plans. The teacher would be using skills such as providing information, feedback and guidance, giving out homework assignments, teaching techniques such as relaxation and role-play (Hill, 2004)

The Skilled Helper Model (Egan, 2002) has also three stages similar to the Hill (2004) framework:

1. Stage 1 which is helping the helpee to tell their story by tuning-in using empathy, listening to verbal and non-verbal communication, and communicating back, highlighting core issues, probing and summarising, identifying problems and opportunities and identifying contradictions in the story and challenging.
2. In Stage 2 the focus is on helping the helpee to determine what they need and want by goal-setting, decision-making, identifying possibilities for a better future and moving towards choices and making a commitment to change.
3. In Stage 3 action strategies are implemented to help the helpee to get what they need and want by identifying and evaluating strategies, making an action plan and implementing it and evaluating the changes.

(Wosket, 2008)

Figure 5.2 Reflection task

Make a list of the helping skills that you use a lot in interaction with other people, and feel confident or competent about, and another list of helping skills that are more problematic for you.

Now using the list taken from McLeod and McLeod (2011) select the five skills that you deem most important in supporting your students and evaluate your competence in using them

Attending, Observing, Attunement, Offering feedback, Bodily awareness Process monitoring, Boundary management, Providing information, Caring Questioning, Challenging, Reflecting/restating, Checking out/clarifying Reframing, Giving advice, Remembering, Immediacy, Self-disclosure, Listening, Self-monitoring, Making sense, Structuring, Naming, Using silence, Witnessing.

Categories of intervention

Heron (2001) attempted to show how the skills fitted together by classifying them into his six-categories of intervention. Heron's model has two basic styles: 'authoritative' and 'facilitative'. An 'authoritative' intervention involves giving information, challenging the other person, or suggesting what the other person should do. A facilitative' intervention involves drawing out ideas from the person, developing their self-confidence and so on. The six categories of intervention and support include:

- Prescriptive. In this form of approach the advice given is designed to explicitly direct and guide someone else's behaviour
- Informative. The role of the intervener is to impart knowledge, information and meaning
- Confrontative. In a confrontative intervention the intervenor seeks to raise someone's awareness about some limiting attitude or behaviour of which they are relatively unaware by challenging them with direct feedback
- Cathartic. In this type of intervention the goal is to enable the individual to release powerful emotions, primarily anxiety, grief and anger
- Catalytic. A catalytic intervention would aim to help the person learn and work through their problems themselves via self-analysis and self-reflection
- Supportive. A supportive intervention would affirm the worth and value of the person to encourage and building up self-belief and confidence in the person

Signs and symptoms of mental health distress in students

Student mental health issues can be complex and far-reaching, but it is widely agreed that earlier intervention is helpful. Below are some of the most common changes in behaviour or personality that could signify struggles with an individual's mental health:

- A change in personality. If a student starts acting out of character, it could suggest poor mental health. Look out for signs of excessive nervousness, anxiety, apathy or dramatic mood swings or anger, particularly if they are constantly occurring... There could also be an abrupt change in manner, style, or personal hygiene (Norwich et al., 2022)
- Changes in behaviour. This could be evidenced by an individual failing to complete work on time, or handing in work that is not to their usual standard. Unexplained absences or lateness could also suggest that the student is experiencing difficulties (Dazzi et al., 2014)
- Additional warning signs include trouble concentrating or remembering things or problems performing familiar tasks. Any significant changes or fluctuations in weight or appetite, or if a student appears to be constantly tired could be underlying issues that could be causes for concern

- If an individual appears to be 'disconnecting' from the world around them, cancelling meetings with friends, or spending an unusual amount of time alone it may be a sign that the student is struggling to cope (Padmore, 2016)
- Lack of self-care or risky behaviours. This can include drug or alcohol abuse, a lack of care with hygiene or lack of concern with appearance. People suffering from poor mental health may also resort to self-harming as a way of controlling or relieving their suffering
- A general sense of hopelessness, guilt, despair or feeling overwhelmed. Depression can present itself in a wide variety of ways such as feeling intensely sad, isolated, unable to cope, upset and tearful, moving slowly or being very agitated
- Disorganised thinking and speech, feelings that are inappropriate to the situation, lack of emotional involvement, or other evidence that student is "out of touch with reality/This can be combined with expression of feelings of persecution, strong mistrust of others"(Pedrelli et al., 2015)
- Increasing dependence on the class teacher (by making excessive appointments, hanging around their office or after class) or others
- Physical complaints without a medical cause, such as headache, stomach pains, etc

Student's background

There may also be background issues which can impact on students' changes in wellbeing (Shelemy et al., 2019) such as

- History of emotional disturbances (e.g., depression, alcohol, drug abuse, eating disorder, anxiety, suicide attempts)
- Traumatic family event(s) such as recent separation or divorce of parents, serious illness or death of family member, physical, emotional, or sexual abuse at home
- Recent loss of an important person (either by death or by separation/break-up)
- Recent loss of esteem
- Previous period of poor functioning
- Breaking up with one's boyfriend or girlfriend
- A change in accommodation
- Rejection by peers
- Loss of family social or financial status
- Failure to achieve/a struggling with coursework
- The adolescent's own pregnancy or illness

Emotional problems

College can be a difficult time of transition. It is not unusual for students to experience problems, frequently related to depression and anxiety. Symptoms of depression are insomnia or change in sleep patterns, inability to concentrate, change in appetite, loss of ability to experience happiness or pleasure, apathy, and many others. It is important to note that having only one symptom usually is not enough to describe someone as depressed, but when multiple symptoms are present for a long period of time, a person may be experiencing severe depression (Norwich et al., 2022).

Anxiety occurs for many during times of high stress at college, and there are some emotional problems related to anxiety. Students who suffer from anxiety can experience panic attacks or extreme fear of specific situations. Traumatic experiences can also cause students to develop anxiety problems whose symptoms include flashbacks, avoiding things associated with the traumatic event, and being easily startled (Pedrelli et al., 2015).

Levels of distress

It is important to be mindful and engaged of student wellbeing on a range of levels in the classroom and beyond. It is important to look to three levels of distress to be aware of it in students in the college (Zacarian and Alvarez-Ortiz, 2017):

- Level one. These behaviours may signal that something is wrong, even if not disruptive to others, changes in performance in class, excessive absences, especially if the student had previously demonstrated good, consistent class attendance. changed patterns of interaction, lethargy, tiredness
- Level two. These indicate stronger emotional distress, as well as a reluctance of the student to seek help/support, requests for extensions of deadlines, disruptive behaviour in class and mood swings
- Level three. These usually indicate that a student is in obvious crisis and needs emergency care. They can be highly disruptive, struggling to communicate, have overtly suicidal thoughts

---

Figure 5.3 Self-reflection exercise

Here are three self-reflection exercises that can help teachers deal with the three levels of distress in their students

Exercise for dealing with mild distress:

Self-reflection: Teachers can reflect on their own communication styles and identify ways they can improve their communication with students experiencing mild distress. They can ask themselves questions like, "How can I be more patient and attentive to students who seem anxious or stressed?" or "What non-verbal cues am I giving to students that may be exacerbating their mild distress?" They can then identify concrete actions they can take to improve their communication with these students.

> *Exercise for dealing with moderate distress:*
>
> *Self-reflection: Teachers can reflect on how they handle situations with students who are experiencing moderate distress. They can ask themselves questions like, "What are my coping mechanisms when dealing with moderate distress in students?" or "What are some ways I can support students who are experiencing moderate distress without overstepping boundaries?" They can then identify areas where they can improve their support for these students, such as seeking additional resources or referrals to mental health professionals.*
>
> *Exercise for dealing with severe distress:*
>
> *Self-reflection: Teachers can reflect on their own self-care practices when dealing with students experiencing severe distress. They can ask themselves questions like, "What are some self-care practices I can implement when dealing with severe distress in students?" or "What boundaries do I need to establish to ensure that I am not personally affected by the severe distress of my students?" They can then identify concrete actions they can take to prioritise their own mental health while still providing support for their students.*

Frames of reference theory

Frames of reference theory is a psychological theory that explains how people make sense of their environment and their behaviour. The theory suggests that people interpret and understand their experiences through a set of frames of reference, or lenses, that are shaped by their past experiences, cultural background, and social environment. These frames of reference influence how people perceive and respond to different situations (Flotman, and Barnard, 2022).

In the context of mental health issues, frames of reference theory can be used to understand how a student's mental health status is shaped by their past experiences, cultural background, and social environment. Understanding different frames of reference can help teachers design interventions that are tailored to the unique needs of each student (Nelson-Jones, 2013).

Frames of Reference theory can be used to support students with mental health issues in several ways:

- In the first instance identifying and understanding the student's frame of reference can enable teachers to better understand the underlying causes of these behaviours and design interventions that address these causes. For example, a student with anxiety may avoid participating in class discussions, while a student with depression may appear disengaged or unmotivated

- By understanding the cultural context in which a student's mental health issues are embedded, teachers can design interventions that are culturally sensitive and effective. For example, in some cultures, mental health issues may be stigmatised, and seeking help may be viewed as a sign of weakness (Gopalkrishnan, 2018)
- Using empathy to build relationships. Teachers can create a safe and supportive environment that promotes learning and growth and build strong relationships that promote trust and open communication by understanding and validating the student's frame of reference, (Rogers, 1980)
- Designing interventions that address the underlying causes of behaviours.

For example, a student with anxiety may benefit from relaxation techniques while a student with depression may benefit from a structured schedule that provides a sense of routine and predictability (King, 1999)

Figure 5.4 Frame of reference tutorial activities

1 *"Observe and Describe" Activity:*
   This activity is great for helping students understand how different frames of reference can affect the way we perceive an object or event. Start by selecting a common object or event, such as a car driving by or a ball bouncing. Ask students to observe and describe what they see from their current frame of reference, whether it's from their desk, the window, or standing up. Then, ask students to change their frame of reference by moving to a different location and repeating the observation and description process. Discuss how the new frame of reference changed their perception of the object or event and what factors might be influencing their observations

2 *"Relative Motion" Experiment:*
   This activity is great for demonstrating how different frames of reference can affect the way we perceive motion. Start by selecting a toy car or ball and setting up a track or ramp. Ask students to predict what will happen when the object is released from a stationary frame of reference, such as the top of the ramp. Then, ask students to predict what will happen when the object is released from a moving frame of reference, such as a toy car that is moving at a constant speed. Have students test their predictions by releasing the object from both frames of reference and observe the results. Discuss how the different frames of reference affected the motion of the object and what factors might be influencing the results

3 *"Working in another's frame of reference":*
   This experiential exercise is useful for developing both listening skills and the ability to reflect back accurately to the speaker what they have said. The exercise is best carried out with an observer. Feedback can be given to both the person who played the role of the 'Client' and the 'Counsellor'. Take turns playing the rolls of Speaker, Listener, and Observer

1 Divide into groups of three. The roles in each group are Speaker, Listener, and Observer
2 Take a few minutes to prepare a statement on an issue that you believe to be important. You may jot down a few notes, but you should not actually read a prepared speech. You should be able to deliver your statement in less than a minute
3 Agree who is to go first. The speaker then delivers her or his statement to the listener. The observer watches
4 The listener listens carefully to what the speaker says, and then summarises her or his point of view. The listener begins with the phrase "This, I believe, is your point of view …"
5 Both the speaker and the observer give feedback to the listener on her or his accuracy
6 Swap roles. Continue until each member of the group has played all three roles
7 In your groups of three, discuss what feelings emerged for you in this exercise:

- Did any role feel more difficult for you?
- How did it feel to be listening so intently?
- Did you disagree or agree with the statements?
- How did it feel to listen without being able to judge

Using congruence

Congruence (also known as genuineness) means demonstrating that the teacher/counsellor is genuine and authentic by showing warmth and understanding. If the student feels that the teacher is genuinely interested in them and that their comments and questions are genuine and authentic, they will feel at ease when talking about difficult or embarrassing subjects (Nelson-Jones, 2013). Congruence, like Unconditional Positive Regard (UPR) (valuing and accepting the person as they are), helps teachers to build a trusting relationship with students in which they feel safe and supported (Rogers, 1980).

Here are some ways a teacher can demonstrate congruence when supporting a student with mental health needs:

- Actively listening to the student's concerns and feelings without judgment or interruption
- Setting realistic expectations and boundaries and communicating with them clearly helps build trust and rapport with the student
- Showing empathy and understanding towards the student's challenges can help them feel seen and heard It is essential to validate their feelings and let them know that they are not alone

- Teachers can model self-care practices, such as taking breaks, seeking support when needed, and prioritising their mental health. This can help students understand the importance of self-care and reduce stigma around seeking help
- Collaborating with mental health professionals, college and school counsellors, and other support staff can demonstrate the teacher's commitment to the student's wellbeing and show that they are working together to support the student

Incongruence

Demonstrating incongruence when supporting a student with mental health needs can be detrimental to their wellbeing and create additional challenges. Incongruence occurs when a person's words, actions, and body language do not match, leading to confusion and mistrust (Rogers, 1980). Here are some ways a teacher can demonstrate incongruence when supporting a student with mental health needs:

- Making promises that cannot be kept. Empty promises that cannot be delivered, such as complete recovery or immediate solutions to problems, can set unrealistic expectations and lead to disappointment and frustration
- Advice or solutions without fully understanding the student's challenges can be unhelpful and make the student feel misunderstood or dismissed
- Being judgmental can create shame and stigmatise the student's struggles
- A teacher can violate a student's trust and create further distress by disregarding a student's boundaries, such as sharing their personal information or forcing them to talk about things they are not comfortable with
- Inconsistency in behaviour or communication can create confusion and mistrust. For example, promising support but failing to follow through can damage the relationship between the teacher and student

---

Figure 5.5 Self-reflection exercises

Here are three exercises that can help teachers develop congruence in working with students with mental health needs:

Reflective journaling: Encourage teachers to take some time each day to reflect on their interactions with students with mental health needs. They can write down their thoughts and feelings about the experience, what they learned, and what they could do differently next time. This exercise can help teachers develop self-awareness and identify areas where they need to improve to better support their students.

> *Role-playing:* Conduct a role-playing exercise where teachers can practice having difficult conversations with students with mental health needs. For example, teachers can role-play a scenario where a student expresses suicidal thoughts, and the teacher can practice responding empathetically and non-judgmentally. This exercise can help teachers build their confidence in handling challenging situations and develop effective communication skills.
> *Mindfulness exercises:* Incorporate mindfulness exercises into teacher training sessions to help them develop self-awareness and reduce stress. These exercises can include meditation, breathing techniques, or body scan exercises. Mindfulness can help teachers become more present and attentive during interactions with students, which can improve the quality of their communication and support.
> *Personal Values Assessment:* Teachers can complete a personal values assessment and reflect on how their values align with their actions when supporting students with mental health needs. They can then identify areas where they need to make adjustments to better align their values with their actions. This exercise can help teachers develop congruence and authenticity in their communication and behaviour with students.

Designing a welcoming physical environment

Creating a supportive physical environment can be important when discussing mental health issues with college students. The physical environment should be a private and quiet space where the student can feel comfortable to speak freely without any distractions or interruptions. (King, 1999).

Seating issues

When discussing mental health issues with a student, a teacher should be mindful of the following seating issues (McLeod and McLeod, 2011):

- Physical Comfort. The seating arrangement should be comfortable for both the teacher and the student. The chairs should be ergonomically designed to support the back, and the height of the desk and chair should be appropriate for the student's size
- Privacy. The conversation should take place in a private setting where the student feels safe and secure. A private area like a counsellor's office or an empty classroom can be used
- Eye Contact. The seating arrangement should allow for eye contact between the teacher and the student. This can help the student feel heard and understood

- Proximity. The teacher should be close enough to the student to convey a sense of caring and concern, but not so close as to invade the student's personal space
  - Body Language. The teacher's body language should convey empathy and understanding. The teacher should sit upright, maintain eye contact, and avoid crossing their arms or legs, which can convey defensiveness
- Distractions. The seating arrangement should minimise distractions that could interfere with the conversation, such as noise or visual distractions
- Accessibility. The seating arrangement should be accessible for students with physical disabilities. Teachers should ensure that students with disabilities have the same opportunities to participate in discussions about mental health as their peers
- Personal space and height. When discussing mental health issues with a student, a teacher should also be mindful of personal space and height issues and cultural differences. For example:
  - The teacher should be mindful of the student's personal space and avoid standing too close or invading their personal space. This can help the student feel more comfortable and safer during the conversation
  - The teacher should consider the student's height when choosing a seating arrangement. If the student is significantly taller or shorter than the teacher, this could create a power dynamic that could be intimidating for the student
  - It is important for the teacher to be mindful of any cultural differences that may affect personal space and height expectations. Some cultures may value more physical closeness or have different expectations around power dynamics, (Hebel, and Rentzsch, 2022) so it is important for the teacher to be respectful of these differences and adjust accordingly
- Student Preferences. It is important to consider the student's preferences when it comes to personal space and height. Some students may feel more comfortable with a closer seating arrangement, while others may prefer more distance. Similarly, some may prefer a seating arrangement that puts them at eye level with the teacher, while others may feel more comfortable with the teacher seated higher or lower
  - The room should also be at a suitable temperature to ensure that the student is comfortable throughout the conversation
  - Minimal Décor with soothing colours can create a calm and peaceful environment, which can help the student feel more relaxed
  - Providing access to pamphlets or brochures, or providing a referral to a mental health professional, can help the student feel supported and empowered

> **Figure 5.6 Self-reflection task**
>
> *Classroom Environment Assessment: In this exercise, teachers can assess their classroom environment and identify potential physical barriers to discussing mental health needs with their students. They can ask themselves questions like, "Is my classroom designed to promote open and honest communication?" or "What changes can I make to the physical environment to create a safe and supportive space for students to discuss their mental health needs?" By identifying potential barriers and making necessary changes, teachers can create a supportive and non-judgmental environment for students to discuss their mental health needs.*
>
> *Personal Space Assessment: In this exercise, teachers can reflect on their own personal space and how it affects their ability to support students discussing their mental health needs. They can ask themselves questions like, "Do I have a designated space in my classroom where students can come and talk to me about their mental health needs?" or "Am I able to create a safe and private space for students to discuss sensitive topics with me?" By identifying any potential issues with their personal space, teachers can make changes to ensure they can provide effective support for their students.*

Dual relationships and boundaries

Where there are 'dual relationship' situations such as in schools and prisons. Taking care around role boundaries is absolutely essential When teachers are supporting students with mental health problems, boundary issues can arise in several ways (Finlay, 2008). Here are a few examples:

- Over-involvement. Teachers may become too involved in a student's personal life, such as trying to solve their problems or becoming their primary emotional support. While it's important for teachers to show empathy and offer support, it's crucial that they maintain a professional distance and avoid taking on the role of a therapist or counsellor
- Lack of boundaries. In some cases, teachers may share too much personal information about themselves, blur the lines between their personal and professional lives, or engage in inappropriate physical contact with their students. This can create confusion and discomfort for the student and may also be a violation of college policies or laws
- Dual relationships: If a teacher has a personal relationship with a student outside of the classroom, such as a family friend or neighbour, this can create a conflict of interest when it comes to supporting the student's mental health needs. The teacher may feel torn between their personal relationship and their professional obligations, and this can impact upon the quality of support they provide

- Overstepping professional boundaries. Teachers may sometimes feel pressure to provide mental health support to students beyond their scope of expertise or training. For example, they may attempt to diagnose a student's condition or recommend specific treatments without consulting a mental health professional. This can be harmful to the student and put the teacher at risk of legal liability.

When supporting students with mental health issues, teachers should be aware of the potential conflicts that can occur because of dual relationships and take steps to manage them appropriately (Nelson-Jones, 2013). Here are some strategies that can help:

- Teachers should make it clear to students and their families what their role is in supporting the student's mental health needs. They should communicate that they are not therapists or counsellors, and that they have a duty to maintain a professional distance. This can help prevent confusion and expectations that may lead to dual relationship issues
- Teachers should be mindful of any personal relationships they have with their students or their families outside of the classroom. If they feel that these relationships may create a conflict of interest when it comes to supporting the student's mental health needs, they should consider referring the student to a different teacher or mental health professional
- Teachers who are supporting students with mental health needs should seek supervision or consultation from mental health professionals or college and school administrators. This can help them navigate complex situations and ensure that they are providing appropriate support while maintaining professional boundaries
- Teachers should familiarise themselves with institutional policies and guidelines that address dual relationship issues and follow them closely

---

Figure 5.7   Self-reflection exercise

Personal Boundaries Assessment: In this exercise, teachers can reflect on their own personal boundaries when supporting students with mental health and well-being issues. They can ask themselves questions like, "What boundaries do I have in place when interacting with students who are experiencing mental health issues?" or "Am I able to recognise when a student's needs exceed my boundaries, and what steps do I take to refer them to the appropriate support services?" By identifying their own boundaries and limitations, teachers can better understand how to support their students effectively while also maintaining their own mental health.

> *Case Study Analysis: In this exercise, teachers can analyse case studies of situations where boundary issues arose in supporting students with mental health and well-being issues. They can reflect on how they would handle the situation and identify any potential boundary violations or issues. They can then compare their approach with their colleagues and receive feedback on how to improve their approach. This exercise can help teachers develop critical thinking skills and learn from each other's experiences*

Nonverbal communication skills

The message teachers send out via their bodies as listeners are important when listening to and responding to students. In these types of contexts, teachers need to evidence their attending behaviour, that is, physically convey their availability and their interest to the student. In essence, they should provide nonverbal rewards to the student for opening up their problems (Nelson-Jones, 2013). These should include some of the following body language strategies:

Open body posture

When discussing mental health issues with a college student, a teacher should aim to project a posture that is open, attentive, and non-judgmental. Some general tips for body posture include:

- Sitting square to students with left shoulder opposite their right or at a slight angle. This can be less pressurising for more anxious students. It is also important to sit upright with an open chest and relaxed shoulders to convey an engaged and approachable demeanour.
- *Mirroring vs Automation*: mirroring is a technique common to preliminary sessions in counselling. Mirroring a student's body language can help to create a certain bond or connection with the student assisting in the process of establishing rapport. Basically, the student both consciously and subconsciously notices the familiar behaviour of the teacher. This 'familiarity' helps the client to relax and trust the teacher. However, mirroring needs to be done mindfully; otherwise, the teacher may think he or she is being mocked or not taken seriously.

(King, 1999)

Figure 5.8 A tip

Be attentive to the signals your own body language gives off

A good way to train your body language to give off an image of confidence, is to imagine that you just received a compliment, one that makes you feel great about yourself, concentrate on the good feelings that arise and you will notice that your body becomes more erect, your chin tilts up and you will have a soft smile. The more you practice having your body display a sign of confidence the more natural it will become. Whenever you need to look confident, imagine the compliments and your body will mould itself into that shape.

Figure 5.9   Self-reflection exercise

Video Analysis: In this exercise, you can record yourself having a conversation with a student about mental health issues and analyse your body language during the conversation. You can ask yourself questions like, "Did I maintain eye contact with the student?" or "Did I use open and inviting body language?" By analysing your body language, you can identify areas for improvement and make necessary changes to ensure you are sending the right signals to the student.

Mindful Body Scan: In this exercise, you can take a few minutes to do a mindful body scan before engaging in a conversation with a student about mental health issues. You can ask yourself questions like, "How does my body feel right now?" or "Am I carrying any tension in my body?" By doing a body scan, teachers can identify any physical cues that might affect their body language during the conversation. They can then take steps to relax and ensure their body language aligns with their intentions.

Role-Play Scenarios: In this exercise, you can role-play different scenarios where you discuss mental health issues with a student. You can practice using different body language strategies, such as active listening, non-judgmental postures, and validating facial expressions. After each scenario, you can reflect on your performance and identify which strategies were effective and which ones need improvement. You can also receive feedback from your colleagues on how to improve your body language when discussing mental health issues with students.

Eye contact

It is important to maintain eye contact to demonstrate active listening and show that the student has your full attention. Here are some tips for using good gaze and appropriate eye contact:

- When listening to the student, you should maintain eye contact to demonstrate that you are fully present and engaged in the conversation. However, you should avoid staring at the student, as this can make them feel

uncomfortable, dominated, or threatened. There is an equilibrium level of eye contact depending on the degree of anxiety in the student, how developed the relationship is between teacher and student.
- It's also essential to look away periodically to avoid making the student feel scrutinised or uncomfortable. But you should adjust your gaze depending on the situation. For example, you may want to maintain more eye contact when the student is sharing something emotional or vulnerable (King, 1999)
- You should avoid being distracted by phones, computers, or other devices during the conversation, as this can signal a lack of interest or respect
- Adjust gaze appropriately
- Different cultures have different norms when it comes to eye contact. You should be aware of the student's cultural background and adjust your eye contact accordingly. For example, some cultures value direct eye contact as a sign of respect, while others consider it rude or aggressive. For instance, in many Western cultures, direct eye contact is seen as a sign of honesty, trustworthiness, and attentiveness. However, in some Asian and African cultures, prolonged eye contact may be perceived as confrontational or impolite (Uono and Hietanen, 2015).
- Be mindful of personal preferences. Some individuals, regardless of cultural background, may have personal preferences or experiences that affect their eye contact behaviour. For example, some people with autism spectrum disorder may find eye contact uncomfortable or overwhelming (Trevisan et al., 2017). However, students may want a reasonable level of eye contact from their teachers otherwise they may perceive them as bored, or tense if they look away too often

---

Figure 5.10 Self-reflection exercise

Here are three self-reflection exercises that teachers can use to improve their eye contact when supporting students with mental health issues:

Mirror Self-Reflection: Stand in front of a mirror and practice making eye contact with your own reflection. During this exercise, focus on maintaining steady eye contact while also being aware of your body language and facial expressions. Some questions to consider during this reflection exercise could include:

- *How comfortable do I feel making eye contact with myself in the mirror?*
- *Am I able to maintain steady eye contact without looking away or becoming distracted?*
- *What facial expressions am I making while maintaining eye contact? Do they convey empathy and understanding?*

> *Role-Playing Self-Reflection: role-play a scenario where you are supporting a student with mental health issues. During the role-play, focus on making steady eye contact with the student and being aware of your own body language and facial expressions. Some questions to consider during this reflection exercise could include:*
>
> - *How comfortable do I feel making eye contact with the student during the role-play?*
> - *Am I able to maintain steady eye contact without looking away or becoming distracted?*
> - *What facial expressions am I making while maintaining eye contact? Do they convey empathy and understanding?*
>
> *Peer Observation: observe a peer while they are supporting a student with mental health issues. During the observation, pay close attention to their eye contact and take notes. After the observation reflect on their own eye contact and consider:*
>
> - *What eye contact techniques did my peer use that were effective in supporting the student?*
> - *Did my peer use any eye contact techniques that were not effective in supporting the student?*
> - *How could I adapt my peer's effective eye contact techniques to better support my own students?*
> - *How can I avoid using ineffective eye contact techniques when supporting my own students?*

Facial expressions

Facial expressions can be a powerful tool for a teacher when discussing mental health issues with college students. This can be particularly problematic for students who have social competence deficits like ASD (Lierheimer and Stichter, 2012). Here are some ideas about how to use facial expressions effectively (Frith, 2009):

- Ensure that your facial expressions are consistent with the message you are trying to convey. For example, if discussing a serious topic, such as depression, it's important to have a calm and empathetic facial expression that conveys concern
- Show empathy and understanding. by using facial expressions such as nodding, smiling, and maintaining eye contact to convey understanding and concern for the student. Avoid judgmental facial expressions such as frowning, rolling eyes, or showing disgust

- Use facial expressions to encourage communication. For example, if a student is hesitant to share their feelings a gentle smile or nod can encourage them to be more open
- Use them also to show support for the student and their journey towards healing such as a gentle smile or a nod
- A gentle smile can help put students at ease and show that you are approachable and caring

---

Figure 5.11   Self-reflective exercise

Ask a person to sit in a chair and think about a person that they like, notice what happens to their posture and any movements that they make with their hands or feet, the head position, the eye movements, whether their mouth changes eg, widens or turns up, if their eyes are focusing in the distance or close-up and the direction in which they are looking.

Then ask them to think about a person that they do not like and notice the same elements but this time also looking at the differences between their appearance when thinking about the first person and when thinking about the second.

Finally ask them to think of either and see if you can guess which of the two they are thinking of. Do this with as many people as you can. Also practice becoming aware of exactly how a person looks and sounds in different states, noting what happens with their voice tone what postures they have when thinking about the second.

Finally ask them to think of either and see if you can guess which of the two they are thinking of. Do this with as many people as you can. Also practice becoming aware of exactly how a person looks and sounds in different states, noting what happens with their voice tone what postures they have when feeling energetic or how they express lethargy in their body, note what eye movements go with past memories and future expectation.

Observing these things can help you to become more sensitive and responsive to other people's experiences, helping to improve communication and understanding.

Using gestures when supporting students

Nodding

Nodding can show that the teacher is actively listening and understanding what the students is saying. It can also encourage them to continue sharing their thoughts and feelings.

Hand gestures can also be an effective way to communicate support and understanding when working with students with mental health issues. Use hand gestures that feel natural and authentic and communicate support and understanding in a way that feels comfortable and appropriate for the situation (Goldin-Meadow and Alibali, 2013). It's important to note however that specific hand gestures may not always be appropriate or effective, as they can be culturally specific and may not be universally understood. Here are some effective hand gestures to consider:

- Placing hand on heart can communicate a deep sense of empathy and connection. This gesture can be especially powerful when expressing sympathy or understanding for the student's situation
- Holding palms up can convey openness and receptivity. This gesture can be useful when trying to create a safe and welcoming space for the student to share their thoughts and feelings
- Folding hands in front of you can convey a sense of attentiveness and focus. This gesture can be useful when actively listening to the student and want to communicate that you are fully present in the moment
- Steepling fingers can convey a sense of calm and confidence. This gesture can be helpful when trying to reassure the student or help them to feel more grounded and centred
- A gentle hand gesture, such as rubbing palms together or rubbing own arm, can be a calming and grounding gesture that encourages relaxation. You could also encourage the student to take slow, deep breaths and hold their hands together in a relaxed manner (Clough and Duff, 2020)

When discussing mental health problems with a student, certain hand gestures could be seen as negative or dismissive, (Van Nispen et al., 2022) including:

- Pointing fingers at a student can be seen as confrontational and accusatory, which may make the student feel judged or defensive
- Crossing arms can create a barrier between you and the student, which may signal a lack of openness or interest in what the student is saying
- Fidgeting, such as tapping fingers or shifting weight from foot to foot, can be distracting and signal a lack of attention or interest in what the student is saying
- Raising eyebrows or rolling eyes:Raising eyebrows or rolling eyes can be interpreted as a sign of disbelief or dismissal, which may discourage the student from sharing more
- Using excessive hand gestures can be distracting and may signal a lack of focus or control, which may make the student feel less comfortable sharing their mental health concerns

Figure 5.12 Self-reflection exercises

Here are two self-reflection exercises that you can use to improve your hand gestures when supporting students with mental health problems:

1 *Video Self-Reflection: record themselves while you are supporting a student. After the interaction, watch the video and reflect on your hand gestures. Some questions to consider during this reflection exercise could include:*

- *What hand gestures did I use during the interaction?*
- *Were my hand gestures supportive and empathetic?*
- *Did I use any hand gestures that may have been perceived as negative or dismissive?*
- *How could I improve my hand gestures to better support the student?*

2 *Peer Observation: observe a peer while they are supporting a student. During the observation, pay close attention to their peer's hand gestures and take notes. After the observation, reflect on your own hand gestures and consider:*

- *What hand gestures did my peer use that were effective in supporting the student?*
- *Did my peer use any hand gestures that were not effective in supporting the student?*
- *How could I adapt my peer's effective hand gestures to better support my own students?*
- *How can I avoid using ineffective hand gestures when supporting my own students?*

Figure 5.13 Good and bad body messages self-reflection exercise

Work with a colleague and ask them to discuss a topic which interests them. Your role is mainly to listen, however:

- *Start by using inappropriate body messages when you respond*
- *Switch to attentive body language*
- *Discuss with your colleague what it felt like to send and receive good and bad body messages*
- *Switch roles and start again*

> **Figure 5.14** Evaluating your own body messages. A self-reflective checklist
>
> *Mark yourself out of 10 (10 being excellent) on each of the following body messages and explain how you will work on this area in the future:*
>
> | Body message | Mark out of 10 | How you will improve on this area |
> |---|---|---|
> | Being available to your student | | |
> | Adopting a relaxed and open body posture | | |
> | Leaning slightly forward | | |
> | Using appropriate gaze | | |
> | Using appropriate eye contact | | |
> | Using appropriate facial expressions | | |
> | Using good gesturesBeing mindful of space and height issues | | |
> | Being culturally sensitive | | |

> **Figure 5.15** Improving your approaches to body messages self-reflection exercise
>
> *Reflect on a body message that you feel that you struggle with when you are working with students in a tutorial. For example, body posture:*
>
> - Hold a conversation with a colleague in which you work on this particular body message.
>
> *Ask your colleague to evaluate your approach and give you targets for improvement*

References

Best, R., Jarvis C., and Ribbens, P. (1985). *Perspectives on Pastoral Care.* London: Heinemann.
British Association for Counselling and Psychotherapy (BACP). (2018). *Ethical Framework for the Counselling Professions.* Lutterworth, Leicestershire: BACP House.

British Association for Counselling and Psychotherapy (BACP). (2020a). *A Guide to the BACP Counselling Skills Competence Framework*. Lutterworth, Leicestershire: BACP House.

British Association for Counselling and Psychotherapy (BACP). (2020b). *Counselling Skills Competence Framework*. Lutterworth, Leicestershire: BACP House.

Chandler, B. (2001). Being a tutor. In: C. Atkinson and B. Chandler (eds.), *Student Support: Tutoring, Guidance and Dealing with Disruption*. Greenwich: Greenwich University Press.

Clough, S., and Duff, M. C. (2020). The role of gesture in communication and cognition: Implications for understanding and treating neurogenic communication disorders. *Frontiers in Human Neuroscience*, 14: 323. doi:10.3389/fnhum.2020.00323

Crosling, F., and Webb, G. (2002). *Supporting Student Learning*. London: Taylor and Francis.

Dazzi, T., Gribble, R., Wessely, S., and Fear, N. T. (2014). Does asking about suicide and related behaviours induce suicidal ideation? What is the evidence? *Psychological Medicine*, 44(16): 3361–3. doi:10.1017/S0033291714001299

Egan, G. (2002). *The Skilled Helper: A Problem Management and Opportunity Development Approach to Helping* (7th edn. Pacific Grove, CA: Brooks Cole.

Finlay, I. (2008). Learning through boundary-crossing: Further education lecturers learning in both the university and workplace. *European Journal of Teacher Education*, 31: 1: 73–87. doi:10.1080/02619760701845024

Flotman, A.-P., and Barnard, A. (2022). The evolution of personal frames of reference: Metaphors as potential space. *International Journal of Doctoral Studies*, 17: 67–86. doi:10.28945/4919

Frith, C. (2009). Role of facial expressions in social interactions. *Philosophical Transactions of the Royal Society of London. Series B, Biological Sciences*, 364(1535): 3453–8. doi:10.1098/rstb.2009.0142

Further Education Development Agency (FEDA). (1995). *Tutoring for Achievement-Frameworks*. London: FEDA and Learning Partners.

Goldin-Meadow, S., and Alibali, M. W. (2013). Gesture's role in speaking, learning, and creating language. *Annual Review of Psychology*, 64: 257–83. doi:10.1146/annurev-psych-113011-143802

Gopalkrishnan, N. (2018). Cultural diversity and mental health: Considerations for policy and practice. *Public Health*, 6. doi:10.3389/fpubh.2018.00179

Hebel, V., and Rentzsch, K. (2022). One, two, three, sit next to me: Personality and physical distance. *Personality and Individual Differences*, 198: 111798.

Heron, J. (2001). *Helping the Client: A Creative Practical Guide*. UK: Sage.

Hill, C. E. (2004). *Helping Skills: Facilitating Exploration, Insight, and Action* (2nd edn). New York: American Psychological Association.

Ivey, A. (1971). *Microcounseling: Innovations in Interviewing*. Springfield, IL: Charles C Thomas.

King, G. (1999). *Counselling Skills for Teachers*. Buckinghamshire: Oxford University Press.

Lierheimer, K., and Stichter, J. (2012). Teaching facial expressions of emotion. *Beyond Behavior*, 21: 20–7.

McLeod, J., and McLeod J. (2011). *Counselling Skills*. Maidenhead: Open University Press.

Nelson-Jones, R. (2013). *Introduction to Counselling Skills*. Los Angeles: SAGE Publications Limited.

Neville, L. (2007). *The Personal Tutor's Handbook*. Basingstoke: Palgrave MacMillan.

Norwich, Brahm, Moore, Darren, Stentiford, Lauren, and Hall, Dave. (2022). A critical consideration of 'mental health and wellbeing' in education: Thinking about school aims in terms of wellbeing. *British Educational Research Journal*, 48. doi:10.1002/berj.3795

Padmore, J. (2016). *The Mental Health Needs of Children and Young People.* Maidenhead: OUP.
Pedrelli, P., Nyer, M., Yeung, A., Zulauf, C., and Wilens, T. (2015). College students: Mental health problems and treatment considerations. *Academic Psychiatry*, 39(5): 503–11. doi:10.1007/s40596-014-0205-9
Rogers, C. (1980). *A Way of Being.* New York: Houghton Mifflin.
Rogers, C. R. (1957). A process conception of psychotherapy. *American Psychologist*, 13(4), 142–149. doi:10.1037/h0042129
Shelemy, L., Harvey, K., and Waite, P. (2019). Supporting students' mental health in schools: What do teachers want and need? *Emotional and Behavioural Difficulties*, 24(1): 100–16. ISSN 1363-2752. doi:10.1080/13632752.2019.1582742. Available at https://centaur.reading.ac.uk/82380/
Trevisan, D. A., Roberts, N., Lin, C., and Birmingham, E. (2017). How do adults and teens with self-declared Autism Spectrum Disorder experience eye contact? A qualitative analysis of first-hand accounts. *PLoS One*, 12(11): e0188446. doi:10.1371/journal.pone.0188446
Uono, S., and Hietanen, J. K. (2015). Eye contact perception in the West and East: A cross-cultural study. *PLoS One*, 10(2): e0118094. doi:10.1371/journal.pone.0118094
van Nispen, K. Sekine, K., van der Meulen, I., and Preisig, B. C. (2022). Gesture in the eye of the beholder: An eye-tracking study on factors determining the attention for gestures produced by people with aphasia. *Neuropsychologia*, 174: 108315. ISSN 0028-3932. doi:10.1016/j.neuropsychologia.2022.108315
Wooton, S. (2013). *Personal Tutoring for the 21st Century.* Further Education Tutorial Network (FETN). https://repository.excellencegateway.org.uk/Personal%20tutoring%20for%20the%2021st%20century.pdf
Wosket, V. (2008). *Egan's Skilled Helper Model: Developments and Implications in Counselling.* Abingdon: Routledge.
Zacarian, D., and Alvarez-Ortiz, L. Haynes J. (2017). *Supporting Students Living with Trauma, Violence, and Chronic Stress.* ASCD. https://files.ascd.org/staticfiles/ascd/pdf/siteASCD/publications/books/Teaching-To-Strengths-Sample-Chapters.pdf

6 The development and usage of basic helping skills to support students' mental health and wellbeing needs

Observation

Observation needs to occur continually, as an ongoing activity, during each support session. By accepting and responding to the façade we demonstrate to the young person that we are accepting of what they are presenting to us, showing them Unconditional Positive Regard (UPR) (Brammer and MacDonald, 2003). In effect, you are showing them that they are believed. It can provide information about the young person with regard to mood, culture, self-esteem, creativity, and social influences. Important attributes of the young people need to be observed include:

- General appearance. A young person's general appearance reflects the way in which they wish to be seen and gives an indication of how they would like to be. It is an outward expression of the internal attempt to form a personal identity. Teachers need to be careful about the way in which they interpret a young person's general appearance. Unfortunately, all have their own personal prejudices and personal stereotypes and should be mindful not to fall into these (Garvey et al., 2010).
- A young person's behaviour can give you useful information about ways in which to support them. Modelling is certainly useful in helping young people to learn new behaviours but can only be effective within the context of an effective relationship. Adolescent behaviours such as restlessness, agitation and lethargy can give you an indication of a young person's current emotional state
- Mood and affect. Mood is the internal feeling or emotion which often influences behaviour and the individual's perception of the world and affect is the external emotional effect of this (Geldard and Geldard, 2015). The mood may be disguised by the presenting affect. For example, a student who has depression may present as hyperactive and agitated
- When observing the speech and language of young people, teachers need to pay close attention to what is said, how it is said and the way it is said.

DOI: 10.4324/9781003424376-7

Figure 6.1 Self-reflective task

Mindfulness Practice:
Incorporate mindfulness practice into your reflective activities to help them develop a more intuitive understanding of the differences between mood and affect. During mindfulness practice, you will be able to focus your attention on your own emotions and physical sensations, and observe how these sensations are connected to your mood and affect.

1. *Start by finding a comfortable position, either sitting in a chair with your feet planted firmly on the floor, or sitting cross-legged on the floor*
2. *Close your eyes and take a few deep breaths to relax your body*
3. *Begin to focus your attention on your breathing. Notice how your breath feels as it enters and leaves your body*
4. *If your mind wanders, simply bring your attention back to your breath*
5. *Visualise a peaceful scene in your mind. It can be a beach, a mountain, a lake, or anything that brings you a sense of peace*
6. *Remain in this meditative state for 10 to 15 minutes*
7. *When you are ready, slowly open your eyes and take a few deep breaths*
8. *Reflect on your experience and how you feel*
9. *Take a few moments to write down your thoughts and feelings in a journal*

Through this practice, you can become more attuned to their own emotional states and develop a more nuanced understanding of the connections between mood and affect. You can then apply this understanding to your interactions with students and be more sensitive to changes in a student's mood and affect

Using active questioning to support students

General information-seeking questions. All people commonly use general information-seeking questions in everyday conversation in order to get information. Young people do the same with their peers. Often, when these questions are prefaced with words that indicate the teacher's genuine curiosity and interest, the young person is likely to feel important as a source of information. There are also questions that have more specific purposes (Renger, 2023). These include the following types:

> Gestalt style questions. Gestalt therapy focuses on the moment, most of the questions the teacher should ask are what and how types of questions, which will often make the patient more aware of their present experiences. These are intended to heighten the students's awareness

and to help the student to become more fully aware of what is happening within them, either somatically or emotionally, so that they can intensify those bodily or emotional feelings, deal with them, and move on to discussing associated thought (Perls and Goodman, 1951). These types of questions include:

> '*What are you feeling emotionally right now?*'
> '*Where in your body do you experience that emotional feeling?*'
> '*Can you tell me what's happening inside you right now?*'
> '*What's happening inside you right now?*
> '*Can you put words to your tears*
> *Can you tell me what is happening inside you right now? What are you experiencing internally?*'
> *What are you seeing at this moment?*
> *What is your facial expression saying right now?*

Circular questions come from the Milan Systemic Model of Family Therapy (Palazzoli et al., 1980). A circular question is a non-threatening way of getting information from a young person. Instead of asking the young person directly about how they feel or what that they think, or what their attitude is, the counsellor asks the young person how someone else feels or thinks or asks what the other person's attitude might be. Often, having answered a circular question, the young person will continue by talking about their own feelings, thoughts, attitudes, or beliefs to make it clear whether they agree or disagree with the person who was mentioned in the circular question.

Transitional questions can be used for the following purposes (McLeod and McLeod, 2014):

- To encourage the young person to return to the discussion of an important topic or issue, particularly after the introduction of a digression
- To encourage the young person to direct the young person from talking about one aspect or topic to another more important one
- To make it clear that the counsellor is an active participant in the conversation.
- To enliven the conversation

Some examples include:

- 'Earlier you mentioned that you had had a troubling experience. I'm wondering whether you would like to tell me more about that?
- Are there any changes you've noticed in your thoughts or feelings that you'd like to talk about?
- "Can you help me understand how [specific issue] is impacting you academically or emotionally?"

Choice or option questioning. These type of questions focus on the past, present, or future and enable the young person to look at the likely consequences of different behaviours. By exploring choices and consequences, they are likely to be better prepared for future situations. They can help the young person to develop ideas about the choices they can about the way they think and behave. These methods are a development of Choice and Reality Therapy (CRT) (Glasser, 1965) which teaches people to gain effective control over their lives after they realise and accept responsibility for the behaviours they choose to take, and then make better choices thereafter (1965).

Here are some of the types of questions you might use in choice or option questioning:

- *What do you seek from the world that you are either getting, partly getting, or not getting?*
- *How much effort are you prepared to exert to satisfy your desire (a score between 1 and 10, or a % of the week)?*
- *What might you have to give up or change to get what you want?*
- *What are you happy to settle for if you are not able to attain everything you wish?*
- *'If the same situation arises during the coming weeks, what do you think you will do? (Will you do this, or will you do that?)'*

Figure 6.2 Self-reflection activity

Here are some of the CRT questions that I have used and some of my justifications for using them. Reflect on the validity of my justifications and evaluate them.

Question	My justification	Your comments
What are your options in this situation?	This question prompts the individual to explore different choices available to them, emphasizing that they have the power to make decisions and take responsibility for their actions.	
How do you think your choice will help you meet your needs?	This question encourages the individual to consider the connection between their choices and the satisfaction of their basic needs. It emphasises the importance of making choices that align with their well-being.	

Question	My justification	Your comments
What are the potential consequences of each option?	By asking this question, the focus is shifted towards considering the potential outcomes of different choices. It helps the individual evaluate the positive and negative consequences, fostering a sense of responsibility and thoughtful decision-making.	
What could you do differently to change the situation?	This question prompts the individual to think about alternative actions or behaviours they can adopt to address the issue at hand. It encourages personal agency and empowers them to make changes that can lead to better outcomes.	
How do your current choices align with your long-term goals?	This question directs the individual to reflect on the congruence between their current actions and their overarching objectives. It helps them assess whether their choices are in line with their desired outcomes and encourages them to take responsibility for shaping their future.	

Figure 6.3 Continuing Professional Development activity

I use the following two activities in CPD sessions to train staff in basic CRT questioning so they can use it in their tutorial sessions:

Case Study Analysis: I provide the teacher with a case study or scenario involving a student who is facing a challenge or deciding. Ask the teacher to analyse the situation and come up with relevant questions that would

> help the student explore their choices and take responsibility for their actions. Encourage the teacher to think about questions that focus on the student's needs, options, and potential consequences.
> Role-Playing Scenarios: I can also organise a role-playing activity where the teacher acts as a student facing a problem, and the other participants (e.g., colleagues, fellow teachers, or students) play the role of a Choice and Reality Therapy counsellor. The teacher can present a scenario, and the "counsellors" can ask questions to help the teacher explore their choices, consequences, and ways to take responsibility. After the role-play, discuss the effectiveness of the questions asked and provide constructive feedback.

Guru questioning. When using these types of questions, the young person is given the opportunity to analyse themselves objectivity and then provide advice to themselves as an impartial expert. It is a method taken from Gestalt therapy (Perls and Goodman, 1951). Young people are asked to imagine themselves in the third person and this technique helps them figure out some of their own faults by giving advice. It is based on the premise sometimes it may be easier to give advice and hear it than it is to take it.

Figure 6.4 Examples of Guru questions

Here are some examples of questions that could be used in this situation:

If you were observing yourself from an outsider's perspective, what advice would you offer to the person you see? This question encourages the student to step outside of their subjective experience and imagine themselves as an observer. It prompts them to provide advice based on this objective viewpoint.

Pretend you are a trusted mentor or friend looking at your situation. What insights or guidance would you offer to yourself? By taking on the role of a trusted mentor or friend, the student can detach themselves from their personal biases and offer advice based on what they would recommend to someone else in a similar situation.

How would you advise a close friend who is facing the same challenge you're currently experiencing? This question prompts the student to view their situation through the lens of advising a close friend. It encourages them to consider what advice they would give to someone else dealing with the same challenge.

> *Imagine writing a letter to yourself, providing guidance and support. What would you say to yourself?* By imagining writing a letter to themselves, the student can create distance and objectivity. They can offer compassionate advice and insights as if they were offering support to a dear friend.
>
> *What alternative perspectives or solutions might you suggest to someone else in a similar situation?* This question encourages the student to explore alternative perspectives and solutions they might recommend to someone else facing a similar challenge. It helps them see their situation from different angles and consider new possibilities.
>
> *If you could step into another person's shoes and advise yourself, what advice would you give from their perspective?* This question invites the student to imagine embodying another person, such as a role model, teacher, or someone they admire. From that person's perspective, they can offer advice to themselves, providing a fresh and unbiased viewpoint.

Narrativising questions function as ways in which the issue can be externalised separating the problem, or central issue, from the person. By doing this, the young person can feel that they can control their problem, or central issue, if they wish, because it is something external to them which can be controlled, rather than something inherent in them which cannot be controlled. The approach is derived from Narrative Therapy which attempts to centre people as the experts in their own lives and views problems as separate from people and assumes people have many skills, competencies, beliefs, values, commitments and abilities that will assist them to change their relationship with problems in their lives (Morgan, 2000).Questions to be posed using this approach can include:

- If we were to give this problem a name, what would you choose to name it?
- How is this (insert a feeling) like? If you were to place it in the room, where would it be and how would it look like?
- What would you like to see happen when your (insert a feeling) is in the room with you?
- If this problem were to be solved, how would you see your life? How would it be different?
- Was there a time when this problem wasn't in your life?
- What was different during that time?
- Was there a time when you managed to deal with the problem successfully?
- What helped you to deal with the problem successfully?
- How would you prefer things to be?
- If you were to stay connected to what you have just said about what you prefer, what next steps could you take?

> **Figure 6.5 A narrative exercise for students**
>
> *Encourage your student to complete the following exercise as homework in order to create emotional distance from their past so that they can become reflective in order to gain perspective on their life as a whole. It's intended to be storytelling outline that helps them organise their life events and gain self-compassion, without going too deeply into the memories.*
>
> **The stages of the narrative**
>
> *Recounting your story is important for creating coherent episodes from chaotic events. This helps you re-establish a sense of identity as well as gaining some control over feelings of helplessness. We all have complicated lives but few of us take the time to truly know ourselves and so are left with a sense of uncertainty. This exercise opens the door to knowing and appreciating ourselves more deeply.*
>
> *The idea is not to add more than seven to ten words for any title, chapter, or line – or for the section, Into the Future. This keeps the exercise more reflective and less emotional, so we can really take over the role of being our own adviser.*
>
> *My life story*
>
> *Write your Book Title below:*
>
> *Write out a minimum of seven Life Chapter Titles below that represent significant life stages and events.*
>
> *For each Chapter, write out one line to describe the Life Chapter (i.e., 1. Life at the college)*
>
> *Write your final chapter and one line description below for:*
>
> *Into the Future*

Solution focused behavioural therapy (SFBT) questioning. According to O'Connor, (2013) Solution Focused Behavioural Therapy (SFBT) seeks to enable individuals to identify current problems and find future solutions often drawing upon past solutions and there are a variety of questions used in this approach to therapy:

- Goal Development Questions. These might variously include asking young people to describe their best hope for what will be different as a result of coming for help and what needs to happen as a result of coming in
- Pre-Session Change Question. It may likely be that the solution-development process has already begun before the first session in which case the SF therapist follows up with questions about the details of how, when and where things have begun to get better and how this might possibly continue

- Looking for previous solutions. Using these type of questions SF therapists probe clients' past experiences in dealing with this problem and evaluate how effective their solutions have been in the past
- Looking for exceptions. SF therapist also discuss times when the problem was less of a problem with clients and what partial solutions may have helped
- Future-focused questions. The therapist uses these to prompt action by the client and to direct them to present and future solutions
- Miracle Question (MQ). This is a central technique in SF and it involves imagining and discussing a possible world where their specific problems have been removed and issues have been addressed. It can often serve as a vehicle to enable people to identify the unique details of the first small behavioural steps that can gradually lead towards a viable solution in the context of their everyday life (De Shazer et al., 2021)
- Scaling Questions. Using Scaling questions, normally from 1–10, simultaneously allows both client and therapist to assess the client's situation, identify their current distance from the goal, what it will to maintain their current level of progress and move forward
- Coping Questions. The function of these to check the progress of the individual and to help develop a progressive narrative where the client's life is pictured as becoming better rather than worse

Figure 6.6 Self-reflection activity

1 *Future Vision Journal:* Create a journaling activity focused on envisioning a positive future. Set aside dedicated time each day or week to reflect on the following questions:

- *Miracle Question:* Imagine you wake up tomorrow, and everything related to your current challenge has been resolved. What does your life look like? Describe it in detail
- *Scaling Questions:* On a scale of 0 to 10, where do you currently stand in terms of progress or satisfaction related to your goal? Reflect on why you chose that number and what it would take to move one point up the scale
- *Goal-Oriented Questions:* What specific steps or actions can you take to move closer to your desired outcome? Identify one small goal that you can work on this week

2 Write down your reflections and thoughts in the journal, and revisit them periodically to track your progress and reassess your goals.
Strengths Inventory Exercise: This activity focuses on exploring and utilizing your strengths to address challenges. Set aside some time to reflect on the following questions:

- *Coping Questions: What strengths or resources have you utilised in the past to overcome challenges? How can you leverage those strengths to tackle your current situation?*
- *Exception Questions: Can you recall a time when the problem you're facing was less severe or absent? What was different about that time? How can you apply the strategies or approaches from that situation to your current challenge?*
- *Scaling Follow-up Questions: On a scale of 0 to 10, where would you rate your current utilisation of your strengths? What would it take for you to move one point up the scale?*

3 Make a list of your strengths and brainstorm specific ways to apply them to your current situation. Consider developing an action plan based on your reflections, focusing on how you can maximise your strengths.
Relationship Reflection Exercise: This activity centers on enhancing relationships and interactions with others. Reflect on the following questions:

- *Relationship Questions: How would you like your relationships with important people in your life to be different? What small changes can you make to move in that direction?*
- *Exception Amplification Questions: Think about a time when your interactions with someone were positive and satisfying. What was different about that interaction? How can you apply those positive elements to your current relationships?*
- *Scaling Questions: On a scale of 0 to 10, where would you rate your current satisfaction or connection in your relationships? What would it take for you to move one point up the scale?*

Take time to write down your reflections and identify specific actions you can take to improve your relationships. Consider reaching out to the people involved, expressing your desires for positive change, and implementing the strategies you've identified.

Figure 6.7 Gestalt style self-reflection activities

1 Empty Chair Technique:
  a Find a quiet and comfortable space where you can be alone
  b Set up two chairs facing each other
  c Sit in one of the chairs and imagine a student sitting in the other chair

d   Begin a dialogue with the imagined student, asking questions such as:
   - How do I currently support your mental health needs in the classroom?
   - What can I do differently to better support your mental health?
   - What emotions or challenges do you often experience that I might not be aware of?
   - How can I create a safe and inclusive environment for you and other students?

e   Respond from the perspective of the student, trying to access your empathy and understanding
f   Switch chairs and respond from your own perspective, reflecting on the insights gained during the dialogue
g   Write down your reflections and action steps you can take to improve your support for students' mental health

2   "I" Statements and Reflection:

a   Take a few minutes to think about a recent classroom situation where you interacted with a student who was struggling with their mental health
b   Write down your observations and thoughts about the situation using "I" statements, such as:
   - "I noticed that…"
   - "I felt…"
   - "I thought…"
   - "I responded by…"

c   Reflect on your responses and ask yourself:
   - How did my own emotions and biases influence my interactions with the student?
   - Did I provide a safe and non-judgmental space for the student to express their feelings?
   - Could I have responded differently to better support the student's mental health?
   - What can I learn from this situation to improve my future interactions with students facing similar challenges?

d   Consider writing down your reflections and any action steps you can take to enhance your support for students' mental health

3   The Five Senses Exercise:

a   Take a moment to focus on your breathing and become present in the current moment

> b Engage your five senses: sight, hearing, touch, taste, and smell
> c Reflect on each sense, asking yourself questions such as:
>
> - What do I see in my classroom environment that may affect students' mental wellbeing?
> - How does the classroom sound, and what impact might it have on students' emotions?
> - Are there any textures or objects in the classroom that can provide comfort or trigger stress?
> - Are there any scents or smells in the classroom that may affect students' mood?
> - How can I use the senses to create a more calming and supportive classroom atmosphere?
>
> d Take notes on your reflections and brainstorm practical ways you can modify the classroom environment to support students' mental health needs

Active listening

According to Alessandra and Hunsaker (1993) when people are listening, they can be placed in one of four general categories, i.e., non-listener, marginal listener, evaluative listener, and active listener. Each category requires a particular depth of concentration and sensitivity from the listener, and trust and effective communication increase as we advance beyond the first type.

Active listening (AL) is the highest and most effective level of listening. AL can improve interpersonal relationships and perception of confidence and respect, lessen tension, and provide a better environment for joint problem solving and sharing the information in organisation (Jahromi et al., 2016).

Active listening requires the listener to pay close attention to what is being communicated verbally and nonverbally. The listener is encouraged to interpret not only the content of what is being said, but also the emotions present and the body language.

In order to achieve this, the listener must be willing to devote energy to the task. They will need to have an excellent attention span and honed empathic abilities. Active listening has even been referred to as the "measurable dimension of empathy" (Olson & Iwasiw, 1987, 104).

There are three main components of successful active listening (Rogers and Farson, 1987):

- Listen for total meaning. When someone is conveying a message, there are two meanings to gather: the content and the feeling or attitude underlying the message. An active listener is not only tuned in to the information conveyed, but also how it is conveyed and any nonverbal cues present

- Respond to feelings. After listening, when a response is appropriate, the listener should respond to the feeling of what was said. In this way, the speaker feels understood and empathy is established
- Awareness of all Non verbal cues which can include tone of voice, facial or body expressions, and speed of speech. All of these taken together can convey a much deeper meaning than merely the content of what was said

Active listening is designed to help the person who is being listened to recognise that the speaker is attending carefully to what is being said, to help the speaker join empathically with the listener and to encourage the listener to continue talking. For Carl Rogers, the ultimate goal of active listening was to foster positive change (Rogers and Farson, 1987). This change can occur in the context of a client/helper relationship or in the context of a group. Active listening is a tool that fosters and supports three important principles in effective counselling: empathy, genuineness, and unconditional positive regard.

According to Pickering (1986) active listening involves the following:

- Non-verbal responses. These include appropriate eye contact, nodding or using appropriate facial expressions, and matching the young person's body posture and movements which is likely to give a student an indication that the teacher is listening, an indication of the teacher's level of interest in what is being said, and information about the teacher's attitude to them
- Encouraging prompts. These can be single word such as yes', 'right', 'really' or short responses such as Tell me more', 'I see', 'I understand', 'Is that so?', 'I hear', and 'Go on. These can signal to the student that the teacher is listening and to encourage them to carry on talking. They need to mirror a student's tone of voice, volume, and speed of delivery and if so, they will serve as indications of a teacher's attitudes, including approval and disapproval
- Accenting and amplifying. This can be done effectively using verbal and nonverbal messages such as a short verbal prompts, gestures, and facial expression to accentuate and feedback when the student has said
- Reflection of content, feelings and meaning. These are key skills originally identified by Rogers (1965). Reflecting content involves repeating back to students a version of what they have just said and shows the student they are being understood and are being listened to. Typically, reflecting content alone is not as powerful as reflecting content with feeling and/or meaning.

When a teacher uses reflection of feeling, they accurately describe the student's affective state from either verbal or nonverbal cues. By listening for and responding to the feelings of the student rather than the content of their statement the teacher is communicating that they can accurately sense the world as they are perceiving it. This can facilitate the student's movement toward greater self-awareness and self-understanding.

Reflecting a student's emotion is often useful for heightening their awareness of and ability to label their own emotions. It is important that teachers

have a wide emotional vocabulary, so they can tailor their word choice to match a level of emotional intensity that is congruent with a client's experience. Feeling word charts are useful for reviewing a wide range of feeling words. Reflecting a student's meaning can increase their self-awareness while encouraging emotional depth in the session
- Matching the young person's language This can include the following three areas: vocabulary including sub cultural slang, representational style such as whether it is visual, verbal, or kinaesthetic and metaphorical.

Figure 6.8 Teaching activity

This role-play helps develop active listening and verbalising skills by encouraging the speaker to use language suited to the listener, and for the listener to imagine themselves in another role. It can work equally well for young adults and for staff training sessions. The 500 years ago worksheet includes six steps and can be used in group sessions:

1 *Divide the group into pairs*
2 *Person A is the speaker. They must describe a modern-day object (either one they have chosen or given to them)*
3 *Person B is the listener and guesser, from 500 years ago. They have no knowledge of the modern world and must listen carefully, considering what is being said. They can ask questions to help them guess but must frame them as though they are from a time without technology or the comforts of modern life. For example, a mobile could be the chosen word (or you could introduce the physical object) for describing*
4 *Afterwards, ask the speaker to describe how it felt to explain something to another person with a very different perspective*
5 *Then ask the listener to explain what it was like to listen while being in the mind of someone other than themselves*

Summarising: This is another key skill highlighted in the work of Rogers (1965) and in it teachers feedback in their own words, a brief and concise summary of what the salient points are that have been said by the student. This can help the student to understand their own thoughts more clearly and also to indicate how much the teacher has understood. It can also give the student the opportunity to recap, and to 'correct' the counsellor if any parts of the summary feel inaccurate and to allow the teacher to realign where they are and make ensure they are still within the student's frame of reference. Summarising can be used at various points of a session with a student to sum up, using the main points, what the client has said

Summaries are therefore useful for starting a session by recapping what they discussed with the teacher in a previous meeting and maybe reviewing targets which can allow them to settle into the session. They can help to clarify emotions for both the teacher and the student and review the work done so far, taking stock and bringing a session to a close by drawing together the main threads of the discussion and in addition, beginning a subsequent session if appropriate. They can also be used for starting the process of focusing and prioritising 'scattered' thoughts and feelings and moving the supporting process forward (Hough, 2014).

Barriers to summarising

Teachers can face several barriers when summarising their students' problems in a counselling session, some of which include:

- Sometimes, students may not provide all the necessary information about their problems, which can make it difficult for teachers to provide an accurate summary
- The teacher may misunderstand or misinterpret what the student is saying, which can result in an inaccurate summary of their problems. This can be exacerbated if teachers may face language and cultural barriers that can make it difficult to accurately summarise their students' problems, particularly if the student is from a different culture or speaks a different language
- Teachers may be affected by their own emotional reactions to their students' problems, which can make it difficult to provide an accurate summary
- Lack of training or experience. Teachers who lack adequate training or experience may find it challenging to summarise their students' problems accurately.
- In addition, in some cases, teachers may be working with students who have complex or multiple problems, and time constraints may make it challenging to summarise all the issues accurately.
- Alternatively, some students may be resistant to sharing information about their problems, which can make it difficult for the teacher to provide an accurate summary

Noticing what is missing

It is important that a teacher is very aware of gaps and unfilled spaces in the student's story, and for evidence of conflicting information and hidden meanings as they can then provide opportunities for them to explore them and find opportunities and alternatives that they had already missed (Weger et al., 2014).

Overall looking for gaps in a student's narratives in supporting them is significant because it can provide important insights into their experiences, thoughts, and emotions (Weger et al., 2014). Here are a few reasons why this is the case:

- Identification of underlying issues. By identifying gaps in their narratives, the teacher can identify underlying issues or problems that the student may not have fully acknowledged or expressed. These may represent areas where the student is avoiding or resisting discussing certain topics or feelings. This can help the teacher explore patterns in the students thinking and behaviour. For example, if a student consistently avoids discussing certain topics or emotions, this may indicate a pattern of avoidance or repression
- Encouraging reflection. When the teacher points out gaps in the student's narratives, it can encourage the client to reflect on their experiences and explore their emotions more deeply. This reflection can be helpful in gaining new insights into their situation. Sometimes, students may not be aware of these gaps and the teacher's perspective can help them see things from a different angle. By pointing them out, the teacher can help the client gain a more complete understanding of their experiences and emotions

---

Figure 6.9 Active listening teaching activities

Mindful listening group practice

In many ways, active listening is a mindfulness practice. The listener is trying to stay focused on the present, with what is being shared. And they are working to accomplish this without judgment.

Here is an excellent activity to practice mindful listening in a group:

1. *Have the group sit in a circle*
2. *Offer an ice breaker question or prompt, such as something they are grateful for today*
3. *Rather than go around the circle, ask participants to share spontaneously when they feel ready*
4. *Invite them to notice if they are thinking about their answer, rather than listening*
5. *Ask them to be present with the person who is sharing*
6. *Challenge them to notice if they are uncomfortable with the silences*

Figure 6.10 Mindful listening

At any moment, you can drop in and practice mindful listening. Simply stop what you are doing, close your eyes, and try to see how many sounds you can hear around you and within you. Notice if there are judgments arising and try not to attach to them. Stay with the flow of sounds for as long as you can.

> *Listening accurately:*
>
> 1 *Step In Their Shoes:* Select someone that you would like to work on your relationship with. When you talk, try your best to take their point of view. For instance, try picturing that you are them, going about their day. Does your capacity to feel empathy change by taking their perspective?
> 2 *Fact-Check Your Interpretations:* Reflect on the dialogues you and that person have had. Make a conscious effort to fact-check your interpretations and assumptions regarding what they said
> 3 *Give Your Full Attention During a Conversation:* Start by giving your full attention to the other person. Before you move on to other things, consider what might occur if you asked: "I would like to clarify that I've understood you correctly. May I?" Almost every time, you'll get a positive response
> 4 *Clarify What They've Said:* Make an effort to clarify what you think you have heard – identify and reflect their emotions. If you are unsure whether you've understood correctly, just ask
> 5 *Clarify What You've Said:* During conversations, you might try asking the speaker if they could share what they've heard from you. How would you clear up any misunderstandings if they arose?

Listening with the third ear

Listening with the third ear involves trying to imagine how the other person feels and listening to the unspoken by allowing the teacher's unconscious to receive their unconscious messages by picking up on nonverbal cues and emotions by being observant, reflective, listening to their own emotional responses and patient (Reik, 1948).

The "third ear" approach to discussing mental health issues with students can be an effective way for teachers to build rapport, gain insight into a student's emotional state, and provide support. However, there are also some potential strengths and weaknesses to consider.

The strategy has a variety of strengths and weaknesses. For example, the approach involves actively listening to a student's spoken and unspoken words, which can help build trust and rapport between the teacher and student. Listening beyond the spoken words can also provide insight into the student's emotional state, which can help the teacher identify areas where the student may need additional support. Therefore, when students feel that they are being heard and understood, they may be more likely to share their thoughts and feelings with the teacher. Active listening and responding with empathy can also help validate a student's emotions and experiences, which can help them feel more supported and understood.

On the other hand, teachers may not receive sufficient training or support in how to use the third ear approach effectively, which could limit its effectiveness.

They may also have limited time to engage in lengthy conversations with students, which could limit the amount of information they are able to gather through the third ear approach.

Figure 6.11 Teacher activities

Here are three potential tasks:

1 *Emotion check-in: Start the conversation by asking the student how they are feeling today. Encourage them to share any emotions they may be experiencing, even if they don't feel comfortable going into detail. Listen carefully to their tone of voice and body language, and make note of any changes you observe throughout the conversation. For example, if the student starts off sounding upbeat but becomes more withdrawn as the conversation continues, you may want to explore why they are feeling this way and if there is anything you can do to help*
2 *Mindfulness exercise: Guide the student through a mindfulness exercise, such as deep breathing or body scanning. Encourage them to focus on the present moment and to let go of any distracting thoughts or worries. As they complete the exercise, listen for any comments they make about their experience, such as "I feel more relaxed now" or "It's hard for me to quiet my mind." These comments can provide valuable insight into the student's current mental state and may help you identify any areas where they need additional support*
3 *Self-reflection exercise: Ask the student to reflect on a recent challenging situation they faced, such as a difficult assignment or social conflict. Encourage them to describe how they felt during the situation and what coping strategies they used to manage their emotions. As they share their story, listen for any signs of negative self-talk or self-blame, such as "I'm not good enough" or "It's all my fault." Use active listening skills to show the student that you are fully present and engaged in the conversation and provide positive feedback and validation where appropriate. For example, you might say something like, "It sounds like you did the best you could in a tough situation" or "I'm proud of you for trying to handle the situation in a constructive way."*

Using pauses and silences

According to Balint (1955) silence in therapy can either be threatening or hostile, or tranquil and harmonious. It is complex in meanings as it is not only the absence of response but is also the presence of a series of complex non-verbal human interactions.

According to Jacobs and Farrell, a teacher will allow 0.9 of a second on average to elapse after asking a question before they answer it themselves and they found that extending the wait time resulted in many of the less confident students being able to contribute (2003).

Gilliland and James, observe that using silence is tricky for teachers as some feel uncomfortable with it whereas others use too much silence as a way of managing their anxiety over not knowing what to do or their fear of doing it wrong (1993).When a student is silent, it is important to assess what it could mean to them. It could mean a variety of things, such as:

- Fear of judgment or stigma. The student may worry that their teacher will judge them or think less of them if they disclose their mental health struggles. This fear could stem from previous negative experiences or societal stigma surrounding mental health. The student also may not feel comfortable opening up to them due to a lack of trust. This could be because the student has had negative experiences with authority figures in the past or does not have a strong relationship with the teacher
- Shame or embarrassment. The student may feel ashamed or embarrassed about their mental health issues and may not want to disclose them to anyone, including their teacher or they may be struggling to articulate how they are feeling, especially if they are experiencing symptoms of anxiety or depression. Or even, they may not recognise that they are struggling with a mental health issue and may not understand the importance of seeking help

Silence can function in a variety of different ways for a teacher when supporting a student (Knol et al., 2020). This includes:

- Playing a structural role in discussions just as it does in every conversation. This role is usually to separate different topics within the discourse between speakers. Alternatively, it can signify a change from one issue to the next. Silence occurs not only between topics, but also within them. This "intra-topic" silence is a therapeutic tool that teachers can use to help their students go deeper into the material by allowing them to think about what to say next.
- Teachers can choose to turn silence into a therapeutic event by bringing it to the student's attention in the conversation. By talking about the silence between them, the silence itself becomes material for the discussion. Therefore, comfortable silence can provide a safe space for the student to do serious introspection
- Silence can slow things down in a productive way. A student who is anxious to solve a problem may land on a solution prematurely or settle on a decision that is borne of that anxiety, not on new understanding. The teacher can suggest that they both take a few minutes to sit quietly and think about the usefulness of such a decision before coming to conclusions
- It can also be used as a way of conveying empathy or for challenging a student to take responsibility for their own mental health and wellbeing and therefore it can encourage self-reflection. After listening to the student, the

teacher or mentor can use silence to encourage the student to reflect on their own thoughts and feelings and to find the words and images to express them This can be done by asking open-ended questions such as "What do you think would help you feel better?" or "What steps do you think you can take to address this situation?" and to help the student develop self-awareness by allowing them to notice their own thoughts and feelings without feeling judged or criticised
- Silence can also be a therapeutic event within itself, a moment in which the student can dig deeper into the emotional experience they are having in the session (Knol et al., 2020)

The uses of pauses

According to Levitt (2001a) there are seven types of pauses, disengaged pauses, emotional pauses, interactional pauses, reflexive pauses, expressive pauses, associational pauses, and mnemonic pauses, all of which have their own characteristics and meanings.

Pausing during a communication can benefit both parties, teacher, and students. It can provide an opportunity to slow down and curb the tendency to jump to conclusions without thinking and create opportunities for more creative understanding of problems. Both parties can notice what is happening within them and outside of them and get in touch with feelings and bodily sensations. This can help develop a thinking space in which they can listen to the pauses and silences, picking up visual cues from body language, expressions, and to interpret the implied, unsaid messages. On a physiological level, pauses cancan release tension. Lower blood pressure and dampen stressful feelings (Levitt, 2001b).

Figure 6.12 Mindful Listening Exercise

In this activity, the teacher will pair up students and have them take turns talking about a mental health issue they are currently facing. The listener's job is to listen mindfully, without interrupting or trying to fix the problem. After a few minutes, the roles will switch. After each round, the teacher will encourage students to take a moment of silence to reflect on what they heard and how they felt during the exercise.

Breath Awareness Exercise: In this activity, the teacher will guide students through a brief breath awareness exercise. Students will sit comfortably, close their eyes, and focus on their breath. The teacher can guide them to count their breaths or simply focus on the sensation of the breath moving in and out of their body. After a few minutes, the teacher will invite students to take a moment of silence before sharing how they feel or any insights they gained during the exercise.

> *The Pause and Reflect Exercise: In this exercise, teachers will practice taking a short pause before responding to their students. The pause will give them time to reflect on what has been said and to respond thoughtfully. Teachers can ask themselves the following questions during the pause: "What did the student say?", "What is the student feeling?", and "What does the student need from me?". Once they have reflected on these questions, they can respond to their student's problem. This exercise will help teachers to be more attentive and empathetic listeners, and to respond more effectively to their students' needs.*

Giving feedback to students

Feedback

Feedback can be descriptive, evaluative, emotional, and interpretive.

- Descriptive feedback. Descriptive feedback refers to a type of feedback that focuses on providing specific, detailed, and objective information to clients about their thoughts, feelings, behaviours, or experiences. It is a crucial aspect of the supporting process as it helps students gain insight, self-awareness, and a deeper understanding of themselves. Descriptive feedback is aligned with the students' goals and objectives in supporting. It assists students in gaining insights into their thoughts, feelings, or behaviours that may hinder their progress. By addressing these areas, it helps students move toward their desired outcomes (Swank and McCarthy, 2013)
- Evaluative feedback recognises and highlights the young person's strengths and positive qualities. It acknowledges areas of progress and growth, providing encouragement and motivation for further development. Evaluative feedback refers to feedback that involves judgment, evaluation, or assessment of the client's thoughts, feelings, behaviours, or experiences. While descriptive feedback focuses on providing objective information, evaluative feedback goes a step further and includes the teacher's assessment or opinion (Ospina Avendano, 2021)
- Emotional feedback refers to the process of acknowledging, validating, and exploring the client's emotions during the therapeutic session. It involves the teacher's response to the client's emotional expressions, allowing for a deeper understanding and exploration of the client's emotional experiences (Lang et al., 2022)
- Interpretative feedback involves the teacher offering explanations, insights, or interpretations of the student's thoughts, feelings, behaviours, or experiences. It goes beyond descriptive feedback and aims to provide deeper understanding and meaning to the client's presenting issues. It may delve

into the exploration of unconscious processes, such as unconscious motivations, defence mechanisms, or unresolved conflicts. It can help young people gain new insights into the hidden aspects of their experiences (Geldard and Geldard, 2005)

Feedback has a wide range of functions including the following:

- Self-awareness. Feedback helps young people gain insight into their thoughts, emotions, and behaviours. It provides them with an external perspective on their experiences, helping them become more self-aware and understand the impact of their actions on themselves and others (Padesky and Mooney, 2012)
- It can validate the young person's experiences and emotions, making them feel heard and understood. When a teacher provides empathetic feedback, it fosters a sense of trust and rapport, creating a safe space for the young person to explore their feelings and challenges (Rogers, 1965)
- It can help young people identify their strengths, talents, and positive qualities. It acknowledges their progress and accomplishments, boosting their self-esteem. Additionally, feedback can highlight areas for growth and improvement, guiding the young person towards developing new skills and strategies (Whitmore, 2002)
- It can challenge cognitive distortions and reframe negative or distorted thinking patterns. It helps young people gain a more realistic and balanced perspective, enabling them to challenge self-defeating beliefs and replace them with more adaptive thoughts (Beck, 1991)
- It can support the process of goal setting. By providing feedback on the young person's progress, the teacher can help them establish realistic and achievable goals. Feedback also serves as a benchmark for tracking progress and celebrating milestones along the supporting journey (Cully and Bond, 2011)
- Feedback can play a vital role in helping young people develop and refine coping skills, communication skills, problem-solving abilities, and other adaptive behaviours and offers guidance and suggestions on how they can navigate challenges more effectively and make positive changes in their lives (Otte et al., 2020)
- It can encourage young people to reflect on their experiences, emotions, and behaviours. It prompts them to examine their patterns and motivations, leading to deeper insights and self-discovery and facilitates the process of connecting the dots and gaining a better understanding of themselves (Prasko et al., 2012).
- It can provide encouragement and support to young people, reinforcing their strengths and resilience. It fosters a sense of belief in their ability to overcome difficulties and make positive changes and serves as a reminder that they are not alone in their journey and that someone is supporting them

It can be done through using the following methods:

- Providing compliments. According to research by Wall et al. (1989) into compliments used in therapeutic contexts, compliments enhance the positions of both the giver and the receiver of the compliment as they can be highly effective means of motivating people while at the same time increasing therapeutic leverage. When given appropriately they can enable the young person to feel OK and to continue developing with confidence and to improve their self-efficacy (Weiste et al., 2022)
- Giving affirmations. When teachers use affirmations, they are acknowledging and reinforcing a personal truth that has been discovered by the student and shared with the teacher. Using an affirmation can help to develop self-belief and self confidence in progress that has been made by a student. Sometimes they have more power than a reflection because they convey a stronger message. For example, a reflection could be: 'You believe that you are coping very well in difficult circumstances' and an affirmation could be, You are obviously coping extremely well under difficult circumstances'.

Figure 6.13 Re-write these examples of affirmative statements given to students making them more concise and less patronising

"I want to acknowledge your incredible strength and resilience in navigating your mental health challenges. Despite the difficulties you face, you continue to show up and give your best effort every day."

"I've noticed your progress in managing your emotions and finding healthy coping mechanisms. Your dedication to your well-being is inspiring, and it's evident that you're making positive changes."

"You should be proud of yourself for seeking support and actively working on your mental health. Your willingness to share your thoughts and feelings with me shows tremendous courage and trust."

"I appreciate your honesty and openness during our sessions. Your willingness to be vulnerable allows us to have meaningful discussions and create a safe space for you to express yourself."

"You have a unique perspective on life that stems from your experiences with mental health. Your insights and observations are valuable, and I encourage you to continue sharing them as they contribute to our discussions."

"Your determination to overcome challenges and achieve your goals is admirable. I see the effort you put into your work, and it's clear that you are committed to your personal growth."

"Your self-awareness is commendable. You've developed a deep understanding of your triggers and patterns, and I've seen you take proactive steps to manage them. Your ability to reflect on your experiences is a valuable skill."

> "I want to acknowledge the progress you've made in developing healthy coping strategies. Your commitment to self-care and implementing the techniques we've discussed is evident, and it's making a positive impact on your overall wellbeing."

- Cheerleading

  Cheerleading is a technique which has been borrowed from Solution-Focused Behavioural Therapy (SFBT) also known as solution-focused brief therapy or brief therapy, which is an approach to psychotherapy based on solution-building rather than problem-solving. While it acknowledges present problems and past causes, SFBT predominantly explores an individual's current resources and future hopes (O'Connor, 2013)

  Teachers use cheerleading by showing enthusiastic reactions of emotional support when students relate that they have used new behaviours which are positive and different from behaviours which they have used before, and it aims to celebrate how they have taken control and are responsible for the changes that have occurred. Some examples of questions include:

  - *How did you manage to make that decision?*
  - *That must have been really tricky to pull off?*
  - *You must have worked hard at that?*

  Statements can include;

  - *This is well planned*
  - *That's a strong response*
  - *That sounds really good*
  - *This is a detailed answer*
  - *You demonstrate strong awareness of this*

- Normalising

  It can be important to remind students that what they are experiencing is not unusual and therefore can be managed by them. It is most commonly used in Cognitive Behavioural Therapy (CBT) and can help with a range of mental health issues including anxiety, social phobia, and panic disorder (Dudley et al., 2007). It can be useful in several ways:
- It can make the experience of distress normal and understandable and therefore it can help young people see that they are not alone in experiencing certain feelings or thoughts. This can enhance their feelings of self-esteem, facilitate improved coping, and reduce stigmatisation.
- This can help to reduce secondary emotional reactions such as being anxious about anxiety or depressed about being depressed.
- It can help the student understand the commonality of their problems and become more actively involved in managing them and used to challenge the views of the students

- It can help them to see that there are different ways of seeing the same problem.
- It can prompt the student to see that their problem is not intractable and that there are other avenues to explore and validate their own experiences by checking out whether their peers have had similar experiences (Svinhufvud et al., 2017
- Reframing
  Reframing is a technique most frequently used in CBT to help clients working with negative thoughts. During reframing the teacher tries to encourage the young person to consider not just the part of the picture that they have been considering, but to see their part of the picture as part of a larger picture. When that frame is shifted, the meaning changes, and thinking and behaviour often change along with it. If used effectively reframing can help young people accept difficult situations or processes by viewing them within a wider, more positive context (Clarke, 1998).

Figure 6.14   Self-reflection question

Here is a question from a counselling associate of mine:

How is the saucer the mother of the cup?
When your mind doesn't know. Your mind will create connections between things, and developing truth, which become our assumptions and our realities.
To what extent is your mind creating connections and developing new truths and assumptions which are negative?

Reframing Negative Thoughts: some Guiding Questions

1 What's your thought? You can also use the terms predictions or guesses
2 How likely do you think this is? Use the five-point scale
3 What are some other thoughts you could have (predictions/guesses)? List as many as possible
4 What evidence do you have for the thought?

- *Has this ever happened to me before?*
- *Is there any evidence that this won't happen?*

Are there any facts to back this up?
5 How likely do you think it is now after coming up with some other possibilities and looking at the evidence?
6 If it happens, could you handle it?
7 What's the evidence that you can handle it?

Challenging and feedback

There are a number of situations where teachers might need to challenge adolescent students. Challenging needs to be done in a way that does not offend them but invites them to question what they have said, what they believe or what they are doing. and need to be direct, but in a way which is not threatening to the young person's ego (Swank and McCarthy, 2013).

Some situations in which challenging might need to occur are:

- Where the young person has been talking about things in a way that is confusing because what they are saying is inconsistent or contradictory. This could be where their non-verbal behaviour does not match their verbal behaviour. Or where they are engaging in behaviour, which is inevitably self-destructive, but they are not recognising this
- When the young person is avoiding a basic issue which appears to be troubling them and excessively and inappropriately locked into talking about the past or the future and is unable to focus on the present. Or where they are going around in circles by repeating the same story
- Where undesirable processes are occurring in the relationship between the teacher and the student for example, where dependency or transference is occurring or where a student withdraws or shows hostility, anger or some other emotion towards the teacher
- When the student is out of touch with reality with regard to a specific situation, but is not exhibiting a mental health problem. Or where the young person is failing to recognise possible serious consequences of their behaviour

Some examples of challenging responses could include:

'You have just told me that ... but I'm puzzled because I've noticed that several times you have briefly talked about your relationship with your sister and then have started to talk about something quite different.'

'You have talked about your relationship with your mother. However, I'm confused; you've told me that you care very much about your mother, but you have also said that you are deliberately planning to try to hurt her.

Figure 6.15   Self-reflection exercise

Find a student who is not very actively engaged in talking to you in a tutorial situation. For example, frequently responding to your questions with 'I don't know'.

Think about the pros and cons of challenging him about this as opposed to encouraging him to be more active

Challenge him and see if his responses reflect your own original evaluation of the strategy

> *When you are supporting student with a different cultural background than you, how important is it for you to find common ground?*
> *Which barriers would you need to overcome?*
> *How might they impact on your teacher/student relationship?*

Figure 6.16   Effective confrontation teaching activity

The group should break into sub-groups of four or five people. Go around the group, with each person taking time speaking about some personal concern for a few minutes.

The next person in line is the listener, who responds to the speaker with a confrontation. The group can then discuss the listener response-- was it a confrontation? Was it effective? What was the focus? What are some alternative confrontations which could be made?

After discussing the response, the listener becomes the next speaker. Move around the circle as time permits, hopefully allowing each person to practice responding with a confrontation.

If there is time, discuss the use of confrontation as a skill of self-expression. What are the possible risks in using this skill? Where might you use this skill in your work or daily life? How could you improve your capacity for self-confrontation (not self- depreciation). What are the benefits of confronting yourself?

References

Alessandra, T., and Hunsaker, P. (1993). *Communication at Work*. New York: Fireside, Simon, and Schuster.

Balint, M. (1955). Friendly expanses – horrid empty spaces. *The International Journal of Psychoanalysis*, 36: 225–241.

Beck, A. T. (1991). Cognitive therapy as the integrative therapy. *Journal of Psychotherapy Integration*, 1(3): 191–198.

Brammer, L. M., and MacDonald, G. (2003). *The Helping Relationship: Process and Skills*. Boston: Allyn & Bacon.

Clark, A. J. (1998). Reframing: A therapeutic technique in group counseling, *The Journal for Specialists in Group Work*, 23(1): 66–73. doi:10.1080/01933929808411382

Cully, S., and Bond, T. (2011). *Integrative Counselling Skills in Action*. Thousand Oaks, CA: Sage Publishing.

de Shazer, S., Dolan, Y., Korman, H., Trepper, T., McCollum, E., and Berg, I. K. (2021). *More Than Miracles*, (2nd edn.). Abingdon: Routledge.

Dudley, R., Bryant, Caroline, Hammond, Katherine, Siddle, Ronald, Kingdon, David, and Turkington, Douglas. (2007). Psykologi. Techniques in Cognitive Behavioural Therapy: Using Normalising in Schizophrenia. https://psykologtidsskriftet.no/2007/05/techniques-cognitive-behavioural-therapy-using-normalising-schizophrenia

Garvey, R., Strokes, P., & Megginson, D. (2010). Coaching and Mentoring: Theory and Practice. *NHRD Network Journal*, 3: 79–81.
Geldard, and Geldard. (2005). *Basic Personal Counseling: A Training Manual for Counselors*. Australia: Pearson.
Geldard, K., and Geldard, D. (2015). *Counselling Skills in Everyday Life*. London: Red Globe Press. doi:10.1007/978-1-4039-9761-6
Gilliland, B. E., and James, R. K. (1993). *Crisis Intervention Strategies*, (2nd edn.). Pacific Grove, CA: Thomson Brooks/Cole Publishing Co.
Glasser, W. (1965). *Reality Therapy. A New Approach to Psychiatry*. New York: Harper & Row.
Hough, M. (2014). *Counselling Skills and Theory*. London: Hodder Education.
Jacobs, G. M., and Farrell, T. S. C. (2003). Understanding and implementtng the CLT (communicative language teaching) paradigm. *RELC Journal*, 34(1): 5–30. doi:10.1177/003368820303400102
Jahromi, V. K., Tabatabaee, S. S., Abdar, Z. E., and Rajabi, M. (2016). Active listening: The key of successful communication in hospital managers. *Electronic Physician*, 8(3): 2123–8. doi:10.19082/2123
Knol, A.S.L., Koole, T., Desmet, M., Vanheule, S., Huiskes, M. (2020). How speakers orient to the notable absence of talk: A conversation analytic perspective on silence in psychodynamic therapy. *Frontiers in Psychology*, 11: 584927. doi:10.3389/fpsyg.2020.584927
Lang, Y., Xie, K., Gong, S., Wang, Y., and Cao, Y. (2022). The impact of emotional feedback and elaborated feedback of a pedagogical agent on multimedia learning. *Frontiers in Psychology*, 13: 810194. doi:10.3389/fpsyg.2022.810194
Levitt, D. H. (2001a). Active listening and counselor self-efficacy: Emphasis on one microskill in beginning counselor training. *The Clinical Supervisor*, 20(2): 101–115. doi:10.1300/J001v20n02_09
Levitt, H. (2001b). Sounds of silence in psychotherapy: The categorization of clients' pauses. *Psychotherapy Research*, 11: 295. doi:10.1093/ptr/11.3.295
McLeod, J., and McLeod, J. (2014). Personal and professional development for counsellors, psychotherapists and mental health practitioners. *UK Higher Education OUP Humanities & Social Sciences Counselling and Psychotherapy*. London: McGraw-Hill Education (UK).
Morgan, A. (2000). *What is Narrative Therapy? An Easy-to-Read Introduction*. Adelaide, SA: Dulwich Centre Publications.
O'Connor, B. (2013). *Solution Focussed Therapy*. Thousand Oaks, CA: Sage Publications.
Olson, J. K., and Iwasiw, C. L. (1987). Effects of a training model on active listening skills of post-RN students. *The Journal of Nursing Education*, 26(3): 104–7. doi:10.3928/0148-4834-19870301-06
Ospina Avendano, D. (2021). STEPPA coaching model. Retrieved 8th march 2024 from toolshero: https://www.toolshero.com/management/steppa-coaching-model
Otte, F. W., Davids, K., Millar, S. K., and Klatt, S. (2020). When and how to provide feedback and instructions to athletes? How sport psychology and pedagogy insights can improve coaching interventions to enhance self-regulation in training. *Frontiers in Psychology*, 14(11): 1444. doi:10.3389/fpsyg.2020.01444
Padesky, C. A., and Mooney, K. A. (2012). Strengths-based cognitive-behavioural therapy: A four-step model to build resilience. *Clinical Psychology & Psychotherapy*, 19(4): 283–90. doi:10.1002/cpp.1795
Palazzoli, M. S., Luigi Boscolo, M. D., Gianfranco Cecchin, M. D., and Giuliana Prata, M. D. F. (1980). The problem of the referring person. *Journal of Marital and Family Therapy*, 6(1): 3–9.
Perls, Hefferline, and Goodman, P. (1951). *Gestalt Therapy: Excitement and Growth in the Human Personality*. London: Souvenir Press.
Pickering, M. (1986). "Communication" in explorations. *A Journal of Research of the University of Maine*, 3(1): 16–19.

Prasko, J., Mozny, P., Novotny, M., Slepecky, M., and Vyskocilova, J. (2012). Self-reflection in cognitive behavioural therapy and supervision. *Biomedical Papers of the Medical Faculty of the University Palacky, Olomouc, Czech Republic*, 156(4): 377–84. doi:10.5507/bp.2012.027

Reik, T. (1948). *Listening with the Third Ear: The Inner Experience of a Psychoanalyst*. New York: Farrar, Straus, & Giroux.

Renger, S. (2023). Therapists' views on the use of questions in person-centred therapy. *British Journal of Guidance and Counselling*, 51(2): 238–50, doi:10.1080/03069885.2021.1900536

Rogers, C. R. (1965). The therapeutic relationship: Recent theory and research. *Australian Journal of Psychology*, 17(2): 95–108. doi:10.1080/00049536508255531

Rogers, C. R., and Farson, R. E. (1987). Active listening [1957]. In: R. G. Newman, M. A. Danziger, and M. Cohen (eds.), *Communication in Business Today*, 589–98. Washington, D.C.: Heath and Company.

Svinhufvud, Kimmo, Voutilainen, Liisa, and Weiste, Elina. (2017). Normalizing in student counseling: Counselors' responses to students' problem descriptions. *Discourse Studies*, 19: 196–215. doi:10.1177/1461445617691704

Swank, Jacqueline M., and McCarthy, Shannon N. (2013). The counselor feedback training model: Teaching counseling students feedback skills. *Adultspan Journal*, 12(2): Article 4. Available at: https://mds.marshall.edu/adsp/vol12/iss2/4

Wall, M. V., Amendt, J. H., Kleckner, T., and Bryant, R. D. (1989). Therapeutic compliments: Setting the stage for successful therapy. *Journal of Marital and Family Therapy*, 15(2): 159–67.

Weger Jr., H. Bell, Gina Castle, Minei, Elizabeth M., and Robinson, Melissa C. (2014). The relative effectiveness of active listening in initial interactions. *International Journal of Listening*, 28(1): 13–31. doi:10.1080/10904018.2013.813234

Weiste, E., Niska, M., Valkeapää, T., et al. (2022). Goal setting in mental health rehabilitation: references to competence and interest as resources for negotiating goals. *Journal of Psychosocial Rehabilitation and Mental Health*, 9: 409–24. doi:10.1007/s40737-022-00280-w

Whitmore, J. (2002). *Coaching for Performance*. London: Nicolas Brealey Publishing. (25th anniversary edition 2017).

7 Harnessing the power of thoughts and feelings

Supporting young people with social and emotional issues through identification and monitoring

Identifying feelings

Plutchik's wheel of emotions

Plutchik proposed a psycho evolutionary classification approach for general emotional responses (2002). He considered there to be eight primary emotions – anger, fear, sadness, disgust, surprise, anticipation, trust, and joy and argued that each one was the trigger of behaviour with a high survival value, such as the way fear inspires the fight-or-flight response.

He also created a wheel of emotions to illustrate different emotions and suggested that at the centre there were eight primary bipolar emotions: joy versus sadness; anger versus fear; trust versus disgust; and surprise versus anticipation. His model made connections between the idea of an emotion circle and a colour wheel as he suggested that like primary colours, primary emotions can be expressed at different intensities and can mix with one another to form different emotions.

The power of the emotion wheel is two-fold. Identifying and naming emotions can help students to self-regulate, even increasing their emotional intelligence and looking at complementary and analogous emotions can help them regain control and redirect their behaviour (Semeraro et al., 2021).

Figure 7.1 Teaching activities

Here are three activities based on Plutchik's wheel of emotions:

Emotional Scavenge Hunt: Create a scavenger hunt that requires students to identify and label different emotions based on Plutchik's wheel of emotions. Provide students with a list of emotions (e.g., joy, sadness, anger, fear, etc.) and ask them to find examples of each emotion in their daily lives. For instance, they can look for examples in the books they read, movies they watch, or interactions they have with friends and family.

> *This activity will help students become more aware of their emotions and recognize them in others, which can be helpful in building empathy and improving social skills*
>
> Emotional Check-In: *At the beginning of each class, ask students to identify and share one emotion they are feeling at that moment. Use Plutchik's wheel of emotions to guide the discussion and encourage students to elaborate on their emotions by sharing why they feel that way. This activity will help students become more comfortable with expressing their emotions and also provide an opportunity for the teacher to check in on their students' mental health and wellbeing*
>
> Emotion Regulation Worksheets: *Provide students with worksheets that focus on different emotions from Plutchik's wheel, such as anger or anxiety. The worksheets can include activities such as identifying triggers that cause the emotion, exploring coping strategies, and practicing mindfulness techniques. These worksheets can be used in individual counselling sessions or as part of a classroom activity, and they can help students develop skills to manage their emotions and improve their mental health and wellbeing*

Reflection of Feeling (RoF) (Lapin, 2016)

When a teacher reflects feelings, they are attempting to mirror the feeling or emotion present in the student's statements and expressing in their words the student's essential feelings that were either stated or implied (Jones-Smith, 2011.

Reflection of feelings means that a teacher helps the student explore their thoughts, feelings, and emotions in depth. This process allows for healing and growth to happen in students. The reflection may be as a result of things that the student has directly told the student or may be the result of non-verbal communication by the student. When teachers use the skill of reflection, they are looking to match the tone, the feeling of the words, and the student's facial expression or body language as they spoke.

Reflecting skills

Types of reflections

There are three broad types of reflection: Reflections of content, reflections of feeling, and reflections of meaning (Moustakas and Callahan, 1956).

- Content. Reflecting content involves repeating back to students a version of what they just said. Reflecting content shows them they are being understand and listened to. Typically, alone it is not as powerful as combining it with emotions and/or meaning

- Emotions. Reflecting a student's emotions is often useful for heightening their awareness of and ability to label their own emotions. It is important that teachers have a wide emotional vocabulary, so they can tailor their word choice to match a level of emotional intensity that is congruent with a student's experience. Feeling word charts can be useful for reviewing a wide range of feeling words
- Meaning. Reflecting a student's meaning can increase their self-awareness while encouraging emotional depth in the session

Emotional heightening

Teachers can intentionally use language to increase or decrease the emotional intensity of their reflections, thereby altering a student's emotional arousal which can encourage them to go deeper into a particular experience or emotion. For example, using evocative language and metaphors (e.g., "walking on eggshells"). It is important that teacher's attempt to match their reflections to the emotional intensity of the student's experience.

Reflection of Feeling helps to:

- Convey understanding
- Gain insight into student's emotional responses to life
- Validate student's emotional response
- Manage the emotions of the student
- Identify feelings and sort out multiple meanings
- Discriminate among various feelings

The cognitive triangle

The cognitive triangle is a diagram that shows the relationship between thoughts, emotions, and behaviour. It indicates how thoughts change the way we feel which in turn has an impact on actions which affect thoughts, and the cycle goes on. This pattern cannot be broken without intervention (Briers, 2009).

The cognitive triangle is one of the most popular and effective methods that cognitive behavioural therapists use to treat mental health disorders. It is used to support people with anxiety, depression, and other day-to-day stressors. The point of the cognitive triangle is to shed light on the connection between feelings, thoughts, and actions (Beck, 1991).

The Sides of the triangle:

- Thoughts. People often have fleeting thoughts that come and go every day, some of which linger more than others. These thoughts can have an impact on people's emotions. There are several sources of recurrent thoughts which are sometimes defined as cognitive distortions (Beck, 1963)

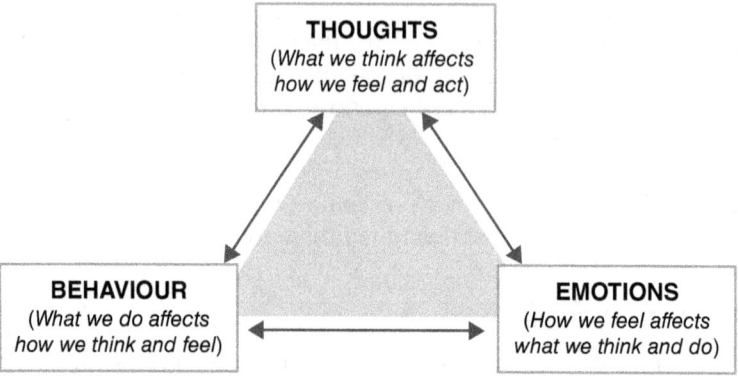

Figure 7.2 An illustration represents the interconnection between thoughts, emotions, and behaviour.

- All-Or-Nothing Thinking. This is black and white thinking that involves thinking in extremes and using absolute terms, such as never or ever (Bonfá-Araujo et al., 2022).
- Overgeneralisation. One negative event is extrapolated it as the way things will always be and is extended beyond the circumstances to which it actually applies (Lissek and Grillon, 2015). With labelling and mislabelling: the generalisation is exaggerated and is fuelled by emotions. and it involves the misrepresentation and inflation of events
- Mental Filter. One negative incident occurs and is fixated upon until it affects how everything is and one small mistake seems to them to represent everything. This is also associated with a process of disqualifying the positive: which involves the excluding of positive incidents and focusing on the negative ones (Beck, 1979)
- Jumping To Conclusions. Negative thoughts become the catalyst to making assumptions. This is sometimes linked to mind reading which involves the interpretations of people's motives or behaviours without a full understanding (Beck, 2012)
- Fortune Telling. With fortune telling predictions become facts. This is often the result of emotional reasoning where negative emotions are believed to show the way things really are (Butler and Beck, 2000)
- Magnification. (Catastrophising) or Minimisation. This is a process of binocular thinking in which the person maximises the positive attributes of other people and shrinks (minimise) their own attributes (Lissek and Grillon, 2015)
- Personalisation. The person sees themselves as the main reason for negative events and places blame on themselves in a way that is disproportionate to the effects of an outcome (Rnic et al., 2016)

Figure 7.3 Cognitive Restructuring Worksheet

Teaching strategy

Provide the student with a list of common cognitive distortions (e.g., all-or-nothing thinking, jumping to conclusions, emotional reasoning, etc.). Ask them to read through the list and identify which distortions are present in their current negative thought.

Ask them to describe the situation that triggered their negative thought. Encourage them to be specific about what happened, who was involved, and how they felt. Then ask them to write down the negative thought that occurred during the situation. Encourage them to be as precise as possible. Encourage them to list the evidence that supports and contradicts their negative thought. This will prompt them to consider alternative perspectives. Based on the evidence, work with the student to reflect on the situation and help them to generate alternative, more balanced thoughts that challenge their cognitive distortion. Ask them to rate the emotional distress associated with the negative thought before and after generating alternative thoughts. This helps them recognise the impact of cognitive restructuring and encourage them to decide on a positive action or coping strategy based on their new, balanced thoughts.

- Behaviour.

Actions are influenced by both thoughts and feelings. Cognitive behavioural therapists use the cognitive triangle to show their clients how thoughts, feelings, and behaviours can be influenced to change the situations around them. This technique can help with mental health issues like anxiety or depression in schools and colleges (Beck, 1991). Feelings differ from thoughts in that they can be described by one word.

Emotions are sometimes easily identifiable in a helping session and they influence how people behave. One way to help students stay in control of their thoughts is to have them write down all the negative ones that come in during their day and categorise them according to the sides of the triangle. This will help them recognise thought patterns and triggers and help them start to avoid these patterns.

In addition, there are underlying emotions connected to the ones felt in the moment. When students uncover underlying emotions and change their thoughts, their actions follow suit. Teachers can help students influence their thoughts and feelings by coaching them on behavioural changes using exercises like the Cognitive wheel (see below).

Figure 7.4 Helping activity

The Cognitive Wheel is a tool that can be used to help students understand their thought patterns and how they impact their emotions and behaviours. Here are two activities that you can do with a student with mental health issues using the Cognitive Wheel:

Identifying thought patterns

You can help the student identify their negative thought patterns by using the Cognitive Wheel. First, the teacher can explain the different sections of the wheel, such as "thoughts," "emotions," "behaviours," and "physical sensations." Next, you can ask the student to think about a recent negative experience they had and write down their thoughts, emotions, behaviours, and physical sensations associated with it in each section of the wheel.

Then, you can work with the student to identify any negative thought patterns that may be contributing to their negative emotions and behaviours. For example, if the student is experiencing anxiety, you can help them identify any catastrophic thinking patterns, such as "I'll never be able to do this," and work with the student to reframe these thoughts in a more positive way.

Developing coping strategies

You can use the Cognitive Wheel to help the student develop coping strategies to manage their mental health issues. First, you can work with the student to identify their triggers and negative thought patterns using the Cognitive Wheel. Next, you can help the student identify coping strategies that work for them, such as deep breathing exercises, journaling, or talking to a trusted friend or family member.

You can then work with the student to create a coping plan using the Cognitive Wheel. The plan should include the student's triggers, negative thought patterns, and coping strategies, as well as a plan for how the student can access these strategies when they are experiencing mental health issues. You can also work with the student to monitor their progress and adjust the coping plan as needed.

Figure 7.5 Self-reflection task

Here are three self-reflection activities that can help you develop your skills in reflecting on students' feelings:

Emotion Journal: Keep an emotion journal, in which you reflect on your interactions with students and the emotions that were present during those

> interactions. For instance, you can note when a student seemed happy, sad, frustrated, or angry, and reflect on what might have caused those emotions. This activity can help you become more aware of your own emotional responses to students and develop empathy towards your students
> Video Reflection: Record a video of yourself teaching and interacting with students. Afterwards, watch the video and pay attention to your tone, body language, and facial expressions to determine if they accurately reflected the students' emotions You can also take notes on their observations and use them to adjust in their teaching style
> Role-Playing: Role-play different scenarios with a colleague or mentor, in which you practice reflecting on students' feelings. For instance, you can role-play a scenario in which a student seems sad or upset and practice asking questions to understand the cause of the emotion. This activity can help you become more comfortable with addressing emotions in the classroom and develop their skills in empathising with their students.

The language of feeling

Choosing the right words to express feelings is complicated and often a struggle for young people and often they resort to acting these out physically with negative consequences. Therefore, it can often be a teacher's responsibility to reconnect students to their feelings and help them develop the ability to express emotion in healthy, satisfying ways and to understand the relationship between thoughts and the emotions and behaviours that result from them. When students realise that they are in charge of how they interpret their world and give it meaning, they become empowered which can lead to positive change(Jones-Smith, 2011).

> **Figure 7.6   Helping activity**
>
> *A feelings chart is a visual tool that can help students with mental health issues identify and communicate their emotions. Here are two activities that you can do with a student using a feelings chart:*
>
> *Emotion Check-In: You can use a feelings chart to help the student check in with their emotions at the beginning of each day or class period. The chart should include a range of emotions, from positive to negative, and the teacher can ask the student to identify and circle the emotions that they are feeling at the moment. The teacher can then ask the student to share their emotions with the class or with a trusted adult, and discuss any emotions that may be causing distress or affecting their ability to learn. This activity can help the student become more aware of their emotions and develop strategies to manage them throughout the day*

> *Emotion Regulation: You can use a feelings chart to help the student learn how to regulate their emotions when they are feeling overwhelmed or distressed. The chart should include a range of coping strategies that the student can use to manage their emotions, such as deep breathing exercises, mindfulness techniques, or talking to a trusted adult. You can work with the student to identify which coping strategies work best for them, and encourage them to use these strategies when they are feeling anxious, depressed, or overwhelmed. The teacher can also help the student create a plan for accessing these coping strategies when they are needed, such as keeping a list of coping strategies in their notebook or posting them on their locker. This activity can help the student develop the skills and strategies they need to manage their emotions in a healthy way*

Figure 7.7 Teaching strategy

Task each student with the responsibility of bringing to each class a list of five feeling words with definitions results in an explosion of vocabulary useful in counselling. Each student is assigned a different letter of the alphabet each time the class meets and is expected to share the definitions with the other class members weekly. This is especially helpful for male students who, having grown up with the stereotype that men keep emotion to themselves, may not have developed a rich vocabulary of feeling words.

The reflecting and summarising micro-skills of listening

The reflective listening skills are used to stimulate deeper exploration of a person's perception of a problem or situation. They can also bring out meanings associated with a problem.

The functions of reflecting

Most statements people make have several levels on which we can understand them:

- The level of facts and thoughts (a cognitive level)
- The person's underlying feelings (an emotional level)
- The level of hidden meanings (an existential level) (Lapin, 2016)

When we use reflective listening skilfully, we can get at all three of these levels. Generally, reflecting consists of feeding back to the person their thoughts, feelings, and implied meanings in a condensed fashion, using our own words.

Reflected statements should show non-evaluative, nonjudgmental understanding sometimes known as Unconditional Personal Regard(UPR) (Rogers, 1957).

Using reflection skills serves four different functions. It is a verbal way of communicating empathy, it is a form of feedback or a mirror, it serves as catalyst stimulating further exploration of what the speaker is experiencing and it can bring out important aspects of the message that otherwise might remain camouflaged(Lapin, 2016).

Reflecting feelings

The purpose of reflecting feelings back to someone is to make these implicit, sometimes hidden emotions clear to the person. Reflecting feelings is a powerful listening tool. If it is done with skill it can do the following: It can bring out the richness of a young person's emotional world, help them sort out conflicting and ambivalent feelings they may they hold towards themselves or others and grounds both the speaker and the listener, in basic experience (Ivey and Ivey, 2003).

Reflecting feelings involves expressing in one's own words the emotions stated or implied by both the verbal and nonverbal responses of the person. A reflection of feelings reflection can make young people more aware of their emotions surrounding a topic, but also can deepen relationships and provide relief for those who have been struggling with conflicting emotions about an experience.

To accurately reflect the strength of a given feeling, you can study (or generate) a list of feeling words. Try to get words of strong, moderate, and weak intensity for each feeling category (Moustakas and Callahan, 1956).

Being able to reflect feelings back to people gives them enormous benefits, and also deepens the relationship between you and reflection of feelings enhances others' awareness.

Methods to reflect a student's feelings

If feeling skills are used effectively, it can help students gain the self-awareness needed to become unstuck and more aware and more able to express those stuck feelings. Four methods are useful in reflecting students' feelings:

- Step into the student's shoes and use emotional recall. This approach involves the teacher stepping inside the student's reality and attempting to experience it. Many individuals have common reference points, past experiences that are similar. For example, if they describe a bereavement the teacher silently asks, "How would I feel if this were going on in my life?" Whatever emotions occur to the teacher are then verbally reflected to the student: "You feel lost and lonely without this person"
- Interpret the student's vocal intonation and body language. Bodily clues to what a student may be feeling should be interpreted and reflected by the teacher "You're feeling overwhelmed and discouraged by the failure of your English exam " is an appropriate counselor reflection of feeling for the student who is sitting slumped with downcast eyes

- Use a synonym for a feeling the student has identified. Students may use feeling words to describe their internal reality. They might share with the teacher that the end of an important relationship leaves them feeling "unhappy." When the teacher reflects a feeling that has a meaning similar to the emotion identified by the student (for example, "There is a lot of sadness in this for you"), the self-awareness of the young person is enhanced.
- Students will often express negative feelings such as. "Well, I don't feel good about it." In cases like this, the teacher may simply reflect any emotions that are the opposite of the emotion the student has rejected. An example would be, "You're feeling bad and worried about this situation"
- Reflect with genuineness and sincerity. One method of helping students release their inhibition about using the reflection of feeling skill is to help them understand that if the reflection of feeling is genuine, then useful information will result. (Plutchik, 2002)

Reflecting meaning

Reflecting meaning is an advanced skill for identifying and responding to the meanings behind what a young person is saying. It is the peeling back of the onion to reveal the deeper layers, and it can only happen if it is possible to provide a safe environment for the increasing depth of disclosure involved with meaning (Rogers, 1957).

Reflecting meaning is a way of re-stating for a young person the personal impact and significance of an event or situation they are describing. Reflecting meaning is one of the most difficult listening skills to learn. The best way to uncover meaning is to use nonverbal behaviour, basic prompting skills (those minimal encouragers), and the reflection of content and feelings. Using these skills creates an environment in which the young person feels safe to give the responses that allow their deepest meanings to be divulged (Lapin, 2016).

Figure 7.8 Self-reflection exercise

Complete the table using your own examples of teachers helping their students reflecting their feelings in each one of the categories:
  Reflecting feelings- words

Example: Student: I'm really pissed
Teacher: You're really angry
Reflecting feelings -phrases
Example: Student I feel there's something special between him and me
Teacher: You feel there is mutual attraction
Reflecting physical reactions

> *If the physical reaction is named, use the same words, otherwise paraphrase it*
> Example: Student: Before I go into the exam I feel butterflies in my stomach
> Teacher: You feel tension in your stomach
> *Searching for feelings that resonate*
> Example: Student: I don't know how to express what I felt toward my mum ...angry, upset ...
> Teacher: Hurt, anxious, confused do any of these words sum it up?
> *Reflecting feelings and reasons*
> Example: Student: Ever since we had a painful break up, I am afraid to go on a date
> Teacher: You're scared about dating again because of you don't want to go through the same pain again

Figure 7.9 Self-reflection exercise

Work with a partner and film yourselves discussing topics in which you can share your feelings. Watch the recording and evaluate the effectiveness of your response strategies, verbal, vocal and body language.

Paraphrasing

Paraphrasing is a skilled process consisting of two steps: (1) listening carefully to what is being said and then (2) feeding back a condensed, nonjudgmental version of the facts and thoughts. Potential problems of paraphrasing include:

- Interrupting the person's flow with too many reflections or paraphrases which are too long
- Overusing certain phrases (for example: "You think ..." or "I gather that ...")
- It is possible to paraphrase something with factual correctness but the wrong intensity, making either too weak or too strong of a reflection
- Getting the language wrong. Things need to be expressed in the teacher's own words in a manner that is non-judgmental, comfortable to the speaker and appropriate to the person you are listening to

Summarising: Pulling themes together

Summarising skills include noticing what the person says (content), how it is said (feelings), and the purpose, timing, and effect of the statements (process). Summarising consists of bringing together in a single statement several ideas and feelings in order to show understanding. It is much broader, than paraphrasing a basic message. The basic idea is to pick out the highlights and general themes of the content and feelings (Lapin, 2016).

Recapping ideas can be very effective because through it, the speaker can absorb and reflect on what they been sharing. They can gain an integrated sense of it and clarify what has been said by putting it into an organised format so that the person is better able to see a clear picture of the situation. It also gives the speaker a feeling of movement in exploring ideas and feelings, as well as awareness of progress in learning and by focusing scattered ideas, summaries make way for new ideas.

Summaries help to reassure speakers that they are being listened and serve as an effective check that the full spectrum of messages from the person have been understood and they can also help to conclude a supporting session in a more structured natural way (Jones-Smith, 2011).

Figure 7.10 Self-reflection activity

Here are two self-reflection exercises for you to develop paraphrasing skills to support students with mental health issues:

Paraphrasing Practice:

Choose a recent conversation you had with a student who shared about their mental health struggles. Take a few minutes to reflect on the conversation and write down the key points that the student shared. Then, try to paraphrase what the student said in your own words. Consider the following questions as you practice paraphrasing: Did you capture the essence of what the student shared? Did you use language that reflects empathy and understanding? Did you use clear and concise language?

After you have finished paraphrasing, take a moment to reflect on the experience. How did it feel to try to put the student's experience into your own words? Did you find any challenges in trying to paraphrase? What can you do to improve your paraphrasing skills in the future?

Self-Reflection on Listening:

Think about a recent conversation you had with a student who was struggling with their mental health. Ask yourself the following questions:

- *Did you actively listen to the student?*
- *Did you interrupt or finish the student's sentences?*
- *Did you jump to conclusions or make assumptions about the student's experience?*

- *Did you show empathy and understanding?*
- *Did you ask clarifying questions to ensure you understood the student's perspective?*

Reflect on your answers to these questions and consider what you could do differently to improve your listening skills. Practice active listening skills by focusing on the student's words, avoiding distractions, and showing empathy and understanding.

Motivation and language

Using a strength-based vocabulary

Supporting students using language based on a knowledge of character, virtue, and strengths has been found to empower students and to develop a stronger rapport with teachers. The concepts of a strength-based vocabulary are derived from positive psychology (Hill and Hall, 2018). The emphasis is placed on stressing positive attributes, proposing solutions that have assisted young person before, and emphasising strengths to help empower for positive change (Peterson and Seligman, 2004). The focus is on encouraging students to believe they have the mental and emotional resources and abilities they can access to help themselves and their relationships.

Peterson and Seligman suggest it is important to use what they call a virtue vocabulary based solely on the character strengths identified in positive psychology literature such as Values in Action (VIA) (2004) which include wisdom, courage, humanity, justice, temperance and transcendence, and to identify these strengths from students' personal narratives and reflect these strengths back to them. They argue that when strengths are highlighted feedback becomes more relevant and motivation is increased (Hill and Hall, 2018).

It has also been argued that by using a virtue vocabulary, a teacher can help set a student on a path towards realising their own strengths and can help suggest ways on how to apply those strengths to present and future challenges, reduce depression and boost wellbeing (Seligman, Steen, Park, and Peterson, 2005) (Table 7.1).

Here are some examples of empathic reflections that use virtue strength affirmations:

"It sounds like your commitment to honesty is really important to you. I admire how you've been able to maintain your integrity, even in difficult situations."

"It seems like your perseverance is one of your greatest strengths. Your determination to keep going despite obstacles is truly inspiring."

Table 7.1 The six virtues and their corresponding strengths. (Peterson & Seligman, 2004 adapted from Hill and Hall, 2018.)

Wisdom & Knowledge	Courage	Humanity	Justice	Temperance	Transcendence
Creativity	Bravery	Love	Citizenship	Forgiveness & Mercy	Appreciation of Beauty & Excellence
Curiosity	Persistence	Kindness	Fairness	Forgiveness/ Modesty	Gratitude
Open Mindedness	Integrity	Social Intelligence	Leadership	Humility	Hope
Love of Learning	Vitality			Self-Regulation	Humour
Perspective					Spirituality

"I can tell that your kindness towards others is a core part of who you are. Your compassion and empathy make a real difference in the lives of those around you."

"Your courage is truly impressive. Facing your fears and taking risks is not easy, but your bravery has led you to some incredible achievements."

"It sounds like your humility is a key aspect of your personality. Your willingness to listen to others and consider different perspectives is a real strength."

"Your sense of justice is truly admirable. Your commitment to fairness and equality has made a real impact on the people around you."

Figure 7.11   Self reflection activity

Using the VIA classification table write an example of a phrase from each one of the 24 strengths that you might use with a student in a tutorial situation

---

Figure 7.12   Helping activity

Here are two activities that I have used to support a student who had issues with their self esteem:

Strengths Exploration:

This activity can help the student recognize their unique strengths and abilities, which can boost their self-esteem. The teacher can ask the student to complete the VIA Survey of Character Strengths and then review their top strengths with them. Together, they can discuss how these strengths relate to the student's interests, goals, and achievements. The teacher can also encourage the student to identify opportunities to use these strengths in the classroom, school, or community.

Gratitude Journaling:

Gratitude is a powerful tool for increasing positive emotions and self-esteem. The teacher can provide the student with a journal or notebook and ask them to write down three things they are grateful for every day. The teacher can also encourage the student to reflect on how these things make them feel and why they are important to them. This activity can help the student focus on positive aspects of their life, which can counteract negative self-talk and improve their overall wellbeing.

Figure 7.13   Self reflection activity

Using the VIA classification table write an example of a phrase from each one of the 24 strengths that you might use with a student in a tutorial situation

Figure 7.14

When one of my students presented to me the problems that she faced going on a work placement for the first time because of her social anxiety I worked with her on the following exercise:

Strengths-Based Self-Talk:

Self-talk can be a powerful tool for managing anxiety and building self-confidence. I encouraged her to identify her top strengths from the VIA classification, and then helped her to create positive affirmations based on these strengths. For example, because she felt that her top strength was perseverance, her affirmation was "I am strong and resilient, and I can handle any challenge that comes my way." I encouraged her to repeat these affirmations to herself when she was feeling anxious or overwhelmed. This activity can help students to reframe negative thoughts and build a more positive self-image.

Monitoring

This is an important skill as using it can assist young people to clarify their problems by monitoring their feelings, thoughts, physical reactions, and behaviours. Monitoring student changes and progress during support treatment and intervention is an essential part of the process. Some of the main purposes of this process monitoring include:

- Assessment. By monitoring the process of sessions, they can gather information about the student's progress, the quality of the tutorial support, and the overall effectiveness of the supporting approach. This can help teachers make informed decisions about the direction and focus of support
- Evaluation. Process monitoring enables teachers to evaluate the outcomes of supportive interventions and to see if adjustments need to be made by tracking the student's progress over time. This evaluation process helps teachers make evidence-based decisions and can ensure that the support is benefiting the student
- Feedback. By reviewing session recordings, session notes, or other monitoring tools, they can gain insights into their supporting skills, areas of improvement, and their impact on the student. It can help teachers enhance their competence and effectiveness as practitioners
- Student Empowerment. Process monitoring involves active collaboration with students, as they are encouraged to participate in monitoring their own progress. This empowers students to become active participants in their therapeutic journey by increasing their self-awareness, identifying patterns or obstacles, and working together with the teacher to set goals and make necessary adjustments
- Quality Assurance. It contributes to ensuring the quality of support services. It allows teachers and student support services to maintain standards of care, adherence to ethical guidelines, and best practices. Monitoring can help identify areas where improvement is needed, leading to ongoing professional development and the provision of high-quality services

Process monitoring can be used at any stage of the support process and can be used to promote, check progress and to motivate and then finally, to evaluate the success of the support given. It works most effectively when combined with a formalised type of self-assessment and feedback approach.

Self-monitoring

Self-monitoring is a practice in which students are asked to systematically observe and record specific targets such as thoughts, body feelings, emotions, and behaviours. It is part of a wider practice of empiricism and measurement that is integral to Cognitive Behavioural Therapy (CBT) (Persons, 2008), and it functions as both an assessment method and an intervention.

Common targets of self-monitoring

These can include any events, emotions, thoughts, memories, bodily sensations, attention, activity and behaviour. For example, monitoring the occurrence, frequency, and content of events and their impact on emotions negative thoughts, memories, bodily sensations. Or situations where a student becomes particularly self-focused, or especially threat-focused (Persons, 2008).

Figure 7.15   Monitoring feelings

One example of how this can be done is via a rating scale in which students can rate feelings of anxiety, stress, mood on scales form 0– 10 or 0–100% on a daily, weekly or monthly, or specific occasion.

A partially completed Student work sheet for monitoring own feelings of stress in a classroom situation:

Situation
Who? What? Where? When?

Monday
9.20 I was late for my Maths class because my bus got cancelled and I had to wait for the next one
Feelings and physical reactions

What did you feel? How did you physically react?
Note down each feeling and rate out of 100%
Out of breath because I rushed – 80%
Annoyed with the bus service – 80%
Anxious that I missed the start of the class and wouldn't be able to follow the rest of the lesson – 90% Thoughts, perceptions and images

What thoughts did you have before you started to feel and physically react this way? Tick the most important ones (hot thoughts)

I was going to get a bollocking because I had been late twice this term already

I was going to struggle throughout the lesson because I didn't know what was going on
She was going to put me on another warning because of my lateness
She was going to phone my mum and ask her why I was late again

---

Monitoring thoughts

This can be done in conjunction with monitoring feelings and physical reactions and it can be useful to encourage your students to classify the most important ones associated with the latter as hot thoughts when presenting them on a worksheet (see the previous figure). One commonly used framework for monitoring thoughts and action is the Situations-thoughts-consequences framework (STC) (Nelson-Jones, 2014). The main stages of this are:

- Situations. In this stage, individuals identify the specific situations or events that trigger their emotional and behavioural responses. It involves recognising the external factors or internal triggers that contribute to their emotional experiences. By becoming aware of the situations that lead to certain thoughts and emotions, young people can start understanding their own patterns and triggers.
- Thoughts. In this stage, automatic thoughts, assumptions, or interpretations thoughts and beliefs that arise in response to the identified situations are explored and examined. This step encourages young people to recognise their cognitive processes, including any negative or distorted thinking patterns. By becoming aware of their thoughts, young people can assess their accuracy and evaluate their impact on their emotions and behaviour. This awareness can enable them to challenge and reframe negative thoughts, leading to better emotional regulation and wellbeing.
- Consequence. This stage involves understanding the emotional and behavioural consequences that result from specific thoughts. Young people explore how their thoughts influence their emotions, actions, and wellbeing. They consider the short-term and long-term consequences of their thoughts and behaviours, both positive and negative. This stage helps young people recognise the impact of their thinking patterns on their emotional experiences and empowers them to make conscious choices for more adaptive and positive outcomes. This empowers them to find alternative solutions, cope effectively with challenges, and improve their decision-making abilities.

References

Beck, A. T. (1963). Thinking and depression: I. Idiosyncratic content and cognitive distortions. *Archives of General Psychiatry*, 9: 324–33. doi:10.1001/archpsyc.1963.01720160014002

Beck, A. T. (1979). Cognitive therapy and the emotional disorders. NY: Meridian Books.

Beck, A. T. (1991). Cognitive therapy as the integrative therapy. *Journal of Psychotherapy Integration*, 1(3): 191–8.

Beck, J. S. (2012). Annual reviews conversations presents: A conversation with Aaron T. Beck. *Annual Reviews*. Retrieved from: https://www.annualreviews.org/userimages/ContentEditor/1351004835908/AaronTBeckTranscript.pdf

Bonfá-Araujo, B., Oshio, A., and Hauck-Filho, N. (2022). Seeing things in black-and-white: A scoping review on dichotomous thinking style. *Japanese Psychological Research*, 64(4): 461–72. doi:10.1111/jpr.12328

Briers, S. (2009). *Cognitive Behavioural Therapy*. London: Pearson Education

Butler, A. and Beck, J. (2000). Cognitive therapy outcomes: A review of meta-analyses. *Journal of the Norwegian Psychological Association.* 37: 1–9.

Hill, P. G., and Hall, M. E. L. (2018). Uncovering the good in positive psychology: Toward a worldview conception that can help positive psychology flourish. In: N. J. L. Brown, T. Lomas, and F. J. Eiroa-Orosa (eds.), *The Routledge International*

Handbook of Critical Positive Psychology, pp 245–62. Routledge/Taylor & Francis Group. doi:10.4324/9781315659794-19

Ivey, A., and Ivey M. (2003). *Intentional Interviewing and Counselling: Facilitating Client Development in a Multicultural Society*. California, USA: Brooks/Cole – Thomson Learning

Jones-Smith, E. (2011). *Theories of Counseling and Psychotherapy: An Integrative Approach*. Los Angeles, CA: Sage Publications.

Lapin, J. (2016). Therapists' use of reflection of feeling with trauma survivors. Unpublished doctoral thesis. Available from: https://www.proquest.com/openview/45d8bff99adcc3f16e76ed38c1f2900d/1?pq-origsite=gscholar&cbl=18750

Lissek, S., and Grillon, C. (2015). Overgeneralization of conditioned fear in the anxiety disorders. *Journal of Psychology*. doi:10.1027/0044-3409/a000022

Moustakas, C. E., and Callahan, R. J. (1956). Reflections on reflection of feelings. *The Journal of Social Psychology*, 43: 323–31. doi:10.1080/00224545.1956.991922

Nelson-Jones, R. (ed.) (2014). *Theory and Practice of Counselling and Therapy*, (6th edn). London: Sage Publications.

Persons, J. B. (2008). *The Case Formulation Approach to Cognitive-Behavior Therapy*. New York, NY: The Guilford Press.

Peterson, C., and Seligman, M. E. P. (2004). *Character Strengths and Virtues: A Handbook and Classification*. Washington, DC: Oxford University Press; American Psychological Association.

Plutchik, Robert. (2002). *Emotions and Life: Perspectives from Psychology, Biology, and Evolution*. Washington, DC: American Psychological Association

Rogers, C. R. (1957). The necessary and sufficient conditions of therapeutic personality change. *Journal of Consulting Psychology*, 21(2): 95–103. doi:10.1037/h0045357

Rnic, K., Dozois, D. J., and Martin, R. A. (2016). Cognitive distortions, humor styles, and depression. *Europe's Journal of Psychology*, 12(3): 348–62. doi:10.5964/ejop.v12i3.1118

Seligman, M. E. P., Steen, T. A., Park, N., and Peterson, C. (2005). Positive psychology progress: empirical validation of interventions. *American Psychologist*, 60(5): 410–21. doi:10.1037/0003-066X.60.5.410

Semeraro, A., Vilella, S., and Ruffo, G. (2021). PyPlutchik: Visualising and comparing emotion-annotated corpora. *PLoS One*, 16(9): e0256503. doi:10.1371/journal.pone.0256503

8 Approaches to teachers' wellbeing

The context of teachers' stress

The teaching profession in England is currently in the midst of a crisis. Although the number of school-aged children is rising year-upon-year (Department for Education, 2023), because of the large numbers of teachers leaving the profession, the number of teachers is struggling to meet the increasing demand(Department for Education, 2023).

On the one hand, it is becoming increasingly difficult to encourage appropriately qualified and skilled young people to enter the teaching profession (Allen et al., 2023). On the other, retention of newly qualified teachers in England is low, with a third of new recruits leaving the job within the first five years (Allen et al., 2023). This is creating a perfect storm for teacher supply in England, with many headteachers suggesting that a lack of suitably qualified staff is hindering the quality of instruction that their school can provide (Jerrim and Sims, 2021).

One potential reason why England is struggling to recruit and retain enough teachers is due to the pressures of the job (Perryman and Calvert, 2020). Teaching demands long working hours, particularly during term-time (Allen et al., 2023), with teachers in England spending more time on lesson planning, marking and administration than teachers in most other countries across the world (Jerrim and Sims, 2019). This may have significant negative implications for teachers' wellbeing, mental health and whether they choose to remain in the profession (Perryman and Calvert, 2020). Indeed, earlier qualitative research drawing on exit interviews with 101 former teachers evidenced a variety of physical and mental health problems that contributed to their decision to leave the profession (DFE, 2018).

Teachers in England are currently leaving the profession at a record pace, with one in three choosing to quit for another job within five years of their initial teacher training (DFE, 2022). Although there are likely to be many factors driving this issue such as pay, increasing workloads, pressure from accountability systems and the resultant stress may play a role. Indeed, job satisfaction amongst the teaching profession in England is low by international standards and has declined rapidly over the last five years (Jerrim and Sims, 2019).

DOI: 10.4324/9781003424376-9

High levels of work-related stress are associated with a range of physical problems, including an increased incidence of cardiovascular disease and psychological issues such as depression, as well as increased rates of absenteeism (Fimian and Fastenau, 1990). In the UK in general, work-related stress, depression or anxiety accounted for more than half (54%) of the working days lost in 2021–22 (HSE, 2022).

Long-term exposure to work-related stressors can lead to burnout, which is characterised by emotional exhaustion, (which can consist of feelings of being emotionally overextended and exhausted because of one's work) a feeling of detachment (depersonalisation), cynical attitudes towards an individual's own job and those around them and a keen sense of professional inefficacy (personal accomplishment and feeling like you are competent and successful at work). Burnout has been linked with physical health issues such as high blood pressure and cardiovascular disease as well as mental health problems such as anxiety and depression. It has been suggested that this is increasingly common amongst teachers (Madigan and Kim, 2021).

Burnout symptoms will have many wide-ranging consequences for teachers as they feed into low job satisfaction. This lack of satisfaction is associated with an increased likelihood of absenteeism and illness low morale and intent to leave teaching (Madigan and Kim, 2021).

Mental health and wellbeing at work is influenced by the relationship between the individual, the nature of their work and their work environment. The Health and Safety Executive (HSE) have identified six key aspects of a working environment that have the potential to contribute to work-related stress (HSE. Online). These include the following:

- Demands which includes workload, work patterns and the work environment
- Control-meaning the level of autonomy and independence that an individual has in their workplace
- Support -which includes the encouragement and resources provided by the organisation, line management and colleagues
- Relationships at work- which involves the promoting of positive working practices to deal with unacceptable behavior and avoid conflict
- Role- which includes whether people understand their role within the organisation and whether the organisation ensures the person does not have conflicting roles
- Change – how organisational change is managed and communicated. Work environments that place high demands on individuals without enough control and support to meet these demands pose risks for mental health and wellbeing

The potential stressors that teachers encounter at work

Teachers face many specific potential stressors in their work environment, including workload pressures as well as relational and external factors. Workload aspects include administrative paperwork, lack of non-contact time for lesson planning and a feeling of responsibility for pupils' educational outcomes.

Relational aspects include the quality of teachers' connections with pupils and their parents as well as with other staff members. For example, student misbehaviour, challenging situations with colleagues and parents of pupils as well as lack of perceived support from management and leaders can impact negatively on teachers' mental health and wellbeing ((Madigan and Kim, 2021).

External influences include policy initiatives and changes to the school and college system. Relationships between teacher wellbeing, the quality of teacher–pupil relationships, pupil wellbeing and educational outcomes is likely to be inter-related and complex. Teachers with poor mental health and wellbeing who continue working are likely to find it more difficult to form positive and supportive relationships with their pupils or to manage classroom behaviour effectively (Miller, 2003).

Burnout in teachers has been linked with reduced quality of teaching and classroom instruction, and an increased risk of poor student classroom behaviour. In a cross-sectional study in 25 secondary schools in England and Wales, better teacher wellbeing and lower depressive symptoms in teachers were found to be associated with better student wellbeing and lower student psychological distress. Young people and children who have higher social and emotional wellbeing tend to do better in colleges and schools (Harding et al., 2019).

Figure 8.1   Self-reflection task

Here is a self-reflection task for you to evaluate your key negative stressors in teaching and how they have impact your mental health and well-being over the past academic year.

1 Take a few moments to think about the past academic year and consider the following questions:

- What were some of the biggest challenges you faced in your teaching role?
- Were there any specific events or situations that caused you stress or anxiety?
- Did you feel overwhelmed or overworked at any point during the year?
- Did you have enough time to complete your tasks and responsibilities?
- Were there any interactions with students, colleagues, or parents that were particularly stressful or negative?

2 Write down your responses to these questions in a journal or notebook
3 Identify the top 3–5 negative stressors that you experienced during the year. These may include workload, lack of support, difficult students, negative colleagues, or other factors

> 4 For each stressor, reflect on how it impacted your mental health and well-being. Did it cause you to feel anxious, stressed, or overwhelmed? Did it affect your sleep or other aspects of your health? Did it impact your relationships with others?
> 5 Think about ways you can address these stressors in the future. Are there specific changes you can make to your workload, schedule, or interactions with others? Can you seek additional support or resources to help manage stress?
> 6 Finally, design a plan for self-care and well-being moving forward. This may include setting aside time for relaxation and hobbies, seeking out support from friends or colleagues, or exploring new ways to manage stress and promote mental health
>
> *Remember, taking care of your mental health is an important part of being an effective and fulfilled teacher. By reflecting on your stressors and taking steps to address them, you can help promote your own wellbeing and better support your students and colleagues.*

According to a National Association of Schoolmasters Union of Women Teachers (NASUWT) Wellbeing at Work Survey of its members in 2022, 90% of teachers have experienced more work-related stress in the last 12 months and in addition:

- Teachers in England are more likely to perceive their job as causing them stress and having a negative impact upon their mental health than teachers in other countries
- As in other professions, over the past five years there has been an increase in the percentage of teachers reporting mental health problems
- 91% report that their job has adversely affected their mental health in the last 12 months
- 64% report that their job has adversely affected their physical health in the last 12 months
- 52% say that workload has been the main factor for increased work-related stress, especially lesson planning and marking followed by the consequences of the pandemic (34%), and worries about pupil behaviour (24%), pupil wellbeing (24%), pupil academic performance (22%) and finances (11%)

Teachers surveyed said that stress was having the following impacts on their lives

- 87% have experienced an increase in anxiousness
- 82% have suffered loss of sleep
- 28% have increased their use of alcohol and 7% have increased their use of prescription drugs

- 10% have had a relationship breakdown
- 3% have self-harmed (NASUWT, 2022)

Their responses were highly critical of how their schools responded to issues around wellbeing and mental health:

- 78% of teachers say that their school does not provide staff with workspaces that promote wellbeing and 66% say that their school does not have measures in place to monitor and manage stress and burnout
- 66% say that their school/college does not have a school-based counsellor who is accessible to both staff and students/pupils
- 63% say that their school does not provide staff with a safe and comfortable space to take time out and debrief outside the classroom environment
- 53% disagree/strongly disagree that their school prioritises staff mental health and only 22% agree/strongly agree
- 50% say that their school does not provide flexible working opportunities
- 48% say that their school does not have staff wellbeing/mental health training in place
- 47% disagree/strongly disagree that their school works with the NASUWT and other trade unions to promote staff wellbeing - only 13% agree/strongly agree
- 42% disagree/strongly disagree that their school is committed to tackling mental health stigmas - only 27% agree/strongly agree
- 37% say that their school does not carry out an annual wellbeing survey, with 39% saying it does and 23% unsure

Overall they suggest that although teachers are more likely to report mental health issues now and to get them treated, there is little evidence to suggest that actual levels of wellbeing and mental health amongst this group has declined or that any trend is specific to those working in the education sector (NASUWT, 2022).

Figure 8.2   Self-reflection task

Here is a sample mental health and burnout self-evaluation checklist that you might want to use to reflect upon:

1 Mental Health

- *Do you feel emotionally stable and able to cope with the demands of your job?*
- *Are you experiencing any symptoms of depression or anxiety, such as low mood, feelings of worthlessness, or panic attacks?*
- *Do you feel comfortable talking about your mental health with colleagues, supervisors, or a mental health professional?*

- *Have you noticed any changes in your sleep patterns or appetite?*
- *Are you experiencing any physical symptoms, such as headaches or muscle tension, that could be related to stress?*
- *Are you engaging in any activities that promote mental wellbeing, such as exercise, socialising, or mindfulness practices?*
- *Do you have a support system in place, such as friends or family members, that you can rely on during difficult times?*

2 Burnout

- *Do you feel exhausted or drained at the end of the day or week?*
- *Are you experiencing any symptoms of burnout, such as cynicism, detachment, or a lack of motivation?*
- *Do you feel that your workload is manageable, or are you consistently overburdened with responsibilities?*
- *Do you feel that your work is meaningful and fulfilling, or are you experiencing a sense of disillusionment or disengagement?*
- *Are you taking breaks throughout the day or week to recharge and reset?*
- *Do you feel that you have a healthy work-life balance, or are you consistently sacrificing personal time and priorities for work?*
- *Are you engaging in any activities outside of work that bring you joy or fulfilment?*

Impact of teacher mental health and wellbeing on student achievement

Impact on achievement

The Teacher Wellbeing Index by the Education Support Partnership in England (ESP, 2022) found that 36% of education professionals believed that taking time off work due to mental health symptoms had a negative impact on their students and a further 15% felt it impacted negatively on their students' results. Furthermore, 40% of both senior leaders and teachers were more likely to believe such absence would have a negative effect on students' studies than colleagues working in other education roles. Senior school leaders and teachers perceived that staff absence due to poor mental health had a detrimental impact on students' studies and their results (ESP, 2022).

According to a study by Glazzard and Rose (2019) teacher absenteeism has a detrimental effect on pupils. This is consistent with research by Jennings and Greenberg (2009). Pupils identified how this impacted negatively on their learning and they responded to the teacher's mood by negotiating their own behaviour. Teachers also identified how their mental health negatively impacted on the way they managed classes, the quality of their relationships with pupils and their teaching. This is consistent with the literature (Harding et al., 2019).

Data in this study seemed to indicate that pupils thought that the use of substitute teachers to cover absent teacher had a detrimental impact on their learning (2019).

Figure 8.3 Self-reflection

Here's a self-reflection task for teachers to examine how your state of mental health and well-being could impact on your teaching and your students' achievements:

1 Take a moment to sit quietly and think about your current state of mental health and wellbeing. Are you feeling stressed, anxious, or overwhelmed? Or are you feeling calm, centred, and energised?
2 Reflect on how your mental state affects your teaching. Consider the following questions:

- When you're feeling stressed or overwhelmed, do you find it harder to focus on your students' needs?
- Does your mental state affect your energy level in the classroom?
- Do you find that you're more likely to snap at students or become frustrated when you're feeling stressed or overwhelmed?
- Are you able to effectively manage the classroom and maintain a positive learning environment when you're feeling mentally drained or unwell?

3 Think about how your mental state impacts your students' achievements. Consider the following questions:

- Do you find that your mental state affects your ability to teach effectively and help your students learn?
- Are your students more likely to be engaged and motivated when you're feeling mentally well and energised?
- Do you notice a difference in your students' achievements when you're feeling mentally unwell compared to when you're feeling mentally well?

Institutional support

There are several ways that schools and colleges can support teachers' mental health and wellbeing. They could:

- Provide access to mental health resources by offering resources such as counselling services, support groups, and workshops that focus on mental health and wellbeing

- Foster a positive work environment by using senior managers to promote a culture of open communication, collaboration, and respect which could include providing opportunities for teachers to provide feedback, encouraging work-life balance, and recognising the achievements of teachers
- Offer professional development as providing teachers with training and professional development opportunities can help them feel more confident and effective in their roles. This can include training on stress management, mindfulness, and other topics related to mental health. Use professional development sessions to enhancing teacher creativity which can help reduce teaching stress
- Reduce workload working to reduce unnecessary paperwork, providing support for lesson planning, and limiting non-teaching responsibilities can help reduce teacher workload
- Encourage self-care by promoting healthy habits such as exercise, healthy eating, and adequate sleep
- Provide strong social support networks (positive feedback, supportive administration and encourage participation in reflective supervision by line managers or peers (Abraham-Cook, 2012)

Self-care

Self-care refers to any activity that helps maintain or improve your physical, emotional, or mental health. It is regarded as essential for teachers because teachers often have demanding schedules that require a lot of mental and emotional energy and therefore in the long run this can lead to burnout, fatigue, and even depression. Taking steps to support your own social and emotional needs can help to manage these negative outcomes and help you feel more refreshed and motivated. As we have previously seen, it can also help to improve your performance in the classroom and modelling self-care for your students can have a positive impact on their own wellbeing. By taking care of yourself, you are teaching your students the importance of prioritising their own needs and taking care of their mental health (Baker, 2020). There are different many self-care methods that teachers can use to benefit their own mental health and wellbeing in UK schools and colleges. Here are some ideas that I promote in staff development sessions to develop self-care in colleagues:

Figure 8.4 Seven teachers' mental health and wellbeing tips

1 Set reminders: very practically, an alarm on your phone will help you remember your boundaries - time to stop marking, time to leave work, time to switch off etc.

2 15 minute clutter buster: there are so many little tasks that stack up. Set a timer and tackle them for 15 minutes each day, to help you then focus on other tasks.

3 *Take back your mornings and weekends:* where possible plan the night before or at the end of the week, so you can approach your mornings (including Monday!) calmly.
4 *Quiet time:* it's hard to think, let alone recharge when you never have any quiet. Create a boundary where you get even a small amount of quiet alone time. Use the win-win approach: if a colleague asks "do you have a minute to talk about something?" and you are focused on another task, offer a response that offers two wins. "I'd love to talk to you. I can speak to you at 10am when I am on my break or at 4pm when I have finished teaching. What would you prefer?"
5 *Lists are your friend:* list people who drain your energy and don't respect your boundaries. Where possible, reduce your contact time with them.
6 *Keep your priorities list up to date:* write down what you 'have to' do, and rank everything on the list by importance. You might not get to everything and that's fine! Fix time boundaries: rather than focus on tasks (e.g. I'll mark until I'm finished) think about time blocks. For example, dedicate a block of time to marking. Do what you can in that time, and then stop. Stick to that time frame. It will help everyone in the long run.
7 *Strict email boundaries:* don't put work emails on your personal phone if you can avoid it.

Figure 8.5 Some self-reflection exercises to help develop approaches to self-care

- *Gratitude Practice:* Start by finding a quiet place to sit and reflect. Think about three things that you are grateful for in your life, and why. It could be something as simple as a beautiful sunrise or the support of a colleague or friend. Write them down in a journal and reflect on how they make you feel. This simple exercise can help you to shift your focus from negative to positive thoughts and emotions, reducing stress and promoting wellbeing
- *Values Assessment:* As a teacher, it can be easy to get caught up in the day-to-day challenges of the job and lose sight of what really matters. Take some time to reflect on your core values and beliefs, and how they align with your work as a teacher. What do you value most about your role? What motivates you to keep going when things get tough? Write down your thoughts and reflect on how you can stay true to your values while also taking care of yourself

- *Mindfulness Practice: Mindfulness is a powerful tool for reducing stress and promoting well-being. Set aside a few minutes each day to practice mindfulness. You can do this by finding a quiet place to sit, closing your eyes, and focusing on your breath. Simply observe your breath as it moves in and out of your body, without judgment or analysis. If your mind wanders, gently bring your attention back to your breath. You can also try guided meditations or mindfulness exercises to help you stay focused and present*

The Joy of practice and self-care

The joys and excitement of teaching can combine in unique forms at different times during a practitioner's life. They can vary in form and intensity across different practitioners and different caring teaching areas. Teachers will always encounter special times when their work felt very helpful to others. This significant helping of others has been called by Becker (1975) the psychic income of the work.

Figure 8.6 A joy of practice self-reflection exercise

Perhaps one or more joy-of-practice experiences were powerful critical incidents or defining moments, which are events that often serve as turning points in our professional lives. We suddenly see ourselves in a new way because the event leads us to view ourselves differently. Sometimes, critical incidents/defining moments lead us to understand theory or practice with sudden insight. Here, describe a joy-of-practice critical incident/defining moment. What happened? How did it impact your life?

If you are a seasoned practitioner, address these questions. Do you judge situations as joy-of-practice experiences in a different way than you did in the past? If so, what has changed? Are you pleased or disappointed with the impact of time and experience on you?

It is important for those of us in the caring professions to have meaningful, positive work experiences. Some practitioners do not have them on a daily basis. However, on a random and intermittent basis, they can be very reinforcing for us. Write below in response to these questions: Are you having a high ratio of positive work experiences in your work life? If not, what is missing? What can you do to increase the ratio of positive experiences in your life as a teacher?

Resilience

Resilience comes from the Latin verb resile, "to leap back" (Cambridge Dictionary online, n.d.). Fletcher and Sarkar (2013) state that most definitions have two aspects: how the individual responds to situations of adversity and to what extent are they equipped to adapt positively to negative events. Within education, many argue that the capacity to be everyday resilient is an important factor in teaching and teacher effectiveness over time (Day et al., 2011).

Resilience is a process rather than an internal trait. Therefore, resilience can change over time depending on the context or situation. Resilience is not a trait that people either have or do not have, it involves behaviours, thoughts and actions that can be learned and developed in anyone. Thus, resilience can be promoted and enhanced (Yates and Masten, 2004).

Impact of poor resilience on teachers

Many studies have confirmed the close relationship between resilience and mental health, showing that resilience had a significant positive impact on mental health symptoms such as loneliness, depression, anxiety (Zhang et al., 2020).

Interestingly, some research suggests that the impact resilience has on multiple mental health issues may be explained by elevated levels of self-esteem among resilient individuals (Ratanasiripong et al., 2022). According to Rossouw et al. (2017) there are six domains of resilience. These are:

- Vision. This relates to a sense of purpose, goal setting and clarity of vision when needing to make tough decisions
- Composure. This is linked to the regulation of emotions under stress and remaining calm and objective under pressure
- Reasoning. This is connected to creativity, planning and organising and resourcefulness under pressure when needed
- Tenacity. This is related to persistency and the ability to learn from mistakes
- Collaboration. This relates working and support others
- Health. This is important because it underpins the other five domains

---

Figure 8.7 Teaching activity

This is an activity I have used in teacher staff development sessions to help develop an understanding of resilience using the six domains of resilience outlined by Rossouw et al. (2017).

1 You begin by introducing the concept of resilience and explaining the six domains of resilience: physical, emotional, cognitive, social, spiritual, and contextual

2 *Provide examples of how teachers can develop resilience within each domain. For example:*
   - *Physical: taking breaks throughout the day to stretch or go for a walk, maintaining a healthy diet and getting enough sleep*
   - *Emotional: practicing mindfulness or meditation, talking with a trusted friend or colleague about challenges, expressing gratitude*
   - *Cognitive: reframing negative thoughts into positive ones, focusing on solutions rather than problems, seeking out professional development opportunities*
   - *Social: building strong relationships with colleagues and students, seeking out mentorship or coaching, participating in professional learning communities*
   - *Spiritual: engaging in activities that promote a sense of purpose or meaning, such as volunteer work or service projects*
   - *Contextual: adapting to changes and challenges in the school environment, seeking out resources and support when needed, maintaining a positive outlook on the future*
3 *Ask teachers to reflect on their own resilience and identify areas where they feel strong, as well as areas where they could improve. They can use the six domains of resilience as a framework for their reflection*
4 *Have teachers share their reflections with a partner or small group, discussing strategies they can use to further develop their resilience in each domain*
5 *As a class, discuss the importance of resilience in teaching and how developing resilience can positively impact both teachers and students*
6 *Finally, encourage teachers to set goals for themselves and create an action plan for how they will work towards developing resilience in each domain*

There are three areas known to be key in enhancing teacher resilience: Belonging, Help-seeking; and Learning (Eldridge, 2016)

- Belonging

Research has identified four important teacher relationships:

1 Teacher and Senior Leadership Team (SLT)):

   This can be enhanced by more effective direct communication, praising effort, and making teachers feel valued by the institution

2 Teacher and colleagues:

   This can be developed through peer mentoring and informal social communication

3 Teacher and Student:

> They can be enhanced by discussing mental health issues with students as a group or on an individual basis and focussing on those who are most vulnerable

4 Teacher and Personal relationships:

> These can be enhanced by developing a more structured work life balance ensuring that more time is spent with family and friends.
>
> (Hartwig et al., 2020)

Help seeking

Staff should model help-seeking behaviour. They could be asked regularly if they need additional help and be encouraged to seek and give help to and from others and engage in activities that promote team reflection.

Learning

Research has clearly indicated the importance of continuing professional development, reflection, and self-study in the development of resilience (Day et al., 2011).

Institutions and resilience

Institutional leadership can create environments where resilience is nurtured, and teachers are able to interact in responsive ways with students without feeling vulnerable to the demands of the work (Day et al., 2011). Their research made several recommendations:

- Resilience develops through interactions between people within organisational contexts and therefore genuine relationships and open, honest yet sensitive communication is essential
- Teachers' resilience can therefore be nurtured at various career stages through initial training, continuing professional development and support networks
- Most crucially, the role of institutional leadership is central to supporting the resilience of its staff through trust, supporting their autonomy, and developing stronger self-efficacy in staff

In addition, there are several other strategies that schools and colleges can implement to develop a teacher's resilience to stress, These include the following approaches:

- Providing teachers with professional development and training opportunities that focus on stress management techniques, such as mindfulness and meditation, can be an effective way to develop their resilience to stress.
- Creating a supportive work environment that includes resources for managing stress, such as an employee assistance program, can help teachers feel supported and better equipped to manage stress.

- Encouraging teachers to connect with one another and providing opportunities for peer support and mentorship can help to build a sense of community and reduce feelings of isolation, which can contribute to stress (Day et al., 2011).
- Ensuring that teachers have reasonable workloads and providing resources to help manage their workload can reduce feelings of overwhelm and burnout and providing flexibility in timetabling and allowing for a healthy work-life balance can also contribute to a teacher's ability to manage stress and maintain resilience.
- Giving teachers the opportunity to develop healthy relationships with their students, contributing to a better understanding of their students' needs which can reinforce self-efficacy among teachers and increase motivation to overcome obstacles within the profession.

(Skovholt and Trotter-Mathison, 2016)

Figure 8.8 Self-reflection task

Self-reflection is an important tool for teachers to evaluate their own mental health and resilience, as well as the level of support provided by their schools and colleges. Here is a self-reflection task that can be used for this purpose:

1. *Take a few deep breaths and find a quiet space where you can reflect without interruption*
2. *Write down three or four stressful situations you have encountered in the past year. These could be related to work, personal life, or a combination of both*
3. *For each situation, ask yourself the following questions:*
    - *How did I react to this situation? Was my reaction helpful or did it make the situation worse?*
    - *What coping strategies did I use to deal with the situation? Were these strategies effective?*
    - *Did I reach out for support from colleagues or supervisors? If so, how did they respond? If not, why not?*
4. *Reflect on the level of support provided by your school or college. Consider the following questions:*
    - *Has your school or college provided any resources or training to support your mental health and resilience?*
    - *Have you felt comfortable reaching out to colleagues or supervisors for support? Why or why not?*
    - *Have you been able to access mental health resources or services through your school or college? If so, how helpful were these resources?*
5. *Based on your reflections, identify any areas where you could improve your own coping strategies or seek additional support. Consider reaching out to colleagues, supervisors, or mental health professionals for assistance*

> 6 Finally, consider any feedback you would like to provide to your school or college regarding their support for mental health and resilience among teachers. Are there areas where you would like to see more resources or training provided? Are there any policies or practices that could be changed to better support teacher wellbeing?

Developing resilience on an individual level

Fletcher and Sarkar (2013) suggest resilience can be built using the following methods: reduce negative thinking and beliefs, manage energy (vitality), learn good problem solving skills, cultivate gratitude, and have strong relationships.

Some researchers have also confirmed that self-awareness and acceptance of own attitudes and an optimistic outlook on life could enhance the flexibility of an individual's psychological responses to daily life, improve their mental symptoms effectively such as anger, sadness, fear, and anxiety, and improve his/her life quality (Zhang et al., 2020).

It was also found in previous research that social support had a significant impact on mental health symptoms and could affect mental health by regulating and managing individual's emotions, cognition, and behaviour, the higher the level of social support, the higher the level of mental health. (Zhang et al., 2020).

According to Skovholt and Trotter-Mathison (2016) what is central to the development of resilience is sustaining the two selves, the professional and the personal self.

The professional self

The professional self is that part of the teacher that is guided and informed by the values, ethics, and principles of the teaching profession. It represents a way of conducting oneself as a teacher. The professional self aims to be trustworthy, reliable, responsible, and accountable. The professional self-engages in self-evaluation and personal growth on an ongoing basis.

According to the researchers (2016) apart from sufficient salary and benefits and manageable workload these are some of the factors that help to sustain the professional self of teachers:

- Increasing cognitive excitement and decreasing boredom by reinventing oneself and enjoyment in participating in others' growth and feeling successful in helping others
- Creating and sustaining an active, individually designed development method and being nurtured from work as mentors, supervisors, or managers. It is also important to be working within a professional greenhouse at work and a learning environment where practitioner growth is encouraged with a constant focus on professional development and avoidance of stagnation and pseudo development

- Professional self-understanding and using professional venting and expressive writing to release distress emotions) and being able to closely observe human life (creativity, courage, ingenuity, tolerance of pain) and meaningful human contact
- Thinking long-term and being able to understand the reality of pervasive early professional anxiety and the importance of being a "good enough" practitioner
- Low level of organisational conflict and professional social support from peers and from mentors, supervisors, or bosses and leadership that promotes balance between caring for others and self

---

Figure 8.9 Self-reflection exercise

Work through the list of factors which contribute to the maintenance of your professional self, such as increasing cognitive excitement, creating and sustaining an active, individually designed development method, and professional self-understanding and identify:

Those which you feel that you have experienced already
Those in need of further work by you
Those on which you need to work from scratch

The personal self and wellness

Teachers need to be assertive about their own personal self and wellness. One way of conceptualising this involves balancing the four dimensions of health: physical, intellectual, emotional/social health and spiritual health. According to Skovholt and Trotter-Mathison (2016) the main dimensions of the personal self can be broken down further into the emotional, the humorous and loving, the physical, and playful. The priority-setting, the recreational and the relaxation/ stress-reduction, the solitary and the spiritual or religious self. All of these selves need to be nurtured as part of building reliance.

Figure 8.10 Self-reflection task

In terms of a self-care action plan for you, which parts of the personal self are in "good shape" in your life, which ones need a "tune-up," and which ones need a "major overhaul"?

1 *Parts of the personal self in good shape:*
2 *Parts of the personal self in need of a tune-up:*

3 Parts of the personal self in need of a major overhaul:

Dimensions of self	What I need to do in these areas	How I will do those things
The emotional self		
The humorous self		
The loving self		
The physical self		
The playful self		
The priority setting self		
The recreational self		
The relaxation/ stress Reduction self		
The solitary self		
The spiritual self/ Religious self		

Figure 8.11 Self-reflective exercises

- *Gratitude journaling:* Teachers can start each day by writing down three things they're grateful for. This can be something as simple as a supportive colleague, a good night's sleep, or a positive interaction with a student. By focusing on the positive, teachers can shift their mindset and develop a more resilient outlook
- *Mindful breathing:* Taking a few minutes each day to focus on deep breathing can help teachers develop a sense of calm and centeredness. They can sit quietly, close their eyes, and breathe deeply in through the nose and out through the mouth. As they breathe, they can visualize themselves releasing any tension or stress and feel their body becoming more relaxed
- *Reflective journaling:* Reflective journaling is a tool for self-reflection and can help teachers develop greater self-awareness and emotional intelligence. Encouraging teachers to write in a journal for a few minutes each day can help them process their thoughts and feelings, identify patterns in their behaviour, and set goals for personal and professional growth. This activity can also help teachers focus on the positive aspects of their job, as they reflect on their successes and achievements
- Teachers can take some time at the end of each day to reflect on their experiences. They can write about any challenges they faced, what went well, and what they could have done differently. By reflecting on their practice in this way, teachers can identify areas where they need to improve and celebrate their successes. This can help them build resilience by developing a growth mindset and a sense of self-awareness

The PERMA model (Seligman, 2011)

The PERMA model derives from the area of Positive Psychology. Seligman et al. (2005) applied this to education and defined positive education as 'education for both traditional skills and for happiness' (p 293). Seligman(2018) suggests that our sense of wellbeing is multi-dimensional and can be promoted by positive actions in five areas: Positive emotion, Engagement, Relationships, Meaning and Accomplishment.

Positive emotion

This involves building positive emotions and is based on finding the ability to stay optimistic and to view the events and circumstances that life presents us in a way that is constructive and positive. This may be structured around spending time experiencing happiness, joy, fun, gratitude, hope etc.

On a practical level this can involve daily exercise, modelling optimism/hope, engaging in calming activities (e.g. yoga or breathing exercises) and noticing and acknowledge your worries.

An important part of discussing positive emotion is the concept of acceptance. By accepting that something negative may have happened in the past or may well be ongoing this can serve to equip ourselves with the abilities to be optimistic and constructive when moving forward with whatever our present and future may hold.

Engagement

This involves identifying individual strengths and talents and immersion in a particular task that is stimulating and absorbing. For example, pastimes, hobbies, volunteering.

Relationships

This is a feeling of being socially integrated, cared about and supported by others, and satisfied with your social connections. promotes feelings of support and security. For example, collaborative work, peer teaching.

Meaning

This refers to believing that one's life is valuable and feeling connected to something and having a clear sense of purpose and acting in accordance with values or goals. For example, setting personal, achievable goals.

Accomplishment

This can involve making progress toward goals, feeling capable to do daily activities, and achieving goals no matter how small and having a sense of purpose. For example, meeting a new exercise target, planning a new lesson.

According to Seligman these pillars contribute to overall wellbeing, are important areas that people pursue for their own sake and can be defined and measured independently of one another (Kern et al., 2015)

Figure 8.12   Self-reflection exercises

PERMA Inventory

The first self-reflection exercise is an inventory based on the PERMA model. In this exercise, teachers can reflect on their daily activities and experiences using the PERMA categories. For each category, teachers can ask themselves the following questions:

- *Positive Emotion: What are some things that make me feel happy, joyful, or grateful? What activities or interactions bring positivity into my day?*
- *Engagement: What tasks or projects do I find engaging and interesting? What activities do I lose track of time doing because I am so absorbed in them?*
- *Relationships: Who are the people in my life that I feel connected to and valued by? How do I cultivate and strengthen these relationships?*
- *Meaning: What are some of my core values and beliefs? How do these inform my teaching practice and interactions with students?*
- *Accomplishment: What are some goals or achievements that I am proud of? What steps did I take to reach them?*

PERMA Action Plan

The second self-reflection exercise is an action plan based on the PERMA model. In this exercise, teachers can identify specific actions they can take to cultivate each of the PERMA categories in their daily life. For each category, teachers can ask themselves the following questions:

- *Positive Emotion: What are some activities or experiences that bring me joy or happiness? What can I do to incorporate more of these activities into my day?*
- *Engagement: What are some tasks or projects that I find engaging and interesting? How can I incorporate more of these into my teaching practice?*
- *Relationships: Who are the people in my life that I want to prioritize and invest in? What actions can I take to strengthen these relationships?*
- *Meaning: What are some of my core values and beliefs that I want to prioritise in my teaching practice? How can I incorporate these values into my interactions with students and colleagues?*
- *Accomplishment: What are some goals or achievements that I want to work towards? What steps can I take to reach these goals?*

Job Crafting

Job crafting is about taking proactive steps and actions to redesign what is done at work, essentially changing tasks, relationships, and perceptions of work (Berg et al., 2013). The main premise is getting more meaning out of jobs simply by changing what is done and the purpose behind it. It has been linked to better performance (Caldwell and O'Reilly, 1990), intrinsic motivation, and employee engagement (Halbesleben, 2010; Dubbelt et al., 2019). It is premised by the concept that perceptions about challenges being faced can drive motivation and, therefore, resilience (Wrzesniewski and Dutton, 2001).

Job crafting has three dimensions, task, relationship, and cognitive crafting. Through using one or more of these activities, researchers claim to be able to provide the job-person fit that might be lacking in current roles (Wrzesniewski and Dutton, 2001; Tims and Bakker, 2010).

Task crafting involves focusing on what can be changed to make and shape the job to make it stimulating and enjoyable. It can involve adding or dropping the responsibilities or changing the nature of certain responsibilities or dedicating different amounts of time to current activities (Berg et al., 2013). It can provide the opportunity for employees to make the necessary changes to their physical work boundaries that can suit personal needs. Employees are provided with the opportunities to modify their task boundaries to try to ensure that work makes sense, fits with individual strengths, and allows for more variety and use of skills (Hackman and Oldham, 1975). Overall, by exerting control over their work experiences, employees begin to own their work.

Relationship crafting can involve changing workplace interactions on different tasks, (Berg et al., 2013). According to their study this can amount to altering the extent or nature of their relationships with others with whom they were connected in the course of their work as well as creating additional relationships and is often adopted in conjunction with task crafting (2013).

Cognitive crafting involves the development of a proactive and positive mind set and a desire to find and create more meaning and purpose in work (Tims and Bakker, 2010). It enables employees to continuously reevaluate how work influences them personally by changing the way they think about it. According to Berg et al. (2013) this can involve redefining what they see as the type or nature of the tasks or relationships that are involved in their job, as well as reframing their job to see it as a meaningful whole that positively impacts others rather than a collection of separate tasks.

According to their research the three aspects of crafting are interrelated and can trigger or be triggered by one another (2013).

The benefits of job crafting

Job crafting presents lots of potential benefits for organisational and positive psychology practitioners. While still relatively young, the approach has been examined empirically. Among the findings, and in addition to more meaningful work as mentioned above, there is evidence for at least five main benefits.

According to Fay and Frese (2001). the act of shaping one's own job is beneficial, innovative, and creative, and is conducive to flexibility and adaptability. It can provide a sense of control over what the tasks do, as well as more fulfilment from the connections made (Wrzesniewski et.al. 2003) and as a result can facilitate personal growth and goal accomplishment (Halbesleben, 2010). It can promote mastery through challenge which can be conducive to wellbeing (Gorgievski and Hobfoll, 2008) and creativity (Goodman and Svyantek, 1999). Job crafting can help individuals experience better person-job fit (Oldham and Hackman, 2010) when tasks are aligned to meet strengths and motives. A study by Slemp and Vella-Brodrick (2014), suggested that job crafting that boosted employees psychological and subjective wellbeing needs. Most importantly, job crafting puts the responsibility for change in employees' hands and the approach is first and foremost about enhancing their wellbeing (Wrzesniewski and Dutton, 2001; Tims et al., 2013).

Figure 8.13 Self-reflection task

The job crafting exercise

This was developed by Berg, Dutton, and Wrzesniewski (2010) to help identify opportunities for people to craft their jobs to better suit their motives, strengths, and passions and to help them develop a framework for job crafting. It is broken into several parts as it is designed to encourage people to think about their jobs as a flexible set of building blocks, rather than just a fixed list of duties.

Step one is to draw a Before Sketch. This helps you understand how you're allocating and spending your time across various tasks. This is achieved by deconstructing your entire job and placing its component tasks into three types of Task Blocks. The biggest of these blocks are for tasks which consume the most of your effort, attention, and time; the smallest blocks are for the least energy-, attention-, and time-intensive tasks, and some will fall into the middle, 'medium-sized' blocks. This will give you an indication of how and where your resources are being utilised and some indication as to where changes could be made. Step two, based on the knowledge of the way you currently distribute your resources, you can now design an accurate After Diagram of what your ideal role will look like. The After Diagram serves as an image of opportunities for how participants can craft their jobs to be more meaningful, and hence more engaging and fulfilling, To create the After Diagram, participants begin by identifying the three Job Crafting aspects of themselves at work, their motives, strengths, and passions and then create three new task blocks which are more relevant and more meaningful using their motives, strengths, and passions as criteria for assessing how well each task included in their jobs suits them.

The final step of creating the After Diagram is drawing "Role Frames" around groups of tasks that participants see as serving a common purpose. Role Frames are intended to help participants engage in cognitive or perceptions crafting, as they help participants mentally label tasks in ways that are meaningful to them. Here, you are recrafting your perceptions so you can label different tasks in reimagined ways.

The last step is where you create an Action Plan to define clear short- and long-term goals and you will be planning how you are going to move from your Before Diagram (current job) to your After Diagram (ideal job)?

References

Abraham-Cook, S. (2012). The Prevalence and Correlates of Compassion Fatigue, Compassion Satisfaction, and Burnout among Teachers Working in High-Poverty Urban Public Schools. ProQuest LLC, Ph.D. Dissertation, Seton Hall University. https://www.proquest.com/docview/1461391768

Allen, J., Quarmby, T., and Dillon, M. (2023). 'To a certain extent it is a business decision': Exploring external providers' perspectives of delivering outsourced primary school physical education. *Sport, Education and Society.* 1–15. doi:10.1080/13573 322.2023.2264319

Baker, Leia. (2020). Self-care amongst first-year teachers. *Networks: An Online Journal for Teacher Research*, 22(2). doi:10.4148/2470-6353.1328

Becker, G. (1975). *Human Capital: A Theoretical and Empirical Analysis, with Special Reference to Education*, 2nd edn. Volume URL: http://www.nber.org/books/beck75-1

Berg, J. M., Dutton, J. E., and Wrzesniewski, A. (2013). Job crafting and meaningful work. In: B. J. Dik, Z. S. Byrne, and M. F. Steger (eds.), *Purpose and Meaning in the Workplace*, pp 81–104. Washington, DC: American Psychological Association.

Caldwell, D. F., and O'Reilly, C. A. III. (1990). Measuring person-job fit with a profile-comparison process. *Journal of Applied Psychology*, 75(6): 648–57. doi:10.1037/0021-9010.75.6.648

Cambridge Dictionary. Online. (n.d.) https://dictionary.cambridge.org/dictionary/english/resilience

Day, C., Edwards, A., Griffiths, A., and Gu, Q. (2011). *Beyond Survival Teachers and Resilience*. Key Messages from an ESRC-funded Seminar Series. Nottingham, UK: Published by the University of Nottingham.

Department for Education (DFE) (2018). Factors affecting teacher retention: qualitative investigation Research report March 2018 CooperGibson Research. https://assets.publishing.service.gov.uk/media/5aa15d24e5274a53c0b29341/Factors_affecting_teacher_retention_-_qualitative_investigation.pdf

Department for Education (DFE) (2022). Reporting year 2022. School workforce in England. https://explore-education-statistics.service.gov.uk/find-statistics/school-workforce-in-england/2022

Department for Education (2023). Measures announced to boost teacher recruitment and retention. https://www.gov.uk/government/news/measures-announced-to-boost-teacher-recruitment-and-retention

Dubbelt, Lonneke, Evangelia, Demerouti, and Sonja, Rispens. (2019). The value of job crafting for work engagement, task performance, and career satisfaction: longitudinal and quasi-experimental evidence. *European Journal of Work and Organizational Psychology*, 28: 1–15. doi:10.1080/1359432X.2019.1576632

Education Support Partnership. (2022). *Teacher Wellbeing Index 2022*. https://www.educationsupport.org.uk/media/zoga2r13/teacher-wellbeing-index-2022.pdf

Eldridge, M. (2016). Understanding the factors that build teacher resilience. Unpublished doctoral thesis. Institute of Education, University of London. https://discovery.ucl.ac.uk/id/eprint/10018166/1/__d6_Shared$_SUPP_Library_User%20Services_Circulation_Inter-library%20Loans_IOE%20ETHOS_ETHOS%20digitised%20by%20ILL_ELDRIDGE,%20M.pdf

Fay, D., and Frese, M. (2001). The concept of personal initiative: An overview of validity studies. *Human Performance*, 14(1): 97–124. doi:10.1207/S15327043HUP1401_06

Fimian, M. J., and Fastenau, P. S. (1990). The validity and reliability of the Teacher Stress Inventory: A re-analysis of aggregate data. *Journal of Organizational Behavior*, 11(2): 151–157. doi:10.1002/job.4030110206

Fletcher, D., and Sarkar, M. (2013). Psychological resilience: A review and critique of definitions, concepts and theory. *European Psychologist*, 18: 12–23. doi:10.1027/1016-9040/a000124

Glazzard, J., and Rose, A. (2019). The Impact of Teacher Well-Being and Mental Health on Pupil Progress in Primary Schools. *Journal of Public Mental Health*. ISSN 1746-5729. doi:10.1108/JPMH-02-2019-002

Goodman, S. A., and Svyantek, D. J. (1999). Person–organization fit and contextual performance: Do shared values matter. *Journal of Vocational Behavior*, 55(2): 254–275. doi:10.1006/jvbe.1998.1682

Gorgievski, Marjan, and Hobfoll, Stevan. (2008). Work can burn us out or fire us up: Conservation of resources in burnout and engagement. *Handbook of Stress and Burnout in Health Care*, 1: 7–22.

Hackman, J. R., and Oldham, G. R. (1975). Development of the job diagnostic survey. *Journal of Applied Psychology*, 60(2): 159–170. doi:10.1037/h0076546

Halbesleben, J. R. B. (2010). A meta-analysis of work engagement: Relationships with burnout, demands, resources, and consequences. In: A. B. Bakker and M. P. Leiter (eds.), *Work Engagement: A Handbook of Essential Theory and Research*, pp 102–117. London: Psychology Press.

Harding, S., Evans, R., Morris, R., Gunnell, D., Ford, T., Hollingworth, W., Tilling, K., Bell, S., Grey, J., Brockman, R., Campbell, R., Araya, R., Murphy, S., and Kidger, J. (2019). Is teachers' mental health and wellbeing associated with students' mental health and wellbeing? *Journal of Affective Disorders*, 242, 180–7. doi:10.1016/j.jad.2018.08.080

Hartwig, A., Clarke, S., Johnson, S., and Willis, S. (2020). Workplace team resilience: A systematic review and conceptual development. *Organizational Psychology Review*, 10(3–4): 169–200. doi:10.1177/2041386620919476

Health and Safety Executive (HSE). (2022). Mental health conditions, work and the workplace. https://www.hse.gov.uk/stress/mental-health.htm

Jennings, P. A., and Greenberg, M. T. (2009). The prosocial classroom: Teacher social and emotional competence in relation to student and classroom outcomes. *Review of Educational Research*, 79(1): 491–525. doi:10.3102/0034654308325693

Jerrim, J., and Sims, S. (2019). *The Teaching and Learning International Survey (TALIS) 2018*. London: Department for Education. https://assets.publishing.service.gov.uk/government/uploads/system/uploads/attachment_data/file/919065/TALIS_2018_research_brief.pdf

Jerrim, J., and Sims, S. (2021). When is high workload bad for teacher wellbeing? Accounting for the non-linear contribution of specific teaching tasks. *Teaching and Teacher Education*, 105, 103395. doi:10.1016/j.tate.2021.103395

Kern, M., Waters, L. Adler, and White, M. (2015). A multidimensional approach to measuring well-being in students: Application of the PERMA framework. *The Journal of Positive Psychology*, 10: 262–71. doi:10.1080/17439760.2014.936962

Madigan, D. and Kim, L. (2021). Does teacher burnout affect students? A systematic review of its association with academic achievement and student-reported outcomes. *International Journal of Educational Research*, 105. doi:10.1016/j.ijer.2020.101714

Miller, A. (2003). *Teachers, Parents and Classroom Behaviour: A Psychosocial Approach*. Maidenhead: Open University Press.

National Association of Schoolmasters Union Women Teachers (NASUWT) Teacher Wellbeing Survey. (2022). https://www.nasuwt.org.uk/static/1ac040a7-96a5-481a-a052ddd850abc476/Teacher-Wellbeing-Survey-Report-2022.pdf

Oldham, G. R., and Hackman, J. R. (2010). Not what it was and not what it will be: The future of job design research. *Journal of Organizational Behavior*, 31(2–3): 463–79. doi:10.1002/job.678

Perryman, J. and Calvert, G. (2020). What motivates people to teach, and why do they leave? accountability, performativity and teacher retention. *British Journal of Educational Studies*, 68(1), 3–23. doi:10.1080/00071005.2019.1589417

Ratanasiripong, P., Ratanasiripong, N.T., Nungdanjark, W., Thongthammarat, Y., and Toyama, S. (2022). Mental health and burnout among teachers in Thailand. *Journal of Health Research*, 36(3): 404–16. doi:10.1108/JHR-05-2020-0181

Rossouw, Jurie, Rossouw, P., Paynter, P. C., Ward, A., and Khnana, P. (2017). Predictive 6 factor resilience scale – Domains of resilience and their role as enablers of job satisfaction. *International Journal of Neuropsychotherapy*, 5: 25–40. doi:10.12744/ijnpt.2017.1.0025-0040

Seligman, M. (2018). PERMA and the building blocks of well-being. *The Journal of Positive Psychology*. doi:10.1080/17439760.2018.1437466

Seligman, M. E. P. (2011). *Flourish: A visionary new understanding of happiness and well-being*, 3–5, London: Nicholas Brealey Publishing.

Seligman, M. E. P., Steen, T. A., Park, N., & Peterson, C. (2005). Positive psychology progress: empirical validation of interventions. *American Psychologist*, 60(5), 410–421. doi:10.1037/0003-066X.60.5.410

Skovholt, T. M., and Trotter-Mathison, M. (2016). *The Resilient Practitioner Burnout and Compassion Fatigue Prevention and Self-Care Strategies for the Helping Professions*. Routledge: Abingdon, Oxon.

Slemp, G. R., and Vella-Brodrick, D. A. (2014). Optimising employee mental health: The relationship between intrinsic need satisfaction, job crafting, and employee well-being. *Journal of Happiness Studies: An Interdisciplinary Forum on Subjective Well-Being*, 15(4): 957–77. doi:10.1007/s10902-013-9458-3

Tims, M., and Bakker, A. (2010). Job crafting: Towards a new model of individual job redesign. *SA Journal of Industrial Psychology*, 36: 1–9. doi:10.4102/sajip.v36i2.841

Tims, M., Bakker, A.B., and Derks, D. (2013). The impact of job crafting on job demands, job resources, and well-being. *The Journal of Occupational Health Psychology*, 18(2): 230–40. doi:10.1037/a0032141

Wrzesniewski, A., and Dutton, J. E. (2001). Crafting a job: Revisioning employees as active crafters of their work. *Academy of Management Review*, 26(2): 179–201.

Yates, T. M., and Masten, A. S. (2004). Fostering the future: Resilience theory and the practice of positive psychology. In: P. A. Linley and S. Joseph (eds.), *Positive Psychology in Practice*, pp 521–539. John Wiley & Sons, Inc.. doi:10.1002/9780470939338.ch32

Zhang, M., Bai, Y., and Li, Z. (2020). Effect of resilience on the mental health of special education teachers: Moderating effect of teaching barriers. *Psychology Research and Behavior Management*, 3(13): 537–44. doi:10.2147/PRBM.S257842

9 Whole college approaches to mental health and wellbeing

Social and emotional wellbeing and crisis narratives

In the past decade, a dominant narrative has emerged across the globe about a student mental health crisis and the need for urgent action, often assumed to entail formal campus-based psychological or psychiatric interventions (Warwick et al., 2006). This narrative of crisis has positioned young people as anxious, depressed, and suicidal, potentially creating the impression that addressing the mental health of students may be one of the most important global priorities in education.

Although the crisis narrative pre-dated COVID-19, it has gained prominence in the wake of the pandemic because the global response to it disrupted students' academic and social lives and heightened peoples' sensitivity to vulnerability (Bantjes et al., 2023).

Over the last two decades, the crisis narrative of college student mental health has slowly but surely taken hold as the dominant conceptual framework. It defines the problem, shapes our student/faculty experiences, motivates institutional reactions and choices, and has led to constantly shifting sands of challenge and mirage (Brown and Carr, 2019).

It has been argued by some researchers that the crisis framework is neither applicable nor helpful and may even have direct negative impacts at individual, systemic, and cultural levels (Glowacki and Taylor, 2020). According to them, seven significant dynamics have contributed to the evolving narrative. Firstly, advocacy from external stakeholders such as local authorities, and mental health but often lacking in clearly defined goals (2020).

Secondly, the pathologising of normative human distress may have helped to result in the building of assumptions that distress equals pathology and that all distress should go to a mental health professional. Student mental health research that frames relatively mild symptoms of distress and everyday stress as pathological can turn attention and resources away from students with serious mental illnesses (Paris, 2015).

Paradoxically, a crisis narrative may also inadvertently discourage some students from seeking treatment. When academics or the media report ubiquitously high rates of mental disorders and very low treatment rates, they could create the impression that having these symptoms is normal for students (Bantjes et al., 2023).

Thirdly, there may often be an over-reliance on quick surveys among many stakeholders that confirm the narrative, too much attention focused on results that support a crisis narrative, and too little attention on results that do not. These may be amplified by the evolution of media over the past decade including the development of pay-per-click and the rise of social media (Feng et al., 2022).

Fifthly, there is also the impact of the rise of the use of pharmaceuticals in non-serious mental-illness, and the rapid and unprecedent investment in the mental health market (Migone, 2017).

It has also been argued that language and subjectivity has played a part in the narrative by the integrating of specialised jargon (psychology) into the popular culture/language and its impact on encouraging the next generation to use mental health language to describe their everyday experiences. This can result in the commonplace framing of students' difficulties in terms of symptoms and illness which may run the risk of pathologising students' everyday struggles (Madsen, 2014).

Finally, government policy agenda has also helped shape the narrative. Over the decade government policy aspirations to redress mental illness are being replaced with a concern over the potential of young people to disrupt further and higher education which has created a situation in which medicine has become part of the fabric of schooling (Bantjes et al., 2023). According to them this signifies a key policy shift that extends the remit of schooling beyond that of knowledge generation and into the realm of psychological functioning.

Students experiencing mental ill-health are positioned as outside of normative human functioning which legitimatises colleges and schools' application of psychological forms of adjustment where learners willingly submit their psyches to the assessment of experts in the form of peer mentors, counsellors, psychologists, educational specialists, and therapists (Rose, 1989).

Some researchers (Bantjes et al., 2023; Brown and Carr, 2019; Rose, 1989) suggest mental health is seen first and foremost as the means to achievement and academic attainment and therefore that colleges and schools' role in the policy route from mental illness to wellness is now through psychologically reprogramming children towards a hardened approach to school failure and the pressures experienced in daily school life.

It has been argued that there are some alternative ways of viewing the narrative (Bantjes et al., 2023; Brown et al., 2021). These include:

- Questioning and critically evaluating the use of the crisis narrative as a framework. Focussing on long term institutional strategies instead of reacting to the crisis of the moment
- Being mindful of the consequences of labelling normative distress as a mental health condition and re-educating students about normative human distress/coping/support, and empowering a wide variety of help-seeking pathways

- Acknowledging that the linking of human distress to "mental health' represents a mass shared experience and that there is also a lack of treatment capacity for those who are most vulnerable (Hayes et al., 2023)
- Moving beyond diagnostic labels in student mental health research to research that explicitly asks students what they are struggling with, what help they need, and how they would like this help provided (Tonks, 2022)
- Considering ways in which students demonstrate character strengths and wellness acknowledges that mental health is shaped by a range of risk and resilience factors spanning the biopsychosocial spectrum and therefore, policy needs to provide a range of different solutions and responses
- Adopting a life-course approach to promoting student mental health which accepts that some of the suffering students experience is due to negotiation of the typical developmental tasks of young adulthood (e.g., formation of self-identity, learning to tolerate frustration and regulate emotions) instead of encouraging all students who experience such distress to seek professional help (Brown et al., 2021)
- Emphasising that a range of interventions are useful for addressing the normal stressors of college life (including developing healthy relationships with peers and mentors), and that more serious mental disorders are responsive to professional intervention (Cefai et al., 2021)

Rebutting traditional approaches to social and emotional issues in colleges

Research has shown that it is paramount that some of the old assumptions surrounding wellbeing in schools and colleges should be challenged (Brown et al., 2021).

Figure 9.1   Reflection task

How would you rebut the following statements?

Mental health problems are only of concern to specific groups of children and young people.

Pastoral teams and specialist staff are the best response, and that teaching staff cannot be expected to learn skills to support wellbeing issues as well.

A college's central business is education, and its focus should be on learning and achievement.

The mental health of staff is a personal issue to be dealt with outside college.

Some answers:

Evidence shows that this can impact on ALL students and that an early intervention is the most effective approach.

Many emotional issues are not clinical in nature and not best served by specialist interventions, but social models offer broad based approaches that act preventatively.

Research suggests that creating a school ethos that promotes wellbeing, resilience and positive skills has proven able to improve the individual and institutional performance (Lindorff, 2021).

Staff wellbeing is increasingly becoming a priority for the whole college and the evidence suggests taking care of staff and offering them positive skills impacts on the staff but also on the learning climate and the students.

The central principles underpinning a whole college approach to wellbeing

A summary of the research evidence can be organised into various framing principles (CYP, 2021). These are:

- Adopting whole institution thinking. This would help to ensure that all parts of the organisation work coherently together, providing a solid base of universal work to promote wellbeing, and developing a supportive institutional and classroom climate and ethos which builds a sense of connectedness, focus and purpose. This would be based upon the acceptance of emotion and vulnerability, warm relationships, and the celebration of difference. According to research by Brown et al. (2021) the creation of safe and confidential areas for students and staff are particularly important to supporting wellbeing. The use of safe, confidential spaces for students to seek help must be balanced with the need to avoid stigma around certain areas of the campus.
- Community involvement. According to the research of Goldberg et al. (2018) everyone who is involved in or in contact with the school or college system has a part to play. This should include within the college, Senior Leadership Team, parents/carers, students, grandparents, estates staff, receptionists, associations, tutors, governors, outside agencies that come into contact with the child, pastoral leads, college counsellors. The external bodies would include Local Authorities, counselling service, Educational Psychologists, Public Health England, third sector mental health services, Police Schools Liaison, CAMHS, Education Welfare Officers in Local Authorities, Additional Learning Needs specialists in Local Authorities.
- Prioritising professional learning and staff development. There would also need to be intensive skills-based programmes of interventions including staff wellbeing. The aim of these would be to enable staff to understand and

reduce the risk factors that can affect wellbeing, and help students develop the emotional and mental skills to overcome adverse circumstances. This would also raise staff awareness about mental health problems and keep them abreast of new challenges posed by technology for example, such as cyberbullying (Brewster and Cox, 2023).
- Implementing targeted programmes and interventions (including curriculum). These would include the teaching of social and emotional skills, attitudes, and values, integrated into the mainstream processes of college life using specialist staff to initiate innovative and specialist programmes to ensure they are implemented authentically. The system-level programmes would also involve young people in classroom sessions, building relationships between schools and communities, having clear underlying theory, and including staff training.
- There would need to be a strategic focus on the mental health needs of vulnerable and marginalised students. Students exposed to risk, disadvantage and marginalisation are at greater risk of developing mental health problems. These include young people coming from low socioeconomic status (SES) or migrant backgrounds, as well as young people exposed to abuse, violence, and bullying, and those who have experienced other forms of trauma (Cefai et al., 2021).

Figure 9.2   Staff development task

- *Here is an idea for staff development session aimed at enabling teaching and support staff to evaluate the mental health needs of vulnerable and marginalized students and engage in proactive discussions about strategies to support them.*
- *Instructions:*
- Preparatory Work (15 minutes):
  - *Provide staff members with background information on the concept of vulnerability and marginalization, including its effects on mental health.*
  - *Share information about common mental health challenges faced by vulnerable and marginalized students*
- Small Group Discussions (30 minutes):
  - *Divide staff members into small groups and assign each group a specific scenario or case study featuring a vulnerable and marginalized student*
  - *In their groups, staff members should discuss the mental health needs and concerns of the student, considering factors such as cultural, socio-economic, and individual experiences*
  - *Encourage participants to thought shower strategies and support mechanisms that can be implemented to address the identified needs and promote the student's wellbeing.*

- *Each group should appoint a member to summarie their findings and recommendations*
- *Large Group Sharing and Reflection (20 minutes):*
  - *Bring all participants together and invite the group representatives to present their small group discussions and recommendations*
  - *Facilitate an open discussion to exchange ideas, insights, and perspectives on the evaluation of mental health needs and strategies to support vulnerable and marginalised students*
  - *Allow staff members to share personal experiences, resources, and successful practices they have employed in similar situations*
- *Action Planning (15 minutes):*
  - *Provide a template or worksheet for staff members to individually or in small groups develop action plans tailored to support vulnerable and marginalised students' mental health needs*
  - *Encourage staff members to consider both short-term and long-term strategies, including referrals, partnerships with community organizations, and ongoing professional development opportunities*
- *Wrap-Up and Next Steps (5 minutes):*
  - *Summarise the key insights and actions discussed during the session*
  - *Outline any future steps or follow-up activities, such as additional trainings or collaborative initiatives, to ensure ongoing support for vulnerable and marginalised students' mental health*
- *Note: This task aims to facilitate a constructive and solution-oriented discussion among staff members concerning the mental health needs of vulnerable and marginalised students. It also encourages collaborative planning and sharing of best practices to enhance support and promote their wellbeing.*

Appropriate policies

These would include policies and practice in key areas such as behaviour, and diversity, including tackling prejudice and stigma around mental health. Research suggests that Senior Management Teams could play a critical role in reviewing school and college policy, alongside parents/families, governors, and students, who are all seen as partners in developing and reviewing both policy and action plans. Cefai et al.'s (2021) European research findings suggest that anti bullying policy should be prioritised as involvement in bullying increases the risk of mental health problems among victims, perpetrators, and bystanders.

A joined-up approach

According to research by Brown et al. (2021) this needed to function both within school and with services/agencies outside school and could include having a team of staff who all understood and promoted it and transparent delegation and shared responsibility throughout the staff and wider partners. Central to this approach would be working with wider members of the community, including health professionals, community organisations and also other inspectorates to provide clear pathways for students to access support. By developing relationships, mental health services can be brought in quickly and effectively to alleviate pressure on schools and colleges when students' mental health needs become greater or more specialised than the skills of the staff. Staff would need to receive training in order to be able to work effectively with external services and have their workloads adjusted accordingly.

Effective whole college approaches

According to research by Warwick et al. (2006) some of the most effective whole college supportive practices would include:

- Offering students, a range of support services. This would be including those related to learning study support as well as emotional support and embedding issues regarding mental health into a range of college policies, including those on disability, equal opportunities, and diversity. This was felt by their respondents to be central to ensuring that young people could choose the type of support they felt was most relevant to them. It also helped the surveyed college to meet the range of mental health problems students were presenting with, and created an ethos of support, trust and inclusiveness within the setting (2006)
- Having in post a professional with a lead responsibility for addressing students' mental health. This person would be able to coordinate activities within the college, liaise with external agencies, provide some direct support to students, and contribute to the professional development of all college staff regarding mental health and emotional wellbeing
- Providing opportunities for staff development regarding mental health issues. Awareness-raising, skills development, and clearer guidance and support structures within colleges were felt to improve the capacity of all staff working in the college to effectively identify, support and refer on young people at risk of, or experiencing, mental health difficulties
- Listening to the Student voice. However, involving students themselves in developing college provision, and promoting students to have a voice or say in service development, provision, and feedback, was invaluable in developing the kind of inclusive college ethos needed to promote students' mental health and emotional wellbeing

Figure 9.3 Teaching task

I tasked a student group to come up with 10 different ways they could become involved in advancing wellbeing policy and practices in the college. This is what they discussed:

Student Advisory Group: Establish a student-led advisory group composed of students interested in mental health and wellbeing. This board can provide input and feedback to senior management on policy development

Surveys and Feedback: Conduct surveys and collect feedback from students on their experiences and suggestions for improving mental health and wellbeing support on campus

Focus Groups: Organise focus groups with students across each curriculum area and have open and facilitated discussions about mental health concerns, existing support systems, and ideas for policy development

Guest Speakers: Invite experts in mental health and wellbeing to speak at the college and engage with students, gathering their perspectives and ideas for policy development

Workshops and Training: Offer workshops and on-line and off-line training sessions for students to learn about mental health first aid, stress management techniques, and self-care practices. This empowers students to be part of the solution and informs policy development

Social Media Campaigns: Encourage students to share their experiences and suggestions for enhancing mental health support on campus via social media platforms, using designated hashtags. This can generate valuable input for policy development

Student-led Initiatives: Support student-led initiatives aimed at promoting mental health and wellbeing. This can include student-run workshops, support groups, or awareness campaigns

Peer Mentoring Programme: Establish a peer mentoring programme where students can support and guide each other in matters related to mental health. Involve students in designing and implementing the programme

Student Surveys and Assessments: Task students with creating and administering anonymous surveys or assessments to gauge the mental health needs of their peers. This data can inform policy development

Collaborative thought shower sessions: Organise collaborative thoughtshowering sessions with students in tutorials or in seminar groups encouraging them to share their ideas and suggestions for policies with the college's Mental Health Team

Why not try a similar task with your own student group and pilot one of their ideas and then evaluate the success of it?

Creating a collegiate environment

Colleges are gathering more data on staff mental health, and many are expanding their support programmes for their employees, including mentoring, counselling, signposting to services and wellbeing sessions.

Support for FE staff is very variable, however, and the Association of Colleges (AoC) survey reports that 62% of colleges have seen a significant or slight increase in staff accessing mental health and wellbeing services, but 35% of colleges admit they don't regularly collate data on staff MH and wellbeing, and therefore it is not surprising that 15% of colleges acknowledged that they do not know if there has been an increase in use of support services (AoC, 2023).

Respondents to the survey said that the main reasons behind the increases include return of an existing mental health problem brought on by stress and increased workload which is echoed in the findings of Education Support's Teacher Wellbeing Index, where 78% of education staff reported that they have experienced poor mental health due to their work, with symptoms including anxiety, exhaustion, burnout, depression, and acute stress (2022).

According to Education and Training Foundation (ETF) research creating a collegiate environment is a fundamental for building protective resilience and improving wellbeing across the further education (FE) workforce. Central to this is building strong workforce relationships which requires trust, respect, and self-awareness (ETF, 2023). These can:

Improve collaboration, communication, and teamwork, leading to better outcomes for learners and the FE settings and therefore lead to a more enjoyable and fulfilling work environment, increasing overall job satisfaction.

Serve as a valuable professional network that can be beneficial throughout your career and provide opportunities for professional development, networking and growth within the FE setting and create a positive and supportive work environment that contributes to the overall learner experience, and which can help with staff retention.

They suggest that barriers to this can include online or remote environments, workload, lack of support and check ins, reliance on technology, structural barriers such as lack of cross departmental working, varying communication skills, management by dictat. (ETF, 2022a).

Figure 9.4 Reflective exercise

A quick and simple reflective exercise you can try with your team is to rank each question below on a scale of 1–10 (feel free to add your own questions as you wish):

- *How satisfied are you in your role?*
- *Do you feel listened to by team members?*

> - *How well does your team work together?*
> - *How valued do you feel?*
> - *What is your level of motivation?*
>
> *Once complete, collate the answers together as a group. This provides the opportunity to discuss each colleague's thoughts without directly confronting individuals and can be used as a basis to start making improvements collectively as a team.*

Psychological safety

Psychological safety is largely a product of an individual's relationships and their environment. the concept highlights the necessity of meeting employees' basic psychological and safety needs before attempting to build in further staff focused initiatives such as coaching or team building days (Broglia et al., 2018). Here are some effective ways to provide psychological safety:

- Encourage open communication. Establish a culture of open dialogue and active listening. Encourage staff members to express their thoughts, concerns, and ideas without fear of judgment or reprisal. Create platforms for staff to provide feedback, share suggestions, and contribute to decision-making processes
- Foster a supportive culture. Encourage collaboration, teamwork, and mutual respect among staff members. Celebrate diversity and create an inclusive environment where everyone feels valued and included. Promote a sense of belonging by organising team-building activities, social events, and recognition programs
- School or college leaders should model the behaviours they expect from their staff. Demonstrate empathy, respect, and vulnerability. Encourage constructive feedback, admit mistakes, and show appreciation for staff contributions. By setting a positive example, leaders can inspire trust and encourage staff to do the same
  - Provide professional development opportunities for staff members. Offer training programs, workshops, and seminars that enhance their skills, knowledge, and confidence. Supporting their growth and career progression sends a message that their development and wellbeing are valued
  - Promote and prioritise work-life balance by implementing policies that support flexible schedules, reasonable workloads, and time off. Encourage staff to take breaks, use vacation days, and engage in self-care activities. By prioritising well-being, you show that you care about their overall happiness and mental health

- Clearly communicate expectations, roles, and responsibilities to staff members. Provide them with the necessary resources, tools, and support to perform their jobs effectively. Offer regular check-ins, mentoring, and coaching to address any challenges they may face and provide guidance when needed
- Actively address conflicts, concerns, and grievances in a timely manner. Provide a fair and transparent process for conflict resolution and ensure confidentiality. When staff members feel that their concerns are taken seriously and resolved appropriately, it contributes to their sense of psychological safety
- Implement initiatives that support staff wellbeing, such as wellness programs, mindfulness sessions, and access to counselling services. Encourage healthy work habits and self-care practices, such as regular exercise, adequate sleep, and stress management techniques

Conclusions

There is much evidence to demonstrate the positive effects of whole school approaches on social, emotional and behavioural adjustment (Bonell et al., 2020; Goldberg et al. 2018), as well as other outcomes including educational attainment but questions still remain as to which structures and processes are needed to embed effective practices into school routines in a sustainable way (Brown et al., 2021).

The recommendations made in this chapter require the transformation of traditional education systems and teaching practices in schools. They entail some significant and widespread changes in the way education systems are conceived, designed, and operationalised, with significant shifts in roles and power relationships. It is clear that many colleges are making the right moves in these directions (AoC, 2023). It is also clear 'Such a change may be potentially threatening to some educational authorities, school staff, parents, professionals and others in the wider community, who may find their understandings, expectations and sense of identity being challenged.' (Cefai et al., 2021).

As suggested in these recommendations, a combination of legislation, advocacy, policy development, education and training, the provision of multi-level support and intersectoral collaboration will therefore be required to help colleges and schools adopt this approach and to implement it in the everyday life of the institution and bottom-up, participatory process involving the whole college and school community would ensure that any changes made would be meaningful, well implemented and sustained in the long term.

This book has aimed to provide educators with comprehensive knowledge and practical strategies to effectively support the social and emotional wellbeing of college students. Throughout the chapters, we have explored various mental health and wellbeing issues that students commonly face, including anxiety, depression, stress, and loneliness. We have also highlighted the importance of having college mental health policies and procedures in place to ensure a safe and supportive environment for all students.

It has emphasised the significance of adopting a whole-college approach to mental health and wellbeing. By implementing a comprehensive and integrated system, colleges can address the diverse needs of their students and provide them with the necessary support. From establishing student advisory boards to conducting regular needs assessments, these approaches can guide colleges in developing effective strategies and initiatives.

Moreover, the book has provided practical strategies to support mental health and wellbeing in college settings. From fostering a sense of belonging through community and connection to promoting self-care and stress-management techniques, educators can implement small changes that have a significant positive impact on student wellbeing. Through providing pastoral care, basic counselling skills, and fostering a culture of empathy and support, college staff members can create a safe space for students to seek help and support.

However, it is important to acknowledge the challenges that educators themselves face in supporting the mental health and wellbeing of college students. In addressing the wellbeing of students, educators must also prioritise their own self-care and wellbeing. Educational institutions should provide ongoing professional development and support systems to help educators build resilience and cope with the emotional demands of their role.

In conclusion, this book has attempted to provide a comprehensive guide for educators in supporting the social and emotional wellbeing of college students. By recognising the main mental health and wellbeing issues, implementing college mental health policies and procedures, integrating practical strategies, and prioritising the wellbeing of educators, colleges can create an environment that fosters the mental health and wellbeing of all students. Through a collective effort and commitment to supporting students, we can contribute to their overall success and future wellbeing.

References

Association of Colleges, (AoC). (2023). *Mental Health Survey Report*. London: AoC.

Bantjes, J., Hunt, X., and Stein, D. J. (2023). Anxious, depressed, and suicidal: Crisis narratives in university student mental health and the need for a balanced approach to student wellness. *International Journal of Environmental Research and Public Health*, 20(6): 4859. doi:10.3390/ijerph20064859

Bonell, C., Dodd, M., Allen, E., Bevilacqua, L., McGowan, J., Opondo, C., Sturgess, J., Elbourne, D., Warren, E., Viner, R.M. (2020). Broader impacts of an intervention to transform school environments on student behaviour and school functioning: post hoc analyses from the INCLUSIVE cluster randomised controlled tria. *IBMJ Open*, 10: e031589. doi:10.1136/bmjopen-2019-031589

Brewster, L., and Cox, A. M. (2023). Taking a 'whole-university' approach to student mental health: The contribution of academic libraries. *Higher Education Research and Development*, 42(1): 33–47. doi:10.1080/07294360.2022.2043249

Broglia, E., Millings, A., and Barkham, M. (2018). Challenges to addressing student mental health in embedded counselling services: A survey of UK higher and further education institutions. *British Journal of Guidance and Counselling*, 46(4): 441–55. doi:10.1080/03069885.2017.1370695

Brown, C., and Carr, S. (2019). Education policy and mental weakness: A response to a mental health crisis. *Journal of Education Policy*, 34(2): 242–66. 10.1080/02680939.2018.1445293

Brown, R., Van Godwin, J., Edwards, A., Burdon, M., and Moore, G. (2021). Development of a theory of change and evaluability assessment for the whole school approach to mental health and emotional wellbeing. Available at: https://gov.wales/whole-school-approach-mental-and-emotional-wellbeing-evaluability-assessment; https://gov.wales/whole-school-approach-mental-and-emotional-wellbeing-evaluability-assessment

Cefai, C., Simões, C., and Caravita, S. (2021). 'A systemic, whole-school approach to mental health and wellbeing in schools in the EU' NESET report. Luxembourg: Publications Office of the European Union. doi:10.2766/50546

Children and Young People's Mental Health Coalition. (2021). Promoting children and young people's mental health and wellbeing: A whole school or college approach. *HM*. https://assets.publishing.service.gov.uk/media/614cc965d3bf7f718518029c/Promoting_children_and_young_people_s_mental_health_and_wellbeing.pdf

Education and Training Foundation. (2022b). *Helping Staff Balance Work and Life. A Guide for FE Managers and Leaders*. London: ETF. https://www.et-foundation.co.uk/wp-content/uploads/2023/02/Helping-Staff-Balance-Work-and-Life.pdf

Education and Training Foundation. (2023). *Building Collegiate Relationships. A Guide for Further Education Staff*. London: ETF. https://www.et-foundation.co.uk/wp-content/uploads/2023/04/Building-Collegiate-Relationships_04.04.23.pdf

Feng, Y., Gu, W., Dong, F., et al. (2022). Overexposure to COVID-19 information amplifies emotional distress: A latent moderated mediation model. *Translational Psychiatry*, 12: 287. doi:10.1038/s41398-022-02048-z

Glowacki, E. M., and Taylor, M. A. (2020). Health hyperbolism: A study in health crisis rhetoric. *Qualitative Health Research*, 30(12): 1953–64. doi:10.1177/1049732320916466

Goldberg, J., Sklad, M., Elfrink, T., Schreurs, K., Bohlmeijer, E., and Clarke, A. (2018). Effectiveness of interventions adopting a whole school approach to enhancing social and emotional development: A meta-analysis. *European Journal of Psychology of Education*, 34. doi:10.1007/s10212-018-0406-9

Hayes, D., Jarvis-Beesley, P., Mitchell, D., Polley M., and Husk K. [On behalf of the NASP Academic Partners Collaborative]. (2023). *The Impact of Social Prescribing on Children and Young People's Mental Health and Wellbeing*. London: National Academy for Social Prescribing.

Lindorff, A. (2021). The impact of promoting student well being on student academic and non academic outcomes: An analysis of the evidence. *Oxford Impact*. https://oxfordimpact.oup.com/wp-content/uploads/2020/10/Wellbeing-Impact-Study-Report.pdf

Madsen, O.J. (2014). Therapeutic Culture. *Encyclopedia of Critical Psychology*. doi:10.1007/978-1-4614-5583-7_313

Migone, P. (2017). The influence of pharmaceutical companies. *Research in Psychotherapy*, 20(2): 276. doi:10.4081/ripppo.2017.276

Paris, J. (2015). *Overdiagnosis in Psychiatry: How Modern Psychiatry Lost Its Way While Creating a Diagnosis for Almost All of Life's Misfortunes*. Oxford, UK: Oxford University Press.

Rose, G. (1989). The mental health of populations. In P. Williams, G. Wilkinson, & K. Rawnsley (Eds.), *The scope of epidemiological psychiatry: Essays in honour of Michael Shepherd* (pp. 77–85). Taylor & Frances/Routledge.

Tonks, A. (2022). Exploring primary school senior mental health leads' experiences of supporting mental health across a school and wider community: An interpretative phenomenological analysis. Unpublished doctoral thesis for the University of Essex. https://repository.essex.ac.uk/33344/

Warwick, I., Maxwell, C., Simon, A., Statham, J., and Aggleton, P. (2006). Mental health and emotional well-being of students in further education – A scoping study. https://discovery.ucl.ac.uk/id/eprint/10000056/

10 General mental health and wellbeing services

National services

Anxiety UK

Anxiety UK was established to promote the relief and rehabilitation of persons living with agoraphobia and associated anxiety disorders, phobias and conditions, in particular, but not exclusively, by raising awareness in such topics. It aims to provide advice, support and information for people who experience anxiety. Includes specific information for people supporting children and young people with anxiety.

03444 775 774
07537 416 905 (textline)
anxietyuk.org.uk/get-help/helping-your-child

Barnardo's

Barnardo's see ourselves as a children's health and social care charity and they provide practical information and emotional support for children, young people and families which includes specific information on mental health problems.

barnardos.org.uk

Beat

Beat is the UK's eating disorder charity. It was founded in 1989 as the Eating Disorders Association, its mission is to end the pain and suffering caused by eating disorders. It provides a helpline, webchat and online support groups for people with eating problems, as well as family and friends. Includes specific information and support for carers

0808 801 0677 (England)
0808 801 0433 (Wales)
beateatingdisorders.co.uk.

Mental Health Direct

This is a local service that be contacted for mental health help and advice 24 hours per day or night. Callers can be given access to speak directly to a mental health professional or provide advice as to what service to contact to get the support they need

Hub of hope

hubofhope.co.uk

They provide UK-wide database of mental health charities and organisations offering advice and support. *MIND* They offer a variety of services:

Mind's helplines provide information and support by phone and email.
Local Minds offer face-to-face services across England and Wales. These services include talking therapies, peer support and advocacy.
Side by Side is our supportive online community for anyone experiencing a mental health problem.

No panic

They supply support for people experiencing panic attacks and obsessive-compulsive disorder (OCD). They provide information and an advice line for parents and carers of young people.

0300 772 9844
nopanic.org.uk/advice-for-parents

Place2Be place

This service offers counselling support for young people in schools helping them to cope with wide-ranging and complex social issues including bullying, bereavement, domestic violence, family breakdown, neglect and trauma.

2be.org.uk

Email: enquiries@place2be.org.uk

Tel: 0207 923 5500

Samaritans

Samaritans are open 24/7 for people to talk about any concerns, worries and troubles they're going through. You can visit some Samaritans branches in person.

Tel: 116 123
jo@samaritans.org
samaritans.org

Student minds

studentminds.org.uk

This is a charity working with students, service users, professionals and academics to develop new and innovative ways to improve the mental health of students. Offers information and support for students.

Time to change

This campaign is run by the leading mental health charities Mind and Rethink Mental Illness and aims to challenges the stigmas attached to mental health issues. It's website includes resources for campaigning against mental health stigma and discrimination.
time-to-change.org.uk

Women's aid (England)

Woman's Aid provides information and support for women and children in England who have experienced domestic abuse. It provides support by live chat, a directory of local services and a forum.

chat.womensaid.org.uk (live chat)
helpline@womensaid.org.uk
womensaid.org.uk

YoungMinds

YoungMinds is the UK's leading charity fighting for a future where all young minds are supported and empowered, It provides mental health information and emotional support for young people, their parents and those who care for them. It also offers a Parents Helpline, email service and webchat for support, signposting and advice.

Tel: 0808 802 5544
youngminds.org.uk

Local services

College mental health and wellbeing services
    These can provide a series of local internal interventions including counselling for students and staff.

Togetherall

Students can access 24/7 mental health and wellbeing support from a safe online community with on hand counsellors and psychotherapists. Togetherall also offers a range of activities and self-help resources that allow students to work through what's troubling them. Students can register using their student email addresses at www.togetherall.com.

Index

Pages in *italics* refer to figures and pages in **bold** refer to tables.

Academy of Learning (AoL) 64
action planning model 123, 125
active listening (AL) 143, 163–166, *167*, *193*, 223
active questioning to support students: choice/option questioning 155; circular questions 154; continuing professional development activity *156–157*; CRT questions 155, **155–156**; Gestalt style questions 153–154; Guru questioning 157, *157–158*; narrativising questions 158, *159*; SFBT questioning *see* solution focused behavioural therapy; transitional questions 154
adolescent behaviours 152
Aggleton, P. 230
Akehurst, Georgie 13
Alessandra, T. 163
Alexander, Kate 13
Allen, J. 5
all-or-nothing thinking 184
Almansa, J. 15
Amendt, J. H. 174
Anglin, K. 50
anorexia nervosa (AN) 43
anxiety disorders: COVID-19 crisis 39; generalised anxiety disorder 39; major depressive disorder 41; obsessive-compulsive disorder 40–41; phobia 40; post-traumatic stress disorder 41–42; social anxiety disorder 39; uncomfortable emotional state 38
Anxiety UK 238
assessment for learning (AFL) 97
Association of Colleges (AoC) 232

Bailey, D. 52
Balint, M. 169
Bandura, A. 92
Bates, R. 75
Baxter, J. 15
Becker, G. 209
Berg, J. M. 219, *220*
Best, R. 125
binge eating disorder (BED) 43
Bohlmeijer, E. 227
Bolton, Paul 99
Boyce, T. 5
Bradbury, A. 13
Brent, D. 35, 53
British Association of Counsellors and Psychotherapists (BACP) 126–127
Broome, M.R. 22
Brown, R. 227, 230
Bryant, R. D. 174
Buchanan, D. 31
bulimia nervosa (BN) 43
Burdon, M. 227, 230
burnout 201–202, 204, *204–205*, 207, 213
Butler, N. 75
Buzzeo, Jonathan 13
Byford, Morwenna 13

Campbell-Jack, D. 77
Caravita, S. 229
Carli, Vladimir 64
Cefai, C. 229
Chandler, B. 123–124
Chen, C. 22
Chen, Guo-Ming 21
Chen, R. 22

Child and Adolescent Mental Health Services (CAMHS) 53, 63, 81
children and young people's mental health (CYPMH) 80
Choice and Reality Therapy (CRT) 155, *155–156*
Clarke, A. 227
cognitive behavioural therapy (CBT) 5, 68, 175–176, 196
Coleman, N. 72, 74
collegiate environment 232–233
Community and Mental Health Services (CAMHS) 80
community-level stressors 33
continuing professional development (CPD) activity *156–157*
Cook, Joseph 13
Corcoran, P. 51
Corrigan, P. W. 104
COVID-19 13, 224; crisis 39; impact of 33; lockdown 73; lockdowns on depression in young people 34–37, 42–43
curriculum teaching and learning 60
cyberbullying 16, 228

Dalton, A. D. 15
Daly, M. 14
Deci, E. L. 93
De Kroon, M. L. A. 15
De Leo, D. 51
descriptive feedback 172
de Wilde, E. J. 51
Diagnostic and Statistical Manual of Mental Health Disorders (DSM-V) 32
disabled students allowances (DSAs) 72
D'Onofrio, B. 15
Drescher, J. 22
Druss, Benjamin G. 104
Duda, B. 105
Dutton, J. E. 219, *220*

eating disorders (ED) 42–43; anorexia nervosa 43; bulimia nervosa 43; in older learners 45; other specified feeding or eating disorders 44
Ebanks-Silvera, De-Jon 13
educational institutions and educators 2
Education and Training Foundation (ETF) 232
Education Support Partnership in England (ESP) 205
Edwards, A. 227, 230

Eirich, R. 39
Elfrink, T. 227
Emery, R. 15
emotional feedback 172
emotional health issues 1, 123–149
emotional resilience 5
Equality Act 2020 7
Erikson, E. H. 20
Etheridge, B. 35
Ethical Framework for the Counselling Professions (EFfCP) 126
evaluative feedback 172
Eyre, O. 35

Fancourt, D. 13
Farrell, T. S. C. 169
fatigue 31–32, 97, 207
Fay, D. 220
fear of judgment/stigma 170, 223
feedback: affirmative statements 174, *174–175*; challenging and 177, *177*; cheerleading 175; descriptive 172; emotional 172; encouragement and support 173; evaluative 172; interpretive 172–173; normalising 175; process of goal setting 173; providing compliments 174; reframing negative thoughts 176, *176*; self-awareness 173
Fekete, S. 51
Fletcher, D. 210, 214
fortune telling 184
Frese, M. 220
Fuller-Thomson, E. 15
further education (FE) 1, 123–149, 232
Further Education Development Agency (FEDA) 123
further education (FE) workforce 1, 232

Gao, Y. 22
Geddes, I. 5
General Data Protection Regulation (GDPR) 103
generalised anxiety disorder (GAD) 39
Gestalt style self-reflection activities *161–163*
Gestalt therapy 153, 157
Gettens, K. 105
Gilliland, B. E. 170
Glazzard, J. 205
Glick, Oliver 75
Goldberg, J. 227
Goldblatt, P. 5

Grady, M. 5
Greenberg, M. T. 205
Groom, Carola 72, 74
Gullone, E. 93

Hadlaczky, Gergö 64
Hart, L. 50
Hawton, K. 51
Health and Safety Executive (HSE) 201
Heinrich, L. M. 93
Heron, J. 131
Hetrick, S. E. 50
Hewitt, A. 51
Hökby, Sebastian 64
holistic approach 3, 97
Houlston, N. 73
Hunsaker, P. 163

identification survey 62
intelligent student referral systems 76–79
interpretive feedback 172–173
Ivey, A. 129

Jacobs, G. M. 169
James, R. K. 170
Jarvis C. 125
Jennings, P. A. 205
Ji, L. 22
job crafting 219–220, *220–221*
Johnson, S. E. 15
jumping to conclusions 184, *185*

Khnana, P. 210
Kleckner, T. 174

Lawrence, D. 15
leadership and management 60
learning development model 123–125
lesbian, gay, bisexual, transgender or of other minority sexualities and sexual identities (LGBT+) 11, 22, 100
Levitt, D. H. 171
Lewis, J. 99
LGBTQ+ 48
listening: accurately *168*; active 163–166, *167*; mindful *168–169*; third ear approach 168–169
Liu, R. T. 47

Madge, N. 51
Madigan, S. 39
magnification 184

major depressive disorder (MDD) 41
Marmot, M. 5, 31
Maxwell, C. 63, 230
McArthur, B. A. 39
McLeod, J. 129
McNeish, D. 5
mental and emotional health (MEH) 12–13
mental disorder 15, 21, 30, 38–39, 53, 224, 226
mental filter 184
mental health 5; access to resources and support 84; attitudes to 8–9; awareness training 70; changing attitudes towards 9–10; college policies and procedures 62–63; continuum of 6; employment transition 86–87; identity and 20–21; impact of academic pressure on 16–18; impact of bullying on well being 16; impact of divorce on young people's 15; impact of tests and examinations on 18–20; impact of the pandemic on 13–15; intelligent student referral systems 76–79; joined-up approach 230; matter to teachers 7–8; parental issues 85; partnership with mental health professionals 84; peer support and 72–76; policies and practice 229; policy 60; proactive communication 83; problems 35; students transition 86; suicide training 71; and wellbeing 61; of young people in education 11–13
mental health and wellbeing: general services 238–240; *see also* national services; institutional support 206–207; self-care methods 207, *207–208*; teachers' *see* teachers' wellbeing approaches; at work 201
mental health first aid (MHFA) 70–71
Mental Health Foundation (MHF) 31
Mental Health Services and Schools Link Expanded Programme 77
Mental Health Support Teams (MHSTs) 80–81
mental illness 7–8, 9, 43, 70, 92, 104–106, 112, 114, 224–225, 240
Mikolajczak Degrauwe, K. 18
Milan Systemic Model of Family Therapy 154
Mkrtchian, Anahit 64
modern peer support 73
Molodynski, A. 15

Moore, G. 227, 230
Morgan, A. 50
multi-disciplinary approach 65
Mustanski, B. 47

Narrative therapy 158
National Association of Schoolmasters Union of Women Teachers (NASUWT) 203
National Autistic Society 49
national services: Anxiety UK 238; Barnardo's 238; Beat 238; hub of hope 239; local services 240; mental health direct 239; nopanic 239; place2be place 239; samaritans 239; studentminds 240; togetherall 240; women's aid (England) 240; YoungMinds 240
Newton, Becci 13
NHS Digital survey 30
nonverbal communication skills: eye contact 143–145; facial expressions 145–146; open body posture 142–143

obsessive-compulsive disorder (OCD) 40–41, 239
O'Connor, B. 159
Oenema, A 18
older adolescents 30
other specified feeding or eating disorders (OSFEDs) 43–44
Ou, J. 22
overgeneralisation 184
Overseas Economic Corporation Development (OECD) 14, 17–18

panic disorder (PD) 39–40, 106, 175
Park, N. 217
Patel, Rakhee 13
Patel, V. 35
Paynter, P. C. 210
peer support 73; programmes 74; types of 73–74
Perales, F. 15
Perlick, Deborah A. 104
personalisation 77, 184
personal self and wellness 215, *215–216*
Peterson, C. 217
phobia 39–40, 175
physical wellbeing and learning 92
Pickering, M. 164
Plutchik's wheel of emotions 181–182

positive actions: accomplishment 217, *218*; engagement 217, *218*; meaning 217, *218*; positive emotion 217, *218*; relationships 217, *218*
positive psychology 193, 217, 219
post-compulsory education 1, 3
post-traumatic stress disorder (PTSD) 13, 41–42
professional self 214–215, *215*
psychological safety 92, 96, 233–234
psychological wellbeing and learning 92–93

Qi, J. 22
Quigg, Z. 75

Racine, N. 39
real-life scenarios 2
reflecting skills 182–183
reflection of feeling (RoF) 164, 182–183, 189–190
Reijneveld, S. A. 15
resilience-building strategies 65
Ribbens, P. 125
Rickard, Catherine 13
Robinson, E. 14
Robinson, J. 50
Rogers, C. R. 164–165
Rose, A. 205
Rossouw, Jurie 210
Rossouw, P. 210
Ryan, R. M. 93

Sarkar, M. 210, 214
Schreurs, K. 227
Schulte-Körne, G. 93
self-awareness 2, 73, 98, 127–128, 137–138, 164–165, 171–174, 183, 189–190, 196, 214, 216
self-care 207; action plan *215–216*; developing approaches to *208–209*; joy of practice and 209, *209*
self-esteem 1, 5, 8, 12, *20*, 22, 42, 47, 51, 69, 73–74, 80–81, 97, 125, 152, 175, 210
self-harming *46–47*, 46–49, *49*; borderline personality disorder 52; distressing emotions 50; exposure to self-harm 50; failed suicide attempt 52; non-specific signs of 50; relationship difficulties 50; school/work difficulties 51; sense of isolation 50; social comparison 50

self-monitoring *130*, 196–197
self-reflection task 61, 67
Seligman, M. E. P. 217
Senior Leadership Team (SLT) 211, 227
Senior Mental Health Lead (SHML) 63–64
sexual identity 21–22
shame/embarrassment 50, 115, 170
silence 130, *167*, 169–171
Simões, C. 229
Simon, A. 230
situations-thoughts-consequences framework (STC) 198
Sklad, M. 227
Skovholt, T. M. 214
sleep difficulties 32
Slemp, G. R. 220
Slimmen, S. 18
sluggishness 32
Smith, C. 73
social anxiety disorder (SAD) 39
social media 3, 12, *36*, 39, 50, 225, *231*
social wellbeing and learning 92–93
socio-economic status (SES) 12, 31, 228
solution focused behavioural therapy (SFBT) 175; coping questions 160, *161*; exception questions *161*; future-focused questions 160; goal development questions 159, *160*; pre-session change question 159; scaling questions 160, *161*
Spantig, L. 35
specialist mental health mentors (SMHMs) 71–72
Standardised Assessment Report (SAR) 123
Staples-Bradley, L. K. 105
Statham, J. 230
Steen, T. A. 217
Steptoe, A. 13
Stöber, J. 19
strength-based vocabulary 193
stress management 1, *36–37*, 65–66, 68, 97
students': attitudes towards education 112; background issues 132; communication styles 112–114; congruence 136–137; counsellors 67–69; cultural boundaries 111; different cultures 112; emotional problems 132–133; expertise and referral 109; frames of reference theory 134–136; impact of mental health stigma on 114–116; incongruence 137–138; independence and engagement 109; language barriers 111; levels of distress 133–134; mental health 1, 3; mental ill-health 225; mental wellbeing 3, 61; in post-compulsory education 3; professional boundaries 110; reflecting skills 182–183; reflection of feeling 183; roles and boundaries 108–109; seating issues 138–140; self-disclosure 105–106; self-reflection 98; services 66; shared and agreed boundaries 110–111; signs and symptoms of mental health distress in 131–132; stigma and discrimination 144; stigma around mental health 111; teacher-student interaction 106; time 109; voice 60
students' mental health support and needs: active listening 163–166; active questioning to support *see* active questioning to support students; barriers to summarising 166; feedback to students *see* feedback; listening with third ear 168–169; noticing what is missing 166–167; observation 152, *153*; using pauses and silences 169–171
Subasinghe, A. 50
suicidal ideation 35, 47, 52–54, 71, *103*, 116
suicidal thoughts 13, 22, 32, 52, 71, 133, *138*
Sutin, A. 14
Sykes, Wendy 72, 74

teacher resilience: belonging 211–212; domains of 210, *210–211*; help-seeking 212; learning 212
teachers': absenteeism 201, 205; burnout 201–202, 204, *204–205*, 207, 213; categories of intervention 131; cognitive triangle 182–188, *184*; context of stress 200–201; and counselling skills 126–128; counselling skills models 129; dual relationships and boundaries 140–142; gestures when supporting students 146–149; gratitude journaling *216*; helping skills model 129–130; key roles and responsibilities 125–126; mental health and burnout self-evaluation checklist *204–205*; methods to reflect a student's feelings 189–190; micro skills model 129;

micro-skills of listening 188; mindful breathing 216; monitoring student 196–198; motivation and language 193–195; nonverbal communication skills 142–146; paraphrasing 191; personal tutoring role 124–125; potential tasks 169; purpose of reflecting feelings 189; reflecting meaning 190–191; reflection of feeling 182; reflective journaling 216; school and college counsellors 126; work-related stress 201–204

teachers' wellbeing approaches: developing resilience on an individual level 214; help seeking 212; impact of poor resilience on teachers 210–212; impact on student achievement 205–206; institutional support 206–207; institutions and resilience 212–213, 213; job crafting 219–220, 220–221; joy of practice and self-care 209, 209; learning 212; The PERMA model 217–218, 218; personal self and wellness 215, 215–216; potential stressors in work environment 201–204; professional self 214–215, 215; resilience 210; self-care 206–207, 207–209

Thapar, A. 35
The Children Act 2004 103
Theodosiou, L. 75
The PERMA model 217–218, 218
The Prevention of Terrorism Act 2005 103
The Proceeds of Crime Act 2002 103
Timmermans, O. 18
Tinto, V. 92
Tonks, A. 64
transgender issues 22–23
Trotter-Mathison, M. 214
Tullius, J. M. 15
Turecki, G. 53

Unconditional Personal Regard (UPR) 189
Unconditional Positive Regard (UPR) 136, 152, 189
University College London (UCL) 16
University of Roehampton 69

Values in Action (VIA) 193
Van Godwin, J. 227, 230
van Heeringen, K. 51
Vella-Brodrick, D. A. 220

Wall, M. V. 174
Ward, A. 210
Warwick, I. 31, 63, 230
Wasserman, Danuta 64
wellbeing: anxiety and learning 95; assessment and 97; assessment methods 98; attainment issues 94; autonomy 101; capacity to consent 101; confidentiality 100; and curriculum 96–97; duty of care 101–102; energy and enthusiasm 94; impact of learning on 93; informed consent 100–101; issues regarding confidentiality 102–104; lack of engagement in class 94; lack of involvement in studies 93; mental health and behaviour in classrooms 94–95; motivation and focus 98–99; progression 94; regular feedback 97; self-disclosure in a public setting 105; sociability and relationships 94; student self-disclosure 104–105; students' self-disclosure 105–106; students' self-reflection 98; supportive learning environment 98; teacher self-disclosure 106–108

White-Smith, George 13
whole college approaches 230–231
World Health Organization (WHO) 17, 30–31, 99
Wright, L. 22
Wright, N. 52
Wrzesniewski, A. 219, 220
Wu, L. 22

Xi, Y. 22

Ying, X. 22
young person's: behaviour 152; body posture and movements 164; confidentiality 104; ego 177; encourage 154, 176; experiences and emotions 173, 189; general appearance 152; language 165; mood and affect 152, 153; opportunity to analyse 157; self-awareness of 190; signs, contemplating suicide 48–49, 54; speech and language 152

Ystgaard, M. 51

Zhao, H. 22
Zhu, J. 39
Zhu X. 22
Zubrick, S. R. 15